Emotional Intelligence and Behavioral Therapies

A 10-Step Guide to Overcoming Stress, Anxiety, and Depression

J.R. Hernández

The book titled "Emotional Intelligence and Behavioral Therapies: A 10-Step Guide to Overcoming Stress, Anxiety, and Depression" is an original work by the author Jesús Ramón Hernández Barrera (J.R. Hernández), whose expertise spans journalism and psychological counseling, supported by a master's degree in Emotional Intelligence and Personal Development. The author reserves all rights related to the publication, reproduction, distribution, and adaptation of this work in any format, both printed and digital. The infringement of these rights will be subject to the penalties stipulated in intellectual property laws.

This volume offers a 10-step program designed to address and mitigate mood disorders. It is based on a combination of techniques and principles drawn from Cognitive Behavioral Therapy (CBT), Rational Emotive Behavioral Therapy (REBT), and Emotional Intelligence (EI). Using a systematic approach and backed by scientific evidence, the reader will embark on a journey of self-discovery and personal development.

It is crucial to emphasize that, although the book's content is based on therapeutic principles and scientific findings, it does not replace professional diagnosis and treatment for the mood disorders described in the Diagnostic and Statistical Manual of Mental Disorders, fifth edition (DSM-5; American Psychiatric Association, 2013). If the reader exhibits symptoms of stress, anxiety, depression, or any other mental disorder that interferes with their functioning, they are strongly urged to seek evaluation and treatment from a qualified mental health professional.

Regarding the scientific foundation supporting the methods and techniques presented in this book, extensive studies have corroborated the effectiveness of behavioral psychotherapies and practices based on Emotional Intelligence in treating mood disorders (Hofmann, Asnaani, Vonk, Sawyer, & Fang, 2012).By reading this book, the reader not only gains empirically validated tools and techniques to enhance their emotional well-being but also a deeper understanding of the cognitive and emotional mechanisms that influence their quality of life.

It should be noted that results may vary among individuals and that this book does not guarantee the complete remission of mood disorders or any other mental health condition. By reading this book, the reader acknowledges that the author is not responsible for the consequences incurred because of using the information contained in this work, including, but not limited to, errors of omission or inaccuracy.

Finally, it is imperative to emphasize that this book is protected by copyright laws and, as such, any unauthorized use of its content is strictly prohibited.

J.R. Hernández

"You cannot heal what you cannot understand"
Carl Jung.

Table of Content

Dedication

I would like to begin by expressing my deepest gratitude to my mentor, Luz Sofía Vilte. Her dedication, guidance, patience, and expert advice throughout this process were fundamental in accomplishing "Emotional Intelligence and Behavioral Therapies: A 10-Step Guide to Overcoming Stress, Anxiety, and Depression". Her enthusiasm and commitment to research have not only marked the quality of this study but also served as a constant source of inspiration and motivation on my academic journey.

Likewise, I wish to express my appreciation to all the teaching staff and my colleagues at the Higher Institute of Psychological Studies (ISEP), located in Barcelona, Spain, especially to my classmates, Vanessa Young and Lourdes Cortijo. Each of you has significantly enriched my learning and personal and academic growth by generously sharing your valuable knowledge, experiences, and unique perspectives.

I cannot fail to mention my family and friends, who have been a pillar of support, understanding, and unconditional love throughout this journey. I want to highlight my mother, Zori Barrera, for instilling Emotional Intelligence in me from an early age; my wife, Thuy-Tien Hoang, who encouraged me to embark on this journey in the field of mental health, and my son Théodore, who is the inexhaustible source of my inspiration.

I would also like to acknowledge all those who, indirectly, have contributed to the realization of this book. To all the authors of the works I have had the opportunity to review and learn from, to the mental health professionals who tirelessly strive to improve the lives of those affected by mood disorders, and finally to the patients who, with their strength and resilience, inspire us to continue searching for new strategies for their treatment and support.

I also wish to express my gratitude to all those who have taken the time to read this work. I hope it can be of some value in understanding and addressing behavioral therapies and emotional intelligence in the treatment of stress, anxiety, and depression.

Lastly, and in a particularly meaningful way, I would like to dedicate this book to all those who bravely fight depression. This academic effort is more than just a research project; it is a tribute to their constant struggle, their unbreakable strength, and their unquestionable courage.

Every page of this study is a show of respect and admiration for their resilience, and every conclusion, a step in our collective search for more effective paths to well-being and recovery. It is my hope that this book serves not only as an academic resource but also as a reminder that you are not alone in your battle.

To you who, amid darkness, continue to seek the light; to you who, despite the pain, never stop fighting; to you who, in adversity, teach the world what true strength means. This work is by and for you.

J.R. Hernández

Abstract

"Emotional Intelligence and Behavioral Therapies: A 10-Step Guide to Overcoming Stress, Anxiety, and Depression" is dedicated to the conceptualization and development of an innovative educational resource for the treatment of stress, anxiety, and depression. This work focuses on the application of principles drawn from Cognitive Behavioral Therapy and Rational Emotive Behavioral Therapy, with techniques and strategies based on Emotional Intelligence. Through a comprehensive review of relevant scientific literature, this study rigorously investigates the relationship between behavioral therapies and Emotional Intelligence in the context of mood disorders.

Empirical evidence suggests that the adoption of techniques and strategies based on Emotional Intelligence and behavioral therapies can play a crucial and effective role in the treatment and management of mood disorders. In response to these findings, a highly practical and accessible guide that incorporates these principles has been developed.

This book represents a significant contribution to the field of stress, anxiety, and depression treatment, with the potential to serve as an invaluable resource for readers. This manual offers a comprehensive and understandable overview of how behavioral therapies and Emotional Intelligence can be effectively employed to address and mitigate mood disorders.

Furthermore, it is hoped that this work can serve mental health professionals as a valuable repository of information and a recommended tool for clinical practice. The findings of the study not only enrich the existing body of literature at the intersection of behavioral therapies and Emotional Intelligence with depressive mood disorder but also underscore the relevance and applicability of these techniques in the intervention and treatment of mood disorders in general.

Introduction

Problem Statement

Depression has emerged as a critical issue in the field of public health globally. According to estimates, approximately one in every 14 people worldwide suffers from this mental disorder. Despite its prevalence and the serious consequences, it can have on both physical and psychological health, quality of life, and daily performance, there is a notable lack of accessibility and effectiveness in treatment for this condition. According to data from the World Health Organization (WHO, 2022), less than half of those affected manage to access the medical and psychological support they require.

In this context, Emotional Intelligence has emerged as an increasingly relevant field of interest. Although initial research on EI focused mainly on its impact on general health and well-being (Salovey, Stroud, Woolery, & Epel, 2002; Zeidner, Matthews, & Roberts, 2012), more recent studies have pointed out the profound implications this construct could have for understanding and treating mood disorders (Extremera & Fernández-Berrocal, 2006; Martins, Ramalho, & Morin, 2010). Thus, individuals with high scores on Emotional Intelligence tests show a greater ability to identify, understand, and manage their emotions, which could act as a mitigating mechanism for depressive symptoms and promote more sustainable emotional well-being (Fernández-Berrocal et al., 2012).

However, despite this potential, there is a notable scarcity of educational resources and intervention programs that integrate Emotional Intelligence as a central element in the treatment of depression, specifically. Many of the existing programs based on EI are directed at general populations and do not explicitly focus on depressive mood states (Zeidner, Roberts, & Matthews, 2002). Moreover, these programs often adopt a predominantly cognitive-behavioral approach, without directly and emphatically addressing the emotional component, which could limit their efficacy in treating emotional disorders like depression (Beck, Rush, Shaw, & Emery, 1979).

Similarly, it is crucial to consider the relevance of other prevalent mental health conditions, such as stress and anxiety, which are also pressing public health issues. These conditions affect the quality of life and emotional well-being of a large part of the global population. According to the WHO (2019), generalized anxiety disorder affects approximately 3.6% of the world's population, and stress-related disorders, such as post-traumatic stress disorder, have an incidence of 0.9%. Although these figures might be interpreted as modest, they are estimated to increase, highlighting the urgent need to develop and apply more effective psychological treatment strategies.

Just as in the case of depression, Emotional Intelligence could play a vital role in managing stress and anxiety. The ability to understand, manage, and regulate emotions can be crucial in facing stressful situations and minimizing anxiety symptoms. Various studies have shown that individuals with high levels of Emotional Intelligence tend to handle these conditions more effectively (Mikolajczak, Roy, Luminet, Fillée, & de Timary, 2007; Salovey, Bedell, Detweiler, & Mayer, 1999).

Therefore, there is a pressing need to design and implement therapeutic programs that incorporate Emotional Intelligence as a fundamental pillar in the treatment of these conditions. Behavioral therapies, such as Cognitive-Behavioral Therapy and Rational Emotive Behavioral Therapy, have proven effective in this context (David, Lynn, & Ellis, 2010). However, the integration of specific Emotional Intelligence skills training could enhance the efficacy of these therapies, providing additional tools to improve emotional self-regulation. This, in turn, would facilitate more effective management of negative or overwhelming emotions, which are intrinsic characteristics of these disorders.

In conclusion, the development and implementation of therapeutic programs that merge the principles of behavioral therapies with Emotional Intelligence training techniques represent a significant opportunity not only to offer patients more effective tools to cope with stress, anxiety, and depression but also to expand the knowledge base at the intersection of Emotional Intelligence and mental health. The multidisciplinary approach presented in this book could not only optimize therapeutic outcomes but also contribute significantly to the scientific literature in this area (Brackett, Rivers, & Salovey, 2011; Fernández-Berrocal & Extremera, 2006).

Background

Emotional Intelligence, initially conceptualized by Peter Salovey and John Mayer (1990) as the ability to recognize, understand, and effectively manage one's own and others' emotions, has gained increasing importance across various disciplines within the psychological and social domain. A robust body of literature has emerged, evidencing its positive impact on variables such as emotional well-being (Salovey et al., 2000), academic performance (Petrides et al., 2004), workplace success (Lopes et al., 2003), and the quality of interpersonal relationships (Brackett et al., 2011).

Similarly, depression, predominantly characterized by a diminished mood, poses a global concern, affecting approximately 262 million individuals worldwide (WHO, 2022). This psychiatric pathology is primarily marked by a chronic depressive mood and a range of symptoms including sadness, loss of interest in daily activities, feelings of guilt, sleep and appetite disorders, fatigue, and decreased concentration (Fernández-Berrocal et al., 2019). Studies like those by Salovey et al. (2002) and Martins et al. (2010) have explored the correlation between low levels of Emotional Intelligence and the presence and severity of depressive symptoms.

Exploratory studies focused on affective disorders, particularly depression and its link with diminished mood, have revealed promising preliminary results. The study by Fernández-Berrocal et al. (2019) found a significant negative correlation between Emotional Intelligence and depressive symptoms in a sample of young adults. These findings are consistent with similar research, including a meta-analysis of 44 studies that concluded there is an inverse relationship between EI and depression (Martins et al., 2010), and a cross-sectional study in a sample of adolescents (Salguero et al., 2010).

Beyond depression, the scientific literature has begun to investigate how Emotional Intelligence might influence other negative emotional aspects such as stress and anxiety. A study by Saklofske et al. (2007) found that individuals with higher levels of EI experience less stress in challenging situations and have better coping strategies. In the context of the professional environment, work-related stress has been inversely associated with levels of Emotional Intelligence across various professions, including medicine (Weng et al., 2008).

Regarding anxiety, Extremera et al. (2007) reported that individuals with higher levels of Emotional Intelligence exhibited lower levels of anxiety, and the authors suggested that developing EI-based training techniques could be a potentially effective intervention to reduce anxious symptoms. This finding is supported by a meta-analysis by Martins et al. (2010), which included both depression and anxiety and concluded that there is a significant negative correlation between Emotional Intelligence and these negative mood states.

However, despite the empirical evidence on how Emotional Intelligence-based interventions could be helpful in mitigating stress, anxiety, and depression, it is crucial to note that most of these studies focus on specific populations and predominantly use self-report measures for their evaluation. While this method has its scientific value, it is also subject to various limitations, such as personal biases, memory distortions, and fluctuations in self-perception, which could question the reliability of the results (Podsakoff et al., 2003).

Given this context, valid questions arise about the applicability of Emotional Intelligence as a tool in treating mood disorders in a more diverse population, as well as about strategies to improve the accuracy in measuring and developing Emotional Intelligence. Despite the accumulated evidence, the practical application of EI in treating depressive states remains an emerging field that requires further research and resource allocation to bridge this significant gap, leaving the path open for more rigorous and specialized future studies (Fernández-Berrocal et al., 2020).

To conclude, it's vital to highlight that while advances in pharmacological and psychotherapeutic interventions for emotional states like depression are undeniably significant, there are clear limitations in their efficacy and accessibility. Not all individuals respond equally to these methods, and consequently, it is crucial to continue exploring alternative or complementary approaches to treating emotional conditions. The development of Emotional Intelligence could, therefore, offer a new path in the quest for more effective and accessible treatments.

Justification

Despite the growing relevance of Emotional Intelligence in the field of mental health, there is a tangible gap in the scientific literature and clinical practice regarding the scarcity of educational resources that focus on integrating EI in the treatment of mood disorders, such as stress, anxiety, and depression. This book aims to fill that gap by providing a theoretical and practical framework in which these crucial elements are intertwined.

Given the high prevalence of mood disorders and their significant impact on individual and collective quality of life, the applicability of Emotional Intelligence in the treatment and prevention of anxiety and depressive disorders represents an unexplored field of immense potential (Caruso, Salovey & Mayer, 2019). This project aims not only to contribute to the academic corpus but also to have a tangible impact on people suffering from these disorders. This imperative becomes more urgent given current trends in clinical psychology, which increasingly highlight the importance of EI in mental health (Goleman, 1995; Mayer, Roberts & Barsade, 2008).

In modern society, stress, anxiety, and depression have become silent epidemics, affecting not only the quality of life of individuals but also representing a high cost for public health systems (WHO, 2020). Multiple studies have documented the correlation between chronic stress and a wide range of health problems, from heart disease and immune system disorders to psychosomatic issues (Cohen, Janicki-Deverts & Miller, 2007).

Anxiety is not only an affliction but can also act as an exacerbating factor in a variety of comorbidities, such as sleep disorders, gastrointestinal problems, and an increased risk of cardiovascular diseases (Remes, Brayne, Linde & Lafortune, 2016). In this scenario, Emotional Intelligence emerges as a resource that is not only valuable but also indispensable for mental health.

Various research bodies have demonstrated that Emotional Intelligence is a cornerstone in the effective management of stress and anxiety (Kotsou, Nelis, Grégoire & Mikolajczak, 2011). The different skills that make up EI, such as emotional perception and regulation, have been linked to better stress adaptation and a lower incidence of anxiety (Mikolajczak, Luminet, Leroy & Roy, 2007). Furthermore, empirical research has established that interventions focused on the development of Emotional Intelligence have been effective in reducing stress and anxiety levels across various contexts and populations (Brackett, Rivers, Shiffman, Lerner & Salovey, 2006).

In summary, given the high prevalence and impact of emotional disorders such as depression, and considering the growing body of evidence supporting the role of Emotional Intelligence in their management, the development of a specialized program that combines behavioral therapies with Emotional Intelligence training is not only justified but crucial. It is hoped that through its development and dissemination, the understanding of the utility of EI in mental health treatment will be enriched, and practical tools that can improve the lives of patients and professional interventions alike will be provided.

The proposed program is structured in 10 stages, each with daily exercises designed for the development of key emotional skills. Based on the principles of behavioral therapies such as Cognitive Behavioral Therapy and Rational Emotive Behavioral Therapy, these exercises are meticulously conceived to progressively cultivate competencies like self-awareness, emotional self-regulation, and self-motivation (Brackett, Rivers & Salovey, 2011).

Included in this program are exercises for the identification and labeling of emotions, as well as tools that facilitate this work, practices of emotional self-observation, analysis of the relationship between thoughts, emotions, and behaviors, and strategies for emotional management and regulation. These techniques, solidified into emotional skills, have proven effective in previous studies, showing encouraging results in reducing symptoms of anxiety and depression, and improving overall quality of life (Greenberg & Watson, 2006).

Study Objectives

The central focus of this research project was to design an educational resource based on an exhaustive bibliographic analysis. This resource particularly emphasizes the practical utility of behavioral therapies and Emotional Intelligence in managing depressive mood disorders. While it also considers the approach and mitigation of stress and anxiety, these elements are treated as secondary yet equally significant aspects.

What elevates the importance of this resource is its dual applicability. It is designed not only to provide patients with a deeper understanding of how the combination of behavioral therapies and Emotional Intelligence can be crucial in treating these complex emotional conditions but also to serve as an invaluable manual for professionals in the mental health field and anyone seeking strategies to cope with mood disorders. This resource can inform and enhance their therapeutic interventions, making their impact both more effective and lasting.

To achieve this objective, the project began with the purpose of conducting a rigorous bibliographic review. A wide range of scientific literature addressing the relationship between behavioral therapies, Emotional Intelligence, and their impact on stress, anxiety, and depression was consulted, aiming to establish clear and predefined inclusion and exclusion criteria to ensure that only the most rigorous and relevant research was incorporated.

Once the most relevant publications were identified, a thorough analysis of the various theories, models, and approaches that have informed the combined application of behavioral therapies and Emotional Intelligence in treating these emotional conditions was conducted. This meticulous analysis allowed for the establishment of a solid theoretical framework upon which the educational resource was built.

Simultaneously, a critical evaluation of therapeutic interventions that have shown promise in the scientific literature was carried out, with the goal of analyzing their efficacy in mitigating symptoms of stress, anxiety, and depression, as well as their impact on improving the quality of life of affected individuals.

One of the major challenges was to synthesize these academic findings into an educational resource that was accessible and clear, dedicating considerable effort to distill and convey in an understandable manner the concepts, techniques, and strategies identified as effective. To conclude this project, it was proposed to present a series of practical recommendations focused on implementing these combined strategies in clinical practice and outline future research directions that could further expand and enrich the field.

This solid foundation serves as a precursor for the following section of this work, which will present a detailed theoretical framework including a deep conceptualization of Emotional Intelligence, its synergy with behavioral therapies, and its applicability in the treatment of stress, anxiety, and depression. This academic and conceptual framework will lay the groundwork for the 30-step guide that will be detailed in the final chapters of this work.

Theoretical Framework

Emotional Intelligence

Emotional Intelligence has established itself as a psychological construct of great relevance since it was conceptualized by Peter Salovey and John Mayer (Salovey & Mayer, 1990). Its significance was further propelled by the seminal work of Daniel Goleman, who popularized the concept beyond academic circles (Goleman, 1995). Since its introduction, EI has demonstrated its applicability and effectiveness across a variety of settings, ranging from personal to professional (Brackett, Rivers & Salovey, 2011).

Emotional Intelligence is understood as the ability to identify, understand, use, and effectively regulate our own emotions and those of others (Brackett, Rivers & Salovey, 2011). Its impact is notable in various fields, such as education, business leadership, and interpersonal relationships. Various studies have linked high levels of EI with benefits such as improved communication, healthier relationships, and a more effective ability to cope with stress, anxiety, depression, and conflict resolution (Lopes, Salovey & Straus, 2003).

In the educational context, research indicates that students with higher levels of Emotional Intelligence tend to exhibit superior academic performance and are less prone to disruptive behaviors (Brackett & Mayer, 2003). In the workplace, leaders with developed emotional skills generally lead teams that display greater commitment and satisfaction, which, in turn, enhances productivity and overall team performance (Lopes et al., 2006).

However, Emotional Intelligence becomes particularly promising in its therapeutic dimension when applied to the treatment of mood disorders. The EI skills model proposed by Mayer and Salovey (1997) suggests a comprehensive approach based on four core competencies: emotional perception, emotional facilitation, emotional understanding, and emotional regulation. These competencies provide a complete framework that enables individuals to interpret and manage their emotions more effectively, as well as those of others (Mayer & Salovey, 1997).

In the treatment of depressive moods, for example, interventions can be implemented to strengthen the ability to recognize and perceive one's own emotions, a skill often compromised in individuals facing these psychological states (Fernández-Berrocal & Extremera, 2006). Additionally, specific techniques have been designed to facilitate greater emotional understanding, allowing people to comprehend how their emotions influence their thought patterns and behavior (Brackett & Mayer, 2003). Finally, effective emotion management through regulation techniques and strategies has been shown to contribute significantly to the reduction of depressive symptoms (Aldao, Nolen-Hoeksema & Schweizer, 2010). This endows this set of emotional skills with robust empirical support, making it a very promising therapeutic approach.

Depression, Anxiety & Stress

Depression

Within the field of mental health, Emotional Intelligence has emerged as a particularly encouraging resource, especially in addressing and mitigating mental health conditions like stress, anxiety, and depression. Specifically, various studies have revealed a significant negative correlation between low levels of EI and the presence of depressive symptoms (Martins, Ramalho, & Morin, 2010). This data suggests that individuals with a higher degree of Emotional Intelligence are less likely to exhibit symptoms of depression.

Furthermore, Emotional Intelligence not only shows a negative correlation with depressive states but also acts as a predictive factor in emotional resilience. For example, a study involving 415 adults showed that individuals with high levels of EI were less susceptible to the adverse effects of stressful situations and more inclined to recover positive moods after experiencing stress episodes (Fernández-Berrocal & Extremera, 2006). This finding highlights the potential of Emotional Intelligence as a crucial resource for moderating emotional responses to stressful events and facilitating effective emotional recovery.

In the context of longitudinal research, Emotional Intelligence has been the subject of studies underscoring its relationship with a notable decrease in perceived stress levels and a substantial improvement in individuals' mental well-being (Extremera, Durán, & Rey, 2007). It is important to note that longitudinal studies allow for tracking subjects over an extended period, providing more reliable data on the evolution of EI's impact on mental well-being. These findings focus not only on the relationship between Emotional Intelligence and overall well-being but also on how this construct influences stress perception. This is crucial, given that perceived stress is not always an accurate reflection of the actual stress faced by the individual, but it is a determining factor in how such a condition affects the person's mental health.

Additionally, another line of research asserts that Emotional Intelligence plays a significant role as a buffering mechanism in the relationship between chronic stress and mental well-being (Martins, Ramalho, & Morin, 2010). In other words, EI not only minimizes the negative impact that stress can have on a person's emotional state but also acts as a protective barrier reducing individuals' vulnerability to the deleterious effects of chronic stress. This "buffering" role is especially relevant in contexts where chronic stress is a constant variable, such as in high-demand jobs or prolonged crisis situations, which can be found in everyday, academic, and professional settings.

In the academic realm, for example, training in Emotional Intelligence skills has proven to be especially beneficial. A study focused on university students highlighted that an EI training program was effective in decreasing anxiety levels (Kotsou, Nelis, Grégoire, & Mikolajczak, 2011), pointing to the efficacy of Emotional Intelligence skills training as an intervention strategy in academic contexts to mitigate anxiety.

However, despite the growing body of evidence highlighting the fundamental role Emotional Intelligence can play in various aspects of life, including mental health (Brackett, Rivers, & Salovey, 2011; Lopes, Salovey, & Straus, 2003), there continues to be a call for more in-depth research and more effective implementation of EI-based strategies, especially in treating depressive mood states (Fernández-Berrocal & Extremera, 2006).

When discussing depressive states, we refer to a sustained emotional state distinguished by manifestations such as sadness, apathy, hopelessness, and a significant decrease in interest or pleasure in activities that would normally be enjoyable (APA, 2013). This state, which can be an indicator of a more serious mood disorder like major depression, distinguishes individuals with depressive tendencies from those experiencing temporary episodes of sadness or discouragement. It is crucial to understand that this depressive emotional state can vary in degrees of intensity, ranging from temporary sadness to more severe forms like clinical depression. In the latter, profound and persistent sadness is often accompanied by a series of cognitive, behavioral, and physiological symptoms that significantly alter the individual's daily functioning (APA, 2013). Among these additional symptoms are changes in appetite, irregular sleep patterns such as insomnia or hypersomnia, decreased energy levels, intense feelings of worthlessness or guilt, and difficulties concentrating. In extreme cases, there may even be thoughts of suicide or self-harm.

According to epidemiological data, it is estimated that approximately 5% of the global population suffers from depression, with depressive mood as a principal characteristic. This figure has remained worryingly stable over the past decades (Ritchie & Roser, 2018). Moreover, it is worth noting that these figures might be underestimated due to diagnostic barriers and the scarce availability of effective treatments in certain regions (WHO, 2017). This lack of resources and specialized medical care not only contributes to the urgency of addressing depression as a global public health issue but also to seeking other alternatives.

Depression transcends the realm of individual suffering, also impacting the social, family, and community environment of the affected person. Moreover, it often presents comorbidity with other medical conditions, both mental and physical, exacerbating both the severity of the disorder and resistance to conventional treatments (Kessler et al., 2003). In this context, Emotional Intelligence emerges as a factor of vital importance, supported by research emphasizing its role in addressing and understanding depressive states. This relevance becomes more acute considering that, according to recent data from the World Health Organization, more than 300 million people worldwide suffer from depression, representing a 13% increase over the last decade (WHO, 2022).

Epidemiological studies also reveal considerable fluctuation in the global prevalence of depression, with percentages ranging between 3% and 17% of the population experiencing depressive symptoms at some point in their lives (Vos et al., 2017). Additionally, there is a notably higher prevalence in women compared to men. For instance, a longitudinal study by Seedat et al. (2009) found that the rates of major depression in women were almost double those in men, suggesting biological, psychological, and sociocultural factors as possible explanations. Meanwhile, young adults, specifically those between 18 and 29 years of age, show up to three times greater propensity to experience depressive episodes compared to adults over 60 years old (Kessler et al., 2020). This is corroborated by research such as that of Auerbach et al. (2018), who found that the prevalence and severity of depressive symptoms in university students are significantly increasing.

These demographic variations highlight the complexity and diversity of depression and emphasize the need to address multiple variables – such as gender, age, and geographical location – when designing and implementing intervention and prevention strategies for this mental health condition. Incorporating the cultural dimension in addressing depression is crucial, especially given global diversity. Research like that of Haroz et al. (2017) underscores the need to modify and adapt interventions to the cultural specificities of each population. Symptoms of disorders like depression can manifest differently depending on the cultural context. In some cultures, somatic symptoms (such as physical pains and discomforts) may be more prominent, while in others, emotional or cognitive aspects may be more evident. Similarly, cultural beliefs, religious practices, and values can play a significant role in how people understand and approach their mental health. An intervention that does not take these factors into account might be less effective or even counterproductive.

In a more contemporary context, it's noteworthy that the COVID-19 pandemic has dramatically intensified the global burden of depression. Factors such as uncertainty and stress, exacerbated by the health crisis, combined with elements like social isolation and economic instability, have heightened the emergence and worsening of depressive states (Xiong et al., 2020). This scenario has amplified both the extent and severity of this pressing public health problem.

A global study conducted by Pfefferbaum and North (2020) reported that the prevalence of depression symptoms increased considerably during the pandemic. For example, in the United States, the prevalence of depressive symptoms was approximately three times higher during the pandemic compared to the pre-pandemic period. Moreover, according to a study published in The Lancet in 2021, the pandemic contributed to an additional 53 million cases of major depressive disorders worldwide in 2020, representing a 28% increase compared to what would have been expected without the pandemic (Smith, 2021). There was also a 25% increase in the prevalence of anxiety and depression worldwide during the first year of the pandemic, which was more pronounced among women and young people (WHO 2021).

It is equally imperative to highlight that the repercussions of depressive disorders and melancholic mood states transcend individual well-being. Depression stands as one of the leading causes of disability worldwide, imposing a significant economic burden manifested in both direct healthcare costs and indirect costs related to decreased work productivity and increased premature deaths (Chisholm et al., 2016).

Anxiety & Stress

Like depression, stress and anxiety are mental health problems with a global impact. In fact, it is estimated that approximately 31% of adults will experience some type of anxiety disorder during their lifetime (Kessler et al., 2005). The prevalence of stress, though more difficult to quantify due to its multifaceted nature, is equally alarming;

various reports suggest that up to 80% of workers feel stress in their work environment (Leka et al., 2003).

It's pertinent to note that, as with depression, there are disparities in the prevalence of stress and anxiety based on gender, age, and sociocultural environment. Women, for example, are more prone to suffer from anxiety disorders than men, with a prevalence that can be up to twice as high (McLean et al., 2011). Additionally, urban environments seem to foster higher levels of stress and anxiety than rural areas. A study found that the prevalence of anxiety disorders in urban settings can be up to 21% higher compared to rural areas, likely due to factors such as the fast pace of life and pollution (Peen et al., 2010). The economic and social burden of stress and anxiety is another point to consider. These conditions contribute to a significant decrease in work productivity and increase healthcare costs. It has been estimated that anxiety disorders cost the global economy more than 42 billion dollars annually, just in the United States (Greenberg et al., 1999).

In this scenario, Emotional Intelligence emerges as an invaluable resource for the treatment of stress and anxiety. As mentioned earlier, studies have shown that developing EI skills, such as self-awareness, emotional self-management, and empathy, can mitigate the effects of stress and anxiety in different contexts (Brackett et al., 2011). Therefore, it becomes indispensable to redouble efforts in the effective prevention and treatment of stress, anxiety, and depression through the potential of Emotional Intelligence as a viable and promising therapeutic strategy. And, although research on this approach is still in an early phase, existing data suggest that this construct could play a crucial role in mitigating symptoms and improving the quality of life for affected individuals.

The fusion of techniques from behavioral therapies with Emotional Intelligence tools emerges as an especially effective approach to this problem. This integrative model allows not only modifying dysfunctional behaviors but also enhancing emotional skills, such as self-awareness and self-regulation, which are essential for more effectively facing mood disorders. However, it is imperative that more rigorous and comprehensive research be conducted to validate the efficacy of this integrative approach and maximize its therapeutic potential.

Interventions Focused on EI

The systematic exploration and effective application of Emotional Intelligence represent an innovative and necessary approach in the prevention and treatment of stress, anxiety, and depression. Various research lines have evaluated the efficacy of intervention programs based on EI with the goal of improving emotional skills and, therefore, attenuating symptoms associated with mood disorders (Nelis et al., 2011; Ruiz-Aranda et al., 2012).

Interventions focused on Emotional Intelligence have been designed to increase emotional recognition, refine the ability for emotional regulation, and promote adaptive responses to negative emotions. Although this area of study is in a phase of constant growth, preliminary results are encouraging regarding the potential efficacy of these interventions in reducing depressive and anxious moods, as well as a better response to stressors (Hodzic et al., 2018).

It is imperative to emphasize that advancements in the formulation, implementation, and evaluation of these interventions represent an evolutionary and continuous process. Future research will allow these programs to be refined and their effectiveness evaluated in a variety of populations and contexts (Rivers et al., 2013). With the accumulation of scientific evidence, there is a real possibility that EI-based interventions could become a fundamental resource in the therapeutic arsenal for the treatment of mood disorders.

In the current landscape of mental health, interventions such as Emotional Intelligence Therapy (EIT; Nelis et al., 2011) and the Applied Emotional Intelligence program (AEI; Ruiz-Aranda et al., 2012) have shown promise. However, they have also posed critical challenges in the field of EI. These challenges are primarily focused on the need for more rigorous evaluations through Randomized Controlled Trials

(RCTs), attention to specific demographic considerations, and the proper incorporation of Emotional Intelligence strategies into existing therapeutic approaches.

Regarding the evaluation of efficacy, although numerous initial studies have been conducted, there has been a highlighted need for more rigorous research. A meta-analysis that examined 24 Emotional Intelligence-based interventions revealed that only 45% of the EI programs were evaluated using an RCT design, thus limiting the ability to infer their genuine efficacy (Hodzic et al., 2018).

Additionally, there is a demographic bias in the application of Emotional Intelligence programs. Although depressive disorders affect individuals of all ages, most interventions have predominantly focused on youth and adult populations, leaving aside the needs of older age groups (Rivers et al., 2013). A systematic review points out that only a scant 10% of Emotional Intelligence interventions are directed at the elderly population (Johnstone et al., 2020). Given that older adults are more susceptible to a series of unique stressors, such as loneliness and the loss of loved ones, the lack of EI programs specifically aimed at this demographic group is particularly problematic. This statistic highlights a concerning gap in access to these services, even more so when depression rates in the elderly population are rising, with figures indicating that around 7% of older adults suffer from major depression (WHO, 2022).

Regarding the implementation of Emotional Intelligence strategies in existing treatments for depression, their incorporation has been notably limited. For example, although Cognitive Behavioral Therapy has proven effective in treating this mental health condition (Butler et al., 2006), only a minority of programs have considered EE in their therapeutic approach. This omission not only limits the therapeutic potential itself but also postpones the comprehensive evolution of treatment strategies for depression (Kotsou & Leys, 2017).

These gaps reinforce the need for additional research and practical development in the field of Emotional Intelligence and its applicability in the treatment of depression. It is crucial to conduct more rigorous evaluations of intervention programs based on this construct, demographically diversify the populations targeted by these interventions, and promote a more complete integration of EI into established therapeutic approaches.

Moreover, other existing treatments have also shown deficiencies. The "Emotion Regulation Skills" (ERS; Berking et al., 2013) program, although it has shown beneficial results to some extent, does not offer a comprehensive approach by focusing solely on managing negative emotions, without fostering the development of a broader emotional repertoire. According to a systematic review covering 75 studies, only 15% of EI interventions explicitly addressed the development of skills to manage a wide spectrum of emotions, whether negative or positive (Sánchez-Álvarez, Extremera, and Fernández-Berrocal, 2016). Although this research offers a series of promising findings, it is recognized that such an approach is limited and might not be sufficient to address depressive disorders, whose complexity demands more rigorous and holistic research and therapeutic approach.

Similarly, the "Emotional Intelligence Training" (EIT; Slaski and Cartwright, 2003) program has also faced criticism regarding its duration and follow-up. It has been documented that, although it confers short-term benefits, the lack of longitudinal follow-up makes it difficult to assess the durability of these effects (Chapman and Hayslip, 2005). Additionally, approximately only 35% of EI-based interventions have conducted follow-ups of participants beyond the six-month post-intervention period (Kotsou et al., 2019).

Another problem lies in the scarce customization of Emotional Intelligence programs. Most interventions adopt a standardized format, omitting to consider individual differences in Emotional Intelligence levels and the specific needs of participants. In fact, less than 20% of the programs have adopted a personalized approach, which decreases their efficacy and ignores the intrinsic complexity of mood disorders (Hodzic et al., 2018). Therefore, these deficiencies underscore the urgency for clinical researchers and policymakers to collaborate in developing and evaluating more precise and personalized interventions, utilizing Emotional Intelligence as a more effective therapeutic resource to combat depression.

Methodology

Documentary Sources

For the comprehensive development of "Emotional Intelligence and Behavioral Therapies: A 10-Step Guide to Overcoming Stress, Anxiety, and Depression", the bibliographic review was established as a fundamental pillar. This process aimed to establish a solid theoretical framework that would support the concepts of Emotional Intelligence, Rational Emotive Behavioral Therapy, Cognitive Behavioral Therapy, and the treatment of depression, anxiety, and stress, as well as the interconnections among these elements.

Regarding the literature, various essential works in the fields of Emotional Intelligence and psychotherapy were consulted. "Emotional Intelligence" by Daniel Goleman (1995) offered crucial perspectives on how emotional skills impact quality of life. "Cognitive Therapy of Depression" by Aaron Beck (1979) provided understanding of the role of cognitive patterns in emotional states. Meanwhile, "The Science of Compassion: A Juxtaposition between Buddhist Psychology and Western Psychology" by Paul Gilbert (2017) offered an intercultural view of emotional well-being.

Especially, "Rational Emotive Behavioral Therapy" by Albert Ellis (1973) stood as a pillar in the treatment of depression, providing a detailed analysis of REBT. Among other works, the review also included "Emotional Agility" by Susan David (2016), about effective emotional navigation; "Nonviolent Communication: A Language of Life" by Marshall B. Rosenberg (2003), focused on communicative skills for conflict resolution; and "Cognitive Behavioral Therapy Made Simple" by James Williams (2019), offering a more accessible approach to CBT.

The review was extended to include texts that specifically addressed the relationship between Emotional Intelligence and phenomena such as stress and anxiety. Among these compendiums, "The Mind-Body Connection: How Emotional Intelligence Can Reduce Stress and Anxiety?" by Richard Davidson (2001) stands out, which explores the neuroscientific interaction between emotions and these phenomena, underlining the regulatory role of EI. Another relevant contribution was "Managing Stress through Emotional Intelligence" by Peter Salovey and Daisy Grewal (2005). This work highlights the importance of emotional competencies in effective stress management, offering an applied and pragmatic view.

All these sources significantly enriched the initial theoretical framework of "Emotional Intelligence and Behavioral Therapies: A 10-Step Guide to Overcoming Stress, Anxiety, and Depression", expanding the understanding of how EI is not only crucial in treating depressive mood but also in the comprehensive approach to stress and anxiety. The selection of these texts strengthens the multidimensional character of this study, emphasizing its relevance and applicability in different aspects of emotional and mental well-being.

Various academic journals were also utilized, highlighting sources such as the "Journal of Rational-Emotive & Cognitive-Behavior Therapy", focused on current research on REBT; "Emotion", which concentrates on the scientific study of emotions; "Journal of Consulting and Clinical Psychology", covering a wide range of studies in clinical psychology; and the "Journal of Positive Psychology", dedicated to well-being and positive psychology.

Finally, for the development of this manual, academic databases such as PsycINFO, PubMed, and Google Scholar were used to conduct an exhaustive search for information that could enrich this study. Search terms included keywords like "Cognitive Behavioral Therapy", "Rational Emotive Behavioral Therapy", "Emotional Intelligence", "Depressive Mood", "Anxiety", "Depression", "Stress", "Depression Treatment", and "Emotional Resilience", in both English and Spanish.

Qualitative Analysis

During the research for the development of "Emotional Intelligence and Behavioral Therapies: A 10-Step Guide to Overcoming Stress, Anxiety, and Depression", a qualitative analysis methodology was applied to the selection of documentary sources. This procedure encompassed the crucial foundations of Emotional Intelligence and focused particularly on relevant literature in the fields of psychology and psychotherapy. Among the works examined, Albert Ellis's seminal work "Rational Emotive Behavioral Therapy" (1973), Aaron Beck's "Cognitive Therapy of Depression" (1979), and Daniel Goleman's "Emotional Intelligence" (1995) were notably included.

After the identification and selection of the most appropriate documents, a thorough reading of each selected material was undertaken. At this stage, key ideas were highlighted, and summary cards were compiled for each document, contributing to an effective consolidation and synthesis of the most relevant information. Concurrently, a conceptual map was designed to offer a visual and structured representation of the relationships between the different concepts and ideas that emerged from the consulted sources.

In the thematic classification process of the sources, the central thematic areas addressed in the documents were highlighted, such as the pillars of Cognitive Behavioral Therapy, the strategies of Rational Emotive Behavioral Therapy, and the techniques of Emotional Intelligence, as well as specific interventions for the regulation of mood disorders. This thematic classification system not only allowed for a more effective organization of the information repository but also facilitated the detection of patterns and themes that frequently recur in the specialized literature.

A deep comparative analysis of the selected sources was also conducted in relation to other guides, manuals, or existing academic resources that address similar themes. In this sense, various relevant materials were compared using a series of criteria that included, among others, the author, the year of publication, the target audience, the purposes, the topics covered, the methodological strategies employed, and the reported results.

This comparison was essential to identify both the strengths and weaknesses of the existing resources in the study area. In this context, Albert Ellis's work served as an invaluable reference framework that, in turn, provided a solid foundation for the conception and elaboration of a new and more effective resource in treating depressive mood.

STRENGTHS:

- *Scientific Rigor:* Ellis's approach is backed by decades of research and clinical practice. It provides a solid theoretical and practical framework to help people understand and change their destructive thought patterns.

- *Active and Directive Approach:* REBT promotes self-understanding and self-management. Patients are seen as active collaborators in the therapy process, aligning well with the self-directed nature of "Emotional Intelligence and Behavioral Therapies: A 10-Step Guide to Overcoming Stress, Anxiety, and Depression".

- *Versatility:* REBT can be applied to a variety of emotional problems, making it relevant to a target audience that may be dealing with issues such as depression, anxiety, and stress.

WEAKNESSES:

- *Demand for Self-reflection:* REBT requires individuals to have the capacity to reflect on their own thoughts and emotions, which can be challenging for some people. "Emotional Intelligence and Behavioral

Therapies: A 10-Step Guide to Overcoming Stress, Anxiety, and Depression" seeks to address this weakness by providing detailed exercises and step-by-step guides to facilitate this process.

- *Time and Effort:* Like any cognitive therapy, REBT requires time and effort from the individual. Although "Emotional Intelligence and Behavioral Therapies: A 10-Step Guide to Overcoming Stress, Anxiety, and Depression" is designed to be completed in at list 30 days. Some people may need more time to process and apply the concepts and techniques presented.

- *Need for Professional Guidance:* Although REBT can be self-applied to a certain extent, the guidance of a professional therapist can be very beneficial. "Emotional Intelligence and Behavioral Therapies: A 10-Step Guide to Overcoming Stress, Anxiety, and Depression" addresses this by suggesting that, although the exercises can be performed individually, the guidance of a professional can be very helpful in overcoming obstacles and deepening the understanding of the concepts.

Following an exhaustive analysis of Albert Ellis's work "Rational Emotive Behavior Therapy," the next phase of the research focused on another seminal work: "Cognitive Therapy of Depression" by Aaron Beck (1979). As was done with Ellis's work, a comparative analysis of Beck's work with other resources, guides, and manuals existing in the scientific literature was also carried out. This comparative exercise provided a comprehensive view of the strengths and weaknesses of Beck's work, which are described below:

STRENGTHS:

- *Solid Empirical Foundation:* Beck's work is built on a robust base of empirical research. This scientific support adds credibility and effectiveness to the therapeutic techniques proposed, aligning with the rigor required for "Emotional Intelligence and Behavioral Therapies: A 10-Step Guide to Overcoming Stress, Anxiety, and Depression".

- *Individualized Approach:* Beck's cognitive therapy places strong emphasis on individualized treatment, allowing for a more personalized approach to depressive mood, something that has also been integrated into "Emotional Intelligence and Behavioral Therapies: A 10-Step Guide to Overcoming Stress, Anxiety, and Depression".

- *Wide Applicability:* Like REBT, cognitive therapy has a broad range of applications, making it relevant for a diverse audience that may be facing multiple emotional challenges.

WEAKNESSES:

- *Accessibility:* Although effective, Beck's cognitive therapy can be complex and somewhat inaccessible for individuals without a background in psychology. "Emotional Intelligence and Behavioral Therapies: A 10-Step Guide to Overcoming Stress, Anxiety, and Depression" seeks to mitigate this barrier by providing simple explanations and practical exercises.

- *Progress Pace:* Cognitive therapy can be a lengthy process that requires the individual's commitment. "Emotional Intelligence and Behavioral Therapies: A 10-Step Guide to Overcoming Stress, Anxiety, and Depression", structured in a 10-step program, attempts to address this challenge by offering a condensed yet comprehensive guide.

- *Limited Clinical Focus:* Although valuable, Beck's work focuses on a clinical approach that might require the intervention of a professional for severe cases of depression. "Emotional Intelligence and Behavioral Therapies: A 10-Step Guide to Overcoming Stress, Anxiety, and Depression" suggests that, although designed for individual use, the guidance of a professional is invaluable for addressing more complex cases.

Incorporating these findings into "Emotional Intelligence and Behavioral Therapies: A 10-Step Guide to Overcoming Stress, Anxiety, and Depression" not only reinforces its scientific basis but also enhances its applicability and effectiveness, thus contributing to the creation of an improved and more comprehensive resource.

A comparative analysis of Goleman's "Emotional Intelligence" with other resources addressing emotional intelligence and the psychology of depressive mood was also conducted, using criteria such as the approach, suggested techniques, and the applicability of concepts in everyday life. Below, the strengths and weaknesses are detailed.

STRENGTHS:

- *Holistic Approach:* Goleman focuses not only on cognitive intelligence but also highlights the importance of emotional skills, which directly aligns with the objectives of "Emotional Intelligence and Behavioral Therapies: A 10-Step Guide to Overcoming Stress, Anxiety, and Depression".

- *General Applicability:* The concepts and techniques introduced by Goleman are applicable in multiple aspects of life, enriching "Emotional Intelligence and Behavioral Therapies: A 10-Step Guide to Overcoming Stress, Anxiety, and Depression" by providing a more versatile set of tools.

- *Scientific Basis and Popularity:* The work is supported by both psychological research and real-life examples, which gives it a balance between scientific rigor and accessibility. A similar strategy is employed in the writing of "Emotional Intelligence and Behavioral Therapies: A 10-Step Guide to Overcoming Stress, Anxiety, and Depression".

WEAKNESSES:

- *Lack of Depth in Therapeutic Techniques:* Although it addresses the importance of emotional intelligence, the book lacks a detailed guide on how to develop these skills, something that "Emotional Intelligence and Behavioral Therapies: A 10-Step Guide to Overcoming Stress, Anxiety, and Depression" seeks to complement.

- *Broad Focus:* Its generalist approach may mean certain topics are not treated with the depth they might require. In this sense, this program focuses on applying emotional intelligence specifically to the treatment of mood disorders, taking depressive mood as a pillar.

- *Subjective Interpretation:* Although Goleman bases his arguments on research, his work has been criticized for certain subjectivity in data interpretation. "Emotional Intelligence and Behavioral Therapies: A 10-Step Guide to Overcoming Stress, Anxiety, and Depression" attempts to mitigate this by referring to multiple sources and approaches.

The inclusion of findings and concepts from Goleman's work in "Emotional Intelligence and Behavioral Therapies: A 10-Step Guide to Overcoming Stress, Anxiety, and Depression" contributes to creating a more comprehensive and robust resource. Its focus on emotional intelligence adds a layer of complexity and depth that is invaluable for addressing depressive mood in a more holistic way.

Results Analysis

Guide Objective

The book "Emotional Intelligence and Behavioral Therapies: A 10-Step Guide to Overcoming Stress, Anxiety, and Depression" focuses on providing a repertoire of strategies and techniques based on the principles of Cognitive Behavioral Therapy, Rational Emotive Behavioral Therapy, and Emotional Intelligence. This approach aims primarily to help individuals effectively address and mitigate mood disorders, such as stress, anxiety, and depression, with a special emphasis on depressive mood. This interdisciplinary approach integrates knowledge and skills from cognitive, behavioral, and emotional psychology, specifically designed to support patients in their pursuit of stronger emotional and mental health.

This material is particularly relevant for a population facing emotional challenges and anxious and depressive mood states. Offering practical and applicable tools for emotional management, it aims to improve the individual's quality of life by strengthening their resilience and increasing their capacity to cope with life's adversities. Additionally, the imparted skills are versatile and applicable across a wide range of contexts, from everyday situations to work, academic, and social challenges.

The pedagogical foundation of this resource lies in its sequential and formative structure. Various techniques are employed, ranging from introspection and self-assessment, through cognitive restructuring, to more dynamic techniques like role-playing. Each step of the program introduces a new concept, breaks it down relying on scientific evidence, and finally suggests a practical exercise for users to apply what they have learned, concluding each section with a final reflection. This methodology, known as "active learning", has been proven effective in retention and the effective application of knowledge, as evidenced by research in the field of pedagogy (Prince, M. 2004).

The writing and structuring of each activity are designed to be clear, didactic, and accessible. Thus, the reader or patient can autonomously carry out the activities and reflect on their personal experiences. However, it is strongly recommended that the activities be conducted in a safe environment and considering the emotional state of the user. Users are also urged to seek advice from a mental health professional. This flexibility gives the resource added value, enabling its use in both clinical and personal development contexts.

In summary, "Emotional Intelligence and Behavioral Therapies: A 10-Step Guide to Overcoming Stress, Anxiety, and Depression" offers a detailed and scientifically evidenced agenda for the treatment of negative emotional states, through the development of Emotional Intelligence skills, as well as CBT and REBT techniques and strategies. Through its implementation, users are expected to achieve a greater understanding of their emotions, acquire significant skills for their management, and, consequently, improve their emotional and mental well-being.

Guide Instructions

"Emotional Intelligence and Behavioral Therapies: A 10-Step Guide to Overcoming Stress, Anxiety, and Depression" is a manual specifically aimed at adults, with a suggested minimum age of 18 years. As previously noted, the importance of this approach lies in its ability to offer strategies and techniques grounded in the fundamentals of behavioral therapies and Emotional Intelligence. This resource is particularly valuable for individuals' exhibiting symptoms associated with depressive mood states and anxiety spectrum disorders, classified according to the Diagnostic and Statistical Manual of Mental Disorders, fifth edition (DMS-5).

For the effective implementation of this program, it is highly recommended to have the supervision of a professional trained in the field of mental health, ideally with a solid foundation in Rational Emotive Cognitive Therapy, Cognitive Behavioral Therapy, and Emotional Intelligence. The role of such a specialist is crucial for the proper introduction and explanation of the material and will provide valuable guidance during the development of the exercises, offering constructive feedback and facilitating a space for reflection on individual progress.

Additionally, the intervention of this professional will allow the program to be adjusted to the specific needs of the user, ensuring that each session is both relevant and enriching. It is important to note that although the guidance of an expert is recommended to maximize the benefits of the program, each exercise has been designed to allow for autonomous execution by the user. This duality—the combination of professional guidance and the option for independent use—adds a layer of versatility to the resource, making it a highly adaptable tool for a wide range of users.

Ultimately, this educational resource is structured to be applied over a period of approximately 30 days, with daily sessions ranging from 30 to 60 minutes, totaling an approximate 15 to 30 hours of work (15 to 30 psychotherapy sessions). The detailed time planning of each session allows the user to advance at their own pace, enabling a better understanding and internalization of the concepts. Emphasis is placed on the user having the freedom to take all the time necessary to complete each exercise, even if this means repeating the same activity for several consecutive days, thus extending its duration.

Guide Description

Here is a summary of the manual "Emotional Intelligence and Behavioral Therapies: A 10-Step Guide to Overcoming Stress, Anxiety, and Depression." The detailed exercises that compose it will be presented in the "Appendix" section (see Appendix 1). This resource is meticulously designed to address the complexities of emotional and mental well-being, specifically focusing on managing mood disorders such as stress, anxiety, and depression. The manual is structured in a progression of 10 steps, each offering another 10 sub-steps, providing the reader with a sequence of practical exercises, theoretical considerations, and data supported by scientific research.

The content is organized into defined segments: "an introduction to each topic, research evidence for each topic, instructions for each exercise, examples based on everyday situations, reflection, and summary for each step". Each of these elements has been carefully created to be both informative and applicable, ensuring that readers acquire and apply theoretical-practical knowledge. Specifically, the instructions for the exercises are aimed at actively involving the reader, encouraging self-analysis and self-reflection as means to identify and confront irrational thoughts and emotions. These exercises are interconnected, facilitating a continuous and cumulative learning process.

Each chapter (or "step") addresses a specific aspect of emotional health, from identifying emotions and irrational beliefs to more advanced strategies such as replacing those beliefs and discriminating between appropriate and inappropriate negative emotions. At the heart of this approach lies the aspiration to enable readers to foster emotional resilience and effective coping skills applicable to everyday situations. It also includes a chapter where a new proposal is presented: Cognitive Emotive Behavioral Therapy, which is basically the therapeutic approach used in the book author's professional practices and encompasses elements of EI, REBT, and CBT.

In compliance with the guidelines of the American Psychological Association, the manual is presented in technical and professional language to ensure the scientific accuracy and ethical solidity of the content. Throughout the resource, examples based on real cases of mental health that have been previously attended to by the book's author are used to facilitate a clearer and more meaningful understanding, allowing a deep connection of the reader with the material. Essentially, this manual is configured as a pedagogical and clinical resource that aspires to be an effective tool for those seeking to improve their mental health, especially those facing symptoms of stress, anxiety, and depression.

Also, in the "Appendix" section, users are provided with additional tools to complement the practice of the topics addressed in the manual, such as the Hernández-Barrera Cognitive Distortions Scale (H-BCDS) (see Appendix 2). It is crucial to understand that the H-BCDS is an indicative self-report tool whose efficacy has not yet been corroborated. The results derived from its use reflect the individual's self-perception and self-evaluation in relation to their thought patterns.

Although this tool offers a valuable first approach, it is advised to use it in conjunction with professional counseling for a more accurate interpretation and appropriate treatment. Finally, it is essential to underline that this scale is a complementary instrument that is not intended to diagnose disorders or conditions but to offer an approximate overview of the thought patterns that could be affecting the user's emotional well-being. If you experience psychological difficulties or seek a more accurate understanding of such patterns, it is recommended to seek the support of a mental health professional.

Conclusions

The book "Emotional Intelligence and Behavioral Therapies: A 10-Step Guide to Overcoming Stress, Anxiety, and Depression" was developed with the primary objective of creating a manual based on an exhaustive bibliographic review. Its focus is on the applicability of Emotional Intelligence in the treatment of mood disorders, with special consideration for depressive mood. This purpose was effectively fulfilled by designing a structured 10-step program that integrates elements of behavioral and emotional therapies, all supported by solid scientific evidence.

In the process of developing this manual, multiple secondary objectives were achieved. Initially, a thorough bibliographic review was carried out, applying specific inclusion and exclusion criteria. This allowed for a rigorous evaluation of the scientific literature related to the confluence between behavioral therapies, Emotional Intelligence, and mood disorders. This review facilitated the identification of critical links between these elements, highlighting their relevance for the improvement of mental health. Thus, a robust empirical basis was established to inform the content of the manual.

Additionally, an in-depth analysis of the main theories and models related to Emotional Intelligence was achieved, including the Salovey and Mayer (1997) skill model as a central axis. These theoretical frameworks were incorporated into the manual to provide solid conceptual support and back the practical applicability of the suggested techniques to address mood disorders.

It is of utmost importance to highlight that a meticulous analysis of interventions based on Emotional Intelligence was also carried out, examining both individual therapies and group programs. This comparative evaluation provided critical information for crafting the manual and validating the utility of EI in clinical contexts. All this contributes to making the 10-step program an effective tool for patients and mental health professionals.

Finally, this work reached its totality by reviewing and validating, through the results of previous research, the positive impact of Emotional Intelligence-based interventions on quality of life and depressive symptoms related to stress, anxiety, and depression. Furthermore, the efficacy and applicability of such interventions in the treatment of these conditions were confirmed. Despite the achievements, some limitations in the study were identified, and a set of recommendations was formulated to overcome these challenges in future research.

Limitations

While "Emotional Intelligence and Behavioral Therapies: A 10-Step Guide to Overcoming Stress, Anxiety, and Depression" represents a significant contribution to the growing body of literature linking Emotional Intelligence with mental health, it is crucial to address certain methodological and conceptual limitations that could affect both the internal and external validity of the presented results.

First, it is important to note that the efficacy of the study still requires more solid empirical validation. Despite being based on a rigorous bibliographic review, the absence of Controlled Clinical Trials diminishes the strength of the evidence supporting its applicability and efficacy in clinical settings. This aspect, in turn, raises questions about its validity in specialized contexts.

Additionally, although the bibliographic review is extensive, it is essential to consider that its scope could be biased by different factors. These include selection biases when including or excluding specific studies and publication biases that could influence the evaluation of the efficacy of interventions based on Emotional Intelligence. The lack of demographic diversity in the samples of previous studies, along with the omission of a focus on comorbidities, may limit the generalization of the results.

Furthermore, although the book examines a variety of theories, models, and approaches in the field of Emotional Intelligence, it does not exhaustively address how these elements could be influenced by contextual and cultural factors, the diversity of affective states, or the scarcity of specialized professionals to implement the program effectively. This heterogeneity and lack of specific training represent limitations in the generalizability of the interventions, which urges the need for contextually adapted versions for different populations and environments.

Finally, the study may have unintentionally omitted fundamental works or emerging research that provides new insights or questions to existing theories, introducing even more biases. It is imperative to note that the manual is primarily based on a bibliographic review and, therefore, does not provide primary empirical data that could offer more conclusive evidence in support or refutation of the theories and models examined. This lack could limit its impact on evidence-based clinical practice.

Future Investigations

To achieve the continuous optimization of "Emotional Intelligence and Behavioral Therapies: A 10-Step Guide to Overcoming Stress, Anxiety, and Depression", it is necessary to explore various highly specialized research paths that could effectively mitigate the limitations detected during its creation. Firstly, it is crucial for future studies to implement Randomized Clinical Trials to corroborate the efficacy of the educational resource in different populations. Such RCTs should include appropriate control groups and be subject to reviews following the PRISMA (Preferred Reporting Items for Systematic Reviews and Meta-Analyses) method, which will help minimize potential biases inherent in the previous bibliographic review.

It is equally vital to establish Longitudinal Studies that assess the sustainability of the resource's impacts on mental health indicators. These studies could incorporate multiple measurement points over time and use validated scales, such as the PHQ-9 or the GAD-7, for tracking depressive or anxious symptoms.

An additional methodological expansion could involve the application of Multivariate Analysis of Covariates to examine how different factors (such as social support, socioeconomic status, or comorbidities) interact and affect the outcomes of "Emotional Intelligence and Behavioral Therapies: A 10-Step Guide to Overcoming Stress, Anxiety, and Depression". In this context, statistical models like the Generalized Linear Mixed Model or Multivariate Analysis of Variance (MANOVA) could be employed for a more comprehensive evaluation of the resource's efficacy.

Incorporating techniques such as Multivariate Regression Analysis would add an additional dimension to data treatment and facilitate the identification of key variables that influence therapeutic outcomes. Likewise, the confluence of demographic, clinical, and psychometric data in predictive models could shed light on individual responses to interventions, favoring a more personalized therapeutic approach.

Finally, the inclusion of Predictive Models based on Machine Learning or Principal Component Analysis to discern specific patient profiles that would benefit most notably from the interventions presented in "Emotional Intelligence and Behavioral Therapies: A 10-Step Guide to Overcoming Stress, Anxiety, and Depression" is suggested. These advanced methodologies would allow for a more finely tuned customization of interventions, attending to demographic, psychometric, and clinical variables.

In summary, these highly specialized research approaches will not only address the shortcomings of "Emotional Intelligence and Behavioral Therapies: A 10-Step Guide to Overcoming Stress, Anxiety, and Depression" but will also significantly contribute to its refinement and evolution, enhancing its efficacy and applicability in the field of mental health and Emotional Intelligence.

Appendices

Emotional Intelligence and Behavioral Therapies

A 10-Step Guide to Overcoming
Stress, Anxiety, and Depression

J.R. Hernández

Step One

Basic and Complex Emotions

Introduction to the Topic

This program begins with a journey towards understanding emotions, distinguishing between basic emotions, essential for our survival, and complex emotions, which reflect our social and personal complexity. Emotions are defined as psychophysiological responses to internal or external stimuli, crucial for both survival and social interaction. Basic emotions, universal and innate, include joy, sadness, anger, fear, surprise, and disgust, all with specific adaptive functions. Complex emotions, such as shame, guilt, pride, and envy, arise from the interaction of basic emotions and are influenced by cultural context and personal experiences, reflecting the complexity of our interactions and social norms.

While basic emotions are automatic and rapid responses essential for environmental adaptation, complex emotions involve a detailed cognitive process, linking to our identity and cultural values. Emotional Intelligence, which involves the recognition, understanding, and management of our emotions and those of others, is vital for social adaptation, well-being, and managing emotional challenges. The study of basic and complex emotions is fundamental for personal and emotional development, and for promoting healthy interpersonal relationships, being especially relevant in the treatment of mood disorders.

Research Evidence

The identification and understanding of basic and complex emotions are crucial for mental health and emotional well-being. Research indicates that greater emotional knowledge is significantly related to the reduction of symptoms of mood disorders (Gross, 1998; Salovey, Bedell, Detweiler, & Mayer, 1999). Furthermore, understanding complex emotions improves the management of interpersonal and social situations, favoring optimal social adaptation and reducing the risk of mood disorders.

On the other hand, positive psychology highlights the role of emotional understanding in increasing well-being, resilience, and the development of strategies to cope with emotional challenges (Fredrickson, 2001). In summary, the ability to recognize and understand emotions, both basic and complex, is essential for fostering adaptive and effective emotional regulation, key in the prevention and management of mood disorders.

This 10-step program for managing mood disorders includes, as an essential recommendation, the use of a personal journal. This tool will allow you to document emotional experiences and daily reflections, facilitating the development of greater emotional awareness and regulation. This tool will be necessary for future exercises.

Instructions

Development of Emotional Awareness and Understanding

Objective

This exercise represents the first step towards a deep understanding of the emotional spectrum, crucial for our existence and influencing every aspect of life. It goes beyond recognizing basic and complex emotions, encouraging us to explore their origin, function, and impact on decision-making and our social interactions. Developing sharp emotional awareness enhances our social skills and assertive communication, laying the groundwork for effective emotional regulation.

Basic emotions, such as fear and joy, are instinctive responses essential for our survival and adaptation, significantly influencing our interactions. Understanding these emotions is fundamental for navigating life's challenges. On the other hand, complex emotions, formed from the interaction of our experiences and basic emotions, reflect our motivations and behavior patterns, enriching our understanding of ourselves and our relationships.

The purpose of this exercise is to establish a solid foundation for the development of Emotional Intelligence, promoting a greater understanding and appreciation of our emotions and those of others. The ability to identify, understand, and manage our own emotions and those of others is vital for informed decisions, conflict resolution, and strengthening meaningful relationships.

By delving into the knowledge of basic and complex emotions, we better prepare ourselves to face daily emotional challenges, from managing stress to improving relationships. Increasing our emotional awareness is key to achieving comprehensive and lasting well-being, living a fuller, more resilient, and happier life.

Step 1: Identification of Basic Emotions

The first step in developing a deep awareness and understanding of emotions is to identify the basic emotions: joy, sadness, fear, surprise, disgust, and anger. These emotions, fundamental to our human experience, are instinctive responses to environmental stimuli and are crucial for our survival and emotional well-being. Recognizing them allows us to understand their impact on our behavior and emotional state.

For a deeper analysis of these basic emotions, consulting Appendix 3 is suggested. This knowledge is vital for identifying how they manifest in different contexts and their possible influence on mood disorders. For example, understanding sadness is essential for relating it to depression if it occurs intensely and continuously.

Knowing the basic emotions is fundamental for recognizing their interaction in stress or conflict situations, with accurate identification being the first step towards effective management. This sets the stage for analyzing more complex emotions, improving our self-knowledge and quality of life.

Example:

Imagine you have been going through episodes of depressive mood that affect your perception and mood. This is the moment when you should write in your personal journal and take some time to reflect on a situation that has left you overwhelmed and discouraged. Upon reviewing your notes, you might realize that sadness is the predominant basic emotion.

By consulting Appendix 3, you understand that sadness often arises from losses or failures. This helps you recognize that your sadness may stem from the perception of missed opportunities or feeling stuck.

Here, accepting sadness as a natural reaction to your circumstances is a crucial step.

Delving into its function, sadness is revealed not only as an indicator of your depressive state but also as a signal of unmet needs and desires requiring attention. This emotion is essential and suggests that something valuable in your life is missing or at risk, prompting you to reflect and reevaluate your circumstances to align them with your needs, promoting introspection and self-knowledge.

Recognizing how a depressive mood can intensify sadness is vital for its proper management. Although this mood can exacerbate the feeling of sadness, understanding its origin and function facilitates a more objective and therapeutic approach. This involves considering sadness not as an obstacle but as an integral part of your emotional experience that deserves understanding and compassion.

Understanding the function of emotions allows us to see them not as adversaries but as allies that inform, guide, and assist in the complexity of life. Integrating this knowledge improves our emotional management and enables us to use emotions as tools for decision-making, promoting emotional and mental well-being.

Step 2: Differentiating Similar Emotions

The second step in developing deep emotional awareness is to learn to distinguish between similar emotions that have different nuances and origins. This discernment enhances our understanding of our emotional experiences and their impact on perceptions and behaviors.

This differentiation process focuses on emotions that are commonly confused or perceived as equivalent, such as anxiety and fear, or sadness and melancholy. Through introspection and analysis, we aim to dissect each emotion, identifying their unique traits, specific triggers, and their influence on our being.

For example, let's explore the distinctions between anxiety, characterized by worry about uncertain future events, and fear, which manifests as an immediate reaction to perceived threats. Similarly, we can discern between sadness, which stems from a concrete loss, and melancholy, which reflects a more generalized state of discontent.

Anxiety and fear, despite their similarities, differ in their causes and manifestations: anxiety arises from the distressing anticipation of the unknown, presenting with symptoms such as restlessness and muscle tension. Fear, on the other hand, is a specific emotional reaction to a direct threat, triggering fight-or-flight responses, as well as significant changes in heart rate and breathing.

Regarding sadness and melancholy, both emotions share a similar emotional tone, but their roots and depths vary. Sadness originates from specific events of loss or failure, accompanied by feelings of pain and regret. Melancholy, in contrast, describes a prolonged state of sadness without an immediate cause, which can lead to profound reflection and personal growth if well addressed.

As a learning technique, reflective writing exercises are recommended, detailing personal experiences where emotions intertwine. Describing the situation, its triggers, and consequences helps to clarify the nature of our emotions in different contexts. The journal suggested at the beginning of this program is a valuable resource for recording these reflections and the emotions that emerge.

This approach not only enriches our understanding of basic emotions but also equips us to manage our emotional responses more effectively. Accurately identifying what we feel allows us to address our emotional needs more promptly and communicate our feelings more clearly to others.

Example:

Imagine that, during a period of low mood, you decide to apply the suggested techniques to distinguish between similar emotions.

Faced with a sensation of restlessness and confusion, you reflect on whether what you're experiencing is anxiety or fear. Turn to your personal journal to unravel these emotions.

By describing the situation that caused discomfort, your thoughts, and sensations, you may realize that your unease is linked to worries about a future event, such as an important work meeting. This introspection leads you to conclude that what you are truly experiencing is anxiety, not fear, as it involves the anticipation of a potential event and not an immediate threat.

Similarly, by examining your feelings of discontent without an apparent cause and comparing them with moments of sadness linked to specific events, such as the loss of a loved one, you recognize that what you feel more closely resembles melancholy than sadness. This is because it is not directly related to a specific loss but reflects a more prolonged and generalized state of dissatisfaction.

This exercise of differentiation brings clarity and understanding to your emotions, facilitating a more constructive handling of them. By identifying the specific nature of your emotions, you open the door to greater self-knowledge and acquire practical tools for managing your emotional states more effectively in the future.

Step 3: Exploration of Complex Emotions

The third step in our journey towards expanded emotional awareness delves into the territory of complex emotions, those woven from the interaction of multiple basic emotions and intrinsically linked to our personal experiences, beliefs, and values. We will focus on emotions such as envy, pride, and gratitude, which encapsulate a more elaborate amalgam of feelings and thoughts compared to basic emotions.

For an in-depth analysis of this, it is advisable to refer to Appendix 3, which provides a more precise description of these complex emotions. This resource clarifies how emotions like envy can arise from comparisons with others as well as our own insecurities and desires. Additionally, it explains that pride encompasses not just a sense of personal satisfaction but also a quest for recognition and validation from others.

The primary purpose of this step is to invite reflection on specific moments when we have experienced complex emotions, analyzing how these formed from the interaction of basic emotions such as joy, sadness, or fear. For example, gratitude, commonly perceived as a positive emotion, can originate from joy but may also be the result of overcoming difficult moments, where sadness and fear play significant roles. Recognizing the interconnection among emotions is crucial.

This analysis invites us to deep introspection about our experiences, aiming not only to identify the complex emotion experienced but also to trace its origin to the underlying basic emotions and how these intertwine with our personal values and beliefs. Thus, we gain a richer understanding of how complex emotions influence our behavior and mood in different contexts.

Furthermore, this step encourages us to appreciate the function and importance of these emotions in the examined events. Understanding how envy relates to our desires and aspirations allows us to begin channeling it as a source of motivation rather than resentment. Similarly, by appreciating the role of pride in the context of our achievements, we find a balance between self-affirmation and humility.

This step not only enriches our understanding of complex emotions but also teaches us to see them as valuable signals of our internal needs and our interactions with the environment. By incorporating this knowledge into our day-to-day life, we begin to manage these emotions consciously and constructively, enriching and enhancing our emotional experience and quality of life.

Example:

Consider a moment when, during a work meeting, you observe a colleague receiving praise for their performance. This situation awakens feelings of envy within you. However, this emotion is not merely superficial, but the result of a complex interaction of basic emotions. Through reflection and guidance from Appendix 3, you understand that your envy might be a combination of sadness, for not having received the desired recognition, and anger, for believing that your efforts also deserved acknowledgment.

This introspective exercise reveals to you that envy, far from being a purely negative response, signals your unmet personal needs and expectations. It reflects your longing to be valued and recognized in your work environment. By understanding this, you find the opportunity to address your emotions more constructively, focusing on strengthening your self-esteem and seeking ways of self-validation beyond external recognition.

Exploring envy allows you to recognize that, despite its negative connotation, it can be a useful tool for self-discovery and personal growth. Identifying and analyzing these complex emotions facilitates an understanding of their origins and purposes, enabling you to use these emotions as guides to improve your emotional well-being and your interactions at work.

Finally, this exercise transcends the simple management of a challenging emotion, becoming an opportunity for deeper personal and professional development. It helps you identify and meet your needs in a healthier and more constructive manner, which is essential for your well-being and success in various aspects of your life.

Step 4: Identifying Emotions in Past Experiences

The fourth step in our journey towards greater emotional awareness invites us to explore the emotions experienced in past events, a fundamental stage to understand how these have influenced our current reactions and perceptions. Before delving into the complexity of the physiological signals of emotions, it is essential to reflect on the feelings experienced during significant moments of our past, especially those that left a deep emotional imprint.

To undertake this task, we propose an exercise in reflective writing. Choose one or several past events that you consider monumental, focusing on those that triggered strong and clearly identifiable emotions. Describe these moments in detail, paying special attention to the emotions that arose and their subsequent effects. Question your memory: What was the dominant emotion, such as sadness, joy, or anger? How did these emotions manifest at that time? What impact have they had in the long term on your life?

This exercise offers a unique opportunity to delve deeper into the understanding of our emotional responses, providing a framework to identify patterns and trends in our emotional behavior over time. By recognizing and accepting the emotions linked to our past experiences, we take an important step towards developing a richer understanding of how these experiences have shaped our present emotional responses, facilitating a more detailed introspection and an enrichment of self-knowledge.

The goal is to establish a conscious and clear connection between our past experiences and our current emotional reactions. This level of understanding is essential for building a solid emotional awareness, a key component for the effective management of our emotions in day-to-day life and in moments of elevated stress.

Example:

Consider revisiting a pivotal moment from the past, such as the loss of your first job, an event that marked a before and after both in your professional career and in your personal life. Writing about that moment, you evoke all the details: the place, the day's events, how you received the news, and your immediate reactions. You focus on discerning the emotions that arose: the disbelief and initial shock, followed by deep sadness for the loss of an opportunity and your routine. Upon further investigation, you identify feelings of betrayal and frustration, emotions you may not have fully recognized at the time.

Reflecting on this event, you perceive how these emotions guided your subsequent decisions. The sadness might have led to reflection and eventually acceptance, while the frustration perhaps drove you to seek new opportunities with renewed determination. This acknowledgment of emotions linked to past experiences provides you with a clear understanding of how these have shaped your current emotional response, highlighting the importance of recognizing and processing these emotions to manage them more effectively in the future.

This introspection process not only enriches your self-awareness and promotes deeper emotional growth but also improves your ability to handle similar emotions in future situations, strengthening your emotional well-being and resilience in the face of life's challenges.

Step 5: Recognizing Physiological Signals

The fifth step towards enriching our emotional awareness and understanding invites us to delve into recognizing the physiological signals that accompany our emotions. This aspect, often underestimated, plays a crucial role in the fabric of our emotional responses, even more so in the context of mood disorders, where the interaction between body and mind becomes fundamental.

Each emotion catalyzes a unique sequence of physiological reactions in our body. Fear, for example, can increase our heart rate, preparing the body to confront or flee the situation. Anger can raise body temperature and increase muscle tension, while sadness often leads to a decrease in energy and a feeling of lethargy.

To deeply explore this step, it is advisable to refer to Appendix 3, which offers a detailed description of these physiological responses. This resource is essential for understanding how emotions not only affect our mental state but also induce significant physical changes. The dynamics between emotions and physiological reactions is an area of interest for both psychology and neuroscience, highlighting the interconnection between our emotional experiences and our biology.

Reflect on a situation where you've experienced intense emotions, whether it was a moment of acute stress, an experience of uncontrollable joy, or an episode of deep sadness. Assess whether the physical sensations experienced during that situation align with what is presented in Appendix 3. In moments of intense anxiety, did you notice an increase in your breathing rate or a sensation of tension in your stomach? How did your body react to a moment of pure happiness?

This step encourages a greater sensitivity towards our emotions and contributes to a more holistic understanding of how they impact our well-being. By linking physical reactions with emotions, we begin to identify and manage our emotions more effectively, especially in situations that trigger strong emotional responses. This knowledge is invaluable for the proper management of mood disorders and for comprehensive health care, providing tools to recognize and appropriately address our body's signals, in favor of our emotional and physical well-being.

Example:

Imagine you recently went through an intense argument with a loved one. In moments of high tension like this, it's vital to observe your physiological reactions. You might have experienced an increase in heart rate, sweating palms, and accelerated breathing. These physical responses are as revealing as the emotions you're experiencing.

By consulting Appendix 3 to deepen your understanding, you recognize that these are typical reactions associated with anger and stress. This discovery allows you to understand that you're not only experiencing intense emotions at a psychological level, but your body is also responding to them physically. The interrelation between your emotional state and bodily responses becomes evident, tangible, and comprehensible.

Reflecting on this experience shows you how the conjunction of your emotional and physiological responses provides a complete perspective on your reactions to stress or conflict situations. The accelerated heart rate and rapid breathing are not mere physical coincidences; they are indicators that your body is activating defense mechanisms against a perceived threat, helping you understand what you feel.

This new understanding equips you with a valuable tool for managing stressful moments. By being more aware of these physiological signals, you can accurately identify the emotions at play and take proactive measures to calm your body, resorting to deep breathing techniques or relaxation exercises, thus facilitating more effective emotional regulation.

Understanding the physical manifestation of your emotions not only helps you better comprehend your emotional reactions but also enables you to manage them with greater skill. Integrating this knowledge into your daily life improves your ability to face stressful situations, mitigate the intensity of your emotional responses, and promote a healthier balance between your emotional and physical well-being.

Step 6: Analysis of the Context of Emotions

The sixth step towards greater emotional awareness and understanding leads us to examine in detail the context in which our emotions, both basic and complex, emerge. This in-depth analysis goes beyond the mere identification of our feelings, delving into the evaluation of the circumstances and the environment surrounding the manifestation of these emotions. The goal of this process is to achieve a complete understanding not only of what we feel but also of why we feel those emotions, emphasizing how specific situations and our surroundings influence our emotional reactions.

This approach is particularly relevant for those dealing with mood disorders, such as anxiety or depression, where emotions can feel overwhelming or disproportionate. By scrutinizing the circumstances surrounding the emergence of an emotion, we begin to discern whether our responses are proportional to the experienced situation. Thus, we might identify that, at times, an intense feeling of sadness can be influenced not only by a particular triggering event but also by other factors such as accumulated stress, seasonal changes, or lack of proper rest.

This analysis also allows us to understand how our daily interactions, significant life events, work pressures, and personal relationships impact our emotional state. We might discover that irritation towards a coworker is not due solely to their actions but also to our own stress or unmet work expectations.

Additionally, this step includes recognizing how cultural and social context shapes our emotions. Cultural norms and social expectations can influence how we experience and express our emotions. In some cultures, for example, openly expressing anger might be frowned upon, which could lead to suppressing this emotion or expressing it in less direct ways.

By analyzing the context of our emotions, we gain a deeper understanding of our emotional experiences, allowing us to see our emotions not as isolated reactions but as integrated responses to a mix of internal and external factors. This understanding is crucial for managing our emotions effectively and helps us to respond more appropriately and healthily to the situations we face daily.

Example:

Imagine a recent situation in your work environment that generated a high level of stress and pressure. At the end of the day, you found yourself immersed in a whirlwind of emotions, primarily dominated by anxiety and frustration. Facing these intense emotions, you reflect on whether they were proportional to the challenge encountered or if your perception of the facts exacerbated your feelings.

Contemplating these questions and analyzing the circumstances of that day carefully, you recognize that, although there were valid reasons to feel pressured, part of your anxiety stemmed from a tendency to negatively anticipate outcomes without justification. You identify that your self-assessment of the ability to meet expectations played a significant role in the intensity of your emotions.

This introspection allows you to see that, while it was natural to experience some concern given the situation, the magnitude of your anxiety possibly did not fully correspond with the reality of the events. You understand that your emotions were shaped, and even exacerbated, by your habitual thought patterns, leading to a disproportionate emotional reaction.

By becoming aware of this dynamic, you gain the ability to modify these thought patterns. This new knowledge provides you with tools to develop more effective strategies in managing your anxiety, marking a crucial step towards healthier emotional management.

Applying this analysis to future situations, you will be able to identify more quickly when your perceptions are unduly influencing your emotional response, allowing you to maintain a more balanced and objective perspective. This skill will not only help you manage stress and anxiety in the workplace better but also lay the foundation for constructively addressing challenges in other aspects of your life, improving your emotional well-being and overall quality of life.

Step 7: Real-Time Emotion Logging

The seventh step towards a deeper emotional understanding involves an exercise of introspection and continuous recording: documenting our emotions in real-time. After exploring our emotions in past experiences and understanding the context in which they arise, the next challenge is to actively capture our emotions as they emerge in the present.

To effectively tackle this stage, it is essential to always have the suggested journal at hand. The goal is to jot down our emotions at the very moment they manifest, detailing the specific circumstances that provoke them, including the context. This method allows us to record the emotional state in its most authentic expression, reducing memory biases and enabling us to observe how certain situations, people, or thoughts trigger varied emotional responses.

Imagine, for example, that during a week you decide to carry your journal or use an app on your mobile phone to document in real-time moments when you experience particularly intense or significant emotions. In each entry, describe the context in detail: Where were you? Who were you with? What were you doing? Was there any specific thought or event that triggered the emotion?

This exercise promotes greater awareness of your emotional patterns in the here and now. Not only will you manage to identify emotions as they occur, but you will also start to notice trends in your emotional responses, their patterns, and connections. You might discover, for example, that certain work environments specifically trigger stress, or that particular social interactions awaken joy or sadness.

Real-time emotion logging becomes an essential tool for self-knowledge and emotional self-management. By reviewing these records and analyzing them in moments of calm, you get the opportunity to reflect on your emotions objectively and evaluate how your reactions to various situations impact your overall well-being. Over time, this journal will transform into an invaluable resource on your emotional patterns, giving you the possibility to take proactive actions to improve your emotional management and, consequently, your quality of life.

Example:

Consider the commitment to use your personal journal to record your emotions as they arise in your daily life, also noting the circumstances that provoke them and the associated thoughts. You decide to carry a small notebook or use an app on your mobile phone for the notes.

Suppose that, during a work meeting on the third day of this exercise, you experience an intense wave of frustration. Right after the meeting, you take out your journal or open the app and write: "Frustration during the work meeting about project X". You detail the situation precisely: "I was discussing an important project and felt that my ideas were not valued by my colleagues". Additionally, you note that the frustration gave way to a feeling of helplessness and sadness.

When reviewing your journal at the end of the week, you identify a pattern: "similar situations at work tend to trigger the same frustration". You also recognize that, when you feel ignored or underestimated, your immediate reaction is frustration, followed by sadness.

This exercise brings clarity about your emotions and the circumstances that trigger them. Identifying these patterns allows you to understand how certain contexts affect your emotional state. This awareness enables you to more effectively address situations that generate adverse emotional responses, looking for ways to manage them appropriately or even to modify the circumstances to mitigate their impact.

The real-time emotion logging, along with the previous steps, makes it easier for you to live your emotions more consciously and reflectively, turning this practice into an essential habit for developing an expanded emotional awareness. This improves your ability to manage your emotions in day-to-day life and in the face of challenges, thereby enhancing your overall well-being.

Step 8: Exploring the Impact of Emotions on Behavior

The eighth step in enriching our emotional awareness invites us to delve into deep self-exploration to analyze how our emotions, both basic and complex, have a decisive influence on our behavior, decisions, and actions. Building upon the foundation of the previous steps, this step offers us the opportunity to deeply understand how our emotions intertwine with our behaviors, examining the direct relationship between what we feel and how these emotions have shaped or can shape the outcomes of various situations in our lives. This analysis is particularly crucial in the context of managing mood disorders.

To embark on this path of introspection and objective observation, let's consider past situations marked by emotions such as anger or frustration. Analyzing them, we can begin to understand how such emotions have led us to respond in certain ways to conflicts, whether by avoiding them or reacting impulsively. Similarly, by reflecting on moments of joy or gratitude, we discover how these positive emotions have reinforced our relationships or guided beneficial decisions.

This step also involves recognizing how certain emotions can trigger behaviors almost automatically, like anxiety that makes us avoid challenging situations or sadness that leads to social isolation. Identifying and understanding these behavioral patterns are fundamental for intervening and modifying those that are counterproductive or detrimental to our well-being.

Additionally, this stage allows us to explore how our emotions relate to our core beliefs and values, influencing our decisions. For example, if we highly value harmony in our relationships, we might opt to suppress the expression of anger or disagreement, even when it would be healthy to express such feelings. Understanding these dynamics helps us to identify opportunities for personal growth and to develop strategies to manage our emotions in a way that supports our long-term values and goals.

By comprehending the significant impact that our emotions have on our behavior and how they shape the outcomes of our experiences, we gain valuable insight that enables us to make more conscious decisions and develop healthier and more constructive responses to life's challenges.

Example:

Consider a recent episode of anxiety experienced before an important work presentation. This scenario offers an ideal context to reflect on how the emotions you experienced influenced your behavior during that critical moment. You identify two predominant emotions: nervousness, common in stressful situations, and insecurity, a complex emotion that encompasses deeper doubts and fears.

Analyzing the presentation, you observe that nervousness prompted you to avoid eye contact with the audience and to speak faster than usual, physical, and behavioral reactions that are typical manifestations of nervousness and are often interpreted as signs of an unconscious desire to flee the situation.

Delving deeper into your analysis, you recognize that insecurity significantly affected your preparation for the presentation. This complex emotion, possibly fueled by negative self-assessments and fears of failure, undermined your confidence, impacting both your preparation and your performance.

By becoming aware of how these emotions affected your behavior, you understand how they could have influenced others' perception of your competence and confidence, interpreting, for example, your lack of eye contact and accelerated speech as a sign of lack of preparation or confidence.

This introspection is vital for developing effective strategies to manage these emotions in the future, focusing on techniques to reduce anxiety and bolster self-confidence. This understanding not only improves your emotional well-being but also your ability to competently face stressful situations, being key to your professional success, personal growth, and overall emotional well-being.

Step 9: In-depth Analysis of Emotional Patterns

The ninth step on the path to greater emotional awareness leads us to conduct an in-depth analysis of our emotional patterns. This process involves identifying recurring trends in our emotional responses, understanding common triggers, and assessing the impact of various contexts on our emotions. This analysis allows us to reach a deeper and more nuanced understanding of our emotional life, crucial for those looking to effectively manage mood disorders or simply improve their emotional well-being.

To carry out this step effectively, it is vital to review the emotional records kept in earlier stages. Here, the suggested journal plays a key role for future events. With a thorough approach, look for patterns that indicate specific situations, people, or thoughts that consistently provoke certain emotions. You might discover, for example, that uncertainty frequently triggers anxiety, or that certain specific social environments evoke joy or sadness.

Once these patterns are identified, the challenge is to delve even deeper, exploring the underlying reasons behind these trends. Ask yourself why certain contexts evoke these emotions and what these patterns reveal about your underlying needs, desires, and fears. This level of introspection might reveal that criticism–even constructive–awakens feelings of inadequacy in you, which could indicate a deep need for validation or a fear of rejection.

This step also involves reflecting on how past experiences and personal beliefs shape these emotional patterns. Childhood experiences, family values, cultural and religious beliefs, as well as previous life experiences, play a significant role in how we emotionally react to various situations. Understanding these influences is essential to start unraveling how our emotions are intertwined with our identity and life experiences.

By analyzing your emotional patterns, you will gain valuable insights that allow you to take conscious and directed actions in the future. This deep understanding of your emotions and their triggers equips you with tools to manage your emotions in a healthier and more constructive way, promoting sustained emotional well-being.

Example:

After weeks of diligently recording your emotions and their triggering circumstances in the journal, you take a moment to analyze the observed patterns, seeking to understand how certain situations, people, or thoughts influence your emotional states.

With the records at hand, you begin a meticulous examination. You observe, for example, that situations of job uncertainty consistently trigger anxiety. Reflecting on these instances, you identify that your anxiety is not only related to the fear of the unknown but also to a deep concern for stability and security, reflecting personal values of protection and foresight.

This introspection exercise allows you to recognize how certain emotional patterns are influenced by your life experiences, values, and beliefs. Understanding these dynamics, you can focus on developing specific strategies to manage your emotions more effectively. For example, realizing that loneliness often triggers sadness, you make efforts to build and maintain meaningful relationships that counteract this feeling.

This analysis of your emotional patterns is a crucial tool for your personal and emotional development. Being aware of how certain situations affect your emotions allows you to take proactive measures to improve your emotional well-being, responding in a way that is more aligned with your values and personal goals, which is essential for an emotionally rich and satisfying life.

Step 10: Creating a Practical Action Plan

The final step in our journey towards an expanded emotional awareness is the formulation of a practical action plan, designed to effectively implement the knowledge gained about your emotions in everyday situations, with the goal of optimizing your emotional response to various scenarios.

This step is an invitation to proactively use your emotional awareness and social interaction skills to anticipate and prepare for different scenarios. If you have detected that certain situations or contexts trigger specific emotions, such as anxiety or frustration, it's time to plan strategies to manage these emotions more appropriately. These strategies can include relaxation techniques, cognitive restructuring to challenge negative thoughts, or mindfulness practice to focus on the present.

The purpose of this plan is to strengthen emotional awareness and regulation. By being more aware of your emotions and their influence on your thoughts and actions, you can begin to use them as constructive guides. For example, if anger or frustration emerges during a conversation, you can choose to take a pause to reflect on the underlying causes of these emotions and decide how to respond optimally, avoiding impulsive reactions.

This plan should also include strategies to promote positive emotions in your daily life, seeking activities that bring you joy, gratitude, or satisfaction. This is key to improving your overall well-being and balancing your emotional responses to challenges. The creation of this plan provides practical tools to apply emotional understanding in specific situations, preparing you to face emotional challenges with greater skill and confidence. Further details on this topic will be explored in future chapters.

Example:

Consider that the work environment represents a recurrent source of stress or anxiety for you. With a better understanding of your emotions, you decide to create an action plan to handle these situations more effectively and constructively, turning this plan into an essential tool for managing intense emotions and improving your performance and well-being at work.

For example, if important meetings are a constant trigger for anxiety, you can prepare specific strategies that include breathing and relaxation techniques before the meetings, which have been proven effective in reducing anxiety. Additionally, you can incorporate positive affirmations and visualization practices to reinforce your self-confidence and visualize yourself handling the meeting successfully. Seeking the support of a trusted colleague before the meeting can also be beneficial, allowing you to express your concerns and receive reassuring feedback in a safe and non-judgmental environment.

This action plan will not only specifically prepare you for the meeting but also promotes a continuous practice of self-awareness applicable in other areas of your life. By anticipating stressful situations and planning how to manage your emotions, you reduce automatic and reactive responses, allowing you to make more balanced and effective decisions. This practical approach to emotional regulation is crucial for managing mood disorders and significantly improving your quality of life.

Conclusion

Summary and Reflection

As we conclude this exercise, we reflect on the impact and relevance of emotions in our lives. This discovery process invites us to establish a more conscious and harmonious relationship with our emotions, both basic and complex.

We have analyzed how our emotions, influenced by the mind, body, and our experiences, are essential components of our being. Understanding the context of our emotional responses offers clarity on the interaction between perceptions, interactions, and environments.

Significant is the recognition of how emotions influence our behavior. This understanding allows us to respond in a conscious and reflective manner, improving our relationships and decision-making.

The creation of a practical action plan marks a significant change in us, preparing us to face day-to-day life with greater emotional awareness. This approach helps us to be guided by our emotions adaptively, promoting lasting emotional well-being.

This exercise goes beyond understanding emotions; it starts a journey towards a fuller and more balanced life. Applying this knowledge daily directs us towards an improvement in our Emotional Intelligence, positively impacting our relationships, decisions, and life management. We transform into more conscious, empathetic, and effective individuals, capable of facing life's challenges and joys with wisdom.

This path towards advanced emotional understanding is key to managing mood disorders and improving our quality of life. Constant practice and reflection are essential for developing solid Emotional Intelligence and sustainable emotional well-being.

Step Two

Appropriate and Inappropriate Negative Emotions

Introduction to the Topic

The exploration of negative emotions, distinguishing between their appropriate and inappropriate manifestations, is a fundamental axis in the emotional psychology. This distinction is of special importance in the field of treatment and relief of mood disorders. Emotions such as sadness, anger, and fear, often labeled as negative, are revalued for their adaptive and functional contribution in specific contexts. It is crucial to identify when these emotions are appropriate and when they are not, to facilitate effective therapeutic decision-making and promote optimal mental health.

Appropriate negative emotions act as signals that indicate problems or challenges in our environment, motivating corrective actions. Sadness can stimulate introspection and empathy; fear can serve as a protection mechanism against potential dangers. In contrast, inappropriate negative emotions, such as excessive anger or prolonged sadness without justified cause, can be harmful, leading to emotional and behavioral disorders.

Keltner and Gross (1999) argue that all emotions, including negative ones, perform adaptive functions from an evolutionary perspective. Anger can be beneficial in confronting injustices, and anxiety can prepare us for future stressful events. However, these emotions are considered inappropriate or maladaptive when they are excessive or interfere with daily functioning.

In clinical practice, it is crucial to distinguish between appropriate and inappropriate negative emotions. Understanding the origin and purpose of these emotions can offer valuable insights for the treatment of mood disorders. Cognitive-behavioral interventions, for example, train patients to identify and modify the thoughts that trigger inappropriate negative emotional responses, and to develop strategies to manage these emotions constructively.

Research Evidence

The functionality of emotions is a central principle in contemporary psychology, arguing that all emotions fulfill adaptive roles. Keltner and Gross (1999) highlight that negative emotions can have positive effects in appropriate contexts; for example, sadness can foster empathy and strengthen interpersonal bonds, while fear can act as an alert and protection mechanism.

Determining whether an emotion is appropriate or inappropriate in each context is fundamental for mental health. Gross (2002) emphasizes the importance of cognitive reappraisal, a strategy that modifies how we interpret situations and their emotional impact. This ability is essential for effectively adapting to stressful situations and minimizing exaggerated negative emotional responses.

Recent studies indicate that ineffective management of negative emotions can be a key factor in the development of mood disorders. Aldao, Nolen-Hoeksema, and Schweizer (2010) demonstrated that poor emotional regulation strategies, such as emotional suppression, can intensify conditions like depression and anxiety. Conversely, effective management of negative emotions can contribute to more positive therapeutic outcomes.

Behavior-based therapies have been shown to be highly effective in treating mood disorders, focusing on identifying and modifying inappropriate negative emotions. Beck (2011) points out that cognitive-behavioral therapy equips patients to challenge thought patterns that provoke maladaptive negative emotions, thus promoting healthier ways of facing challenges.

The ability to recognize and properly manage negative emotions, whether appropriate or inappropriate, plays a crucial role in the treatment of mood disorders. Identifying these emotions and applying effective regulation strategies can significantly improve mental health and well-being, directing interventions towards more effective approaches for those facing these challenges.

Instructions

Identification and Management of Negative Emotions

Objective

This module is designed to cultivate essential skills in the identification and discrimination of negative emotions, fundamental components in promoting robust mental health. It will focus on the ability to discern between negative emotions that are adaptive and functional under certain circumstances and those that are inappropriate or excessive. This knowledge is crucial for effective decision-making and for the development of healthy social interactions.

Accepting that negative emotions such as sadness, anger, or frustration can be indicative of important aspects of our environment and individual reactions, the challenge, as Lazarus (1991) suggests, lies in recognizing when these emotions exceed the bounds of reasonableness and begin to hinder our daily well-being.

During the development of this module, greater awareness of personal emotional patterns will be encouraged, and learning techniques to observe emotions from a more objective perspective will be promoted. Gross (1998) emphasizes that this awareness is key to assessing the relevance of our emotional responses and for their effective management.

Additionally, the impact of negative emotions on decision-making processes will be addressed. Findings by Lerner, Li, Valdesolo, and Kassam (2015) suggest that intense emotions can distort our judgment, leading us to make decisions that may not align with our values and long-term goals. Accurate identification and effective regulation of these emotions are fundamental to achieving more informed and balanced decisions.

This module also aspires to comprehensively strengthen mental health. By delving into the understanding and management of negative emotions, it seeks to promote expanded emotional well-being, greater resilience, and an enhanced ability to face adversities. Competent emotional management facilitates more effective communication and the development of more satisfying interpersonal relationships.

This exercise represents a valuable opportunity to enrich Emotional Intelligence and self-knowledge, increasing competence in navigating the complexity of human emotions. Upon completion, you will be better equipped to identify, understand, and regulate negative emotions in a way that positively contributes to decision-making and overall mental and emotional well-being.

Step 1: Identification of Negative Emotions

The first step on this journey toward strengthened mental health involves a detailed and reflective identification of the negative emotions experienced. This fundamental step demands sincere and deep introspection, utilizing memories or entries in personal journals to revisit past experiences. The goal is to isolate and name each negative emotion, ranging from the most basic to the most complex, such as sadness, anger, or frustration.

This process is essential for a deep understanding of how emotions influence behaviors and decisions. Accurately naming these emotions provides clarity about our reactions to different situations and allows us to identify those that predominate in our emotional spectrum. This is fundamental for the development of more refined and effective emotional management strategies.

The competence to recognize and label emotions, known as "emotional literacy" (Appendix 4) in the field of psychology, is a pillar of emotional intelligence and is closely linked to psychological well-being. Research suggests that individuals capable of discerning their emotions accurately enjoy better emotional regulation, as well as a superior ability to manage stress and emotional challenges.

Thus, this initial step is not only critical for developing greater emotional awareness but also for refining our coping skills. Upon completing this phase, we will be in a better position to recognize, understand, and manage negative emotions constructively, significantly contributing to our mental and emotional well-being.

Example:

Consider the case of a recent dispute with a close friend. Reflecting on this incident, it's possible to identify negative emotions such as anger and sadness, experienced both during and after the altercation. By reviewing your journal, where you've detailed the event, you can recognize these emotions clearly.

In this record, you specifically name these emotions and contemplate how they manifested: anger, perhaps, through a raised voice and hurried reactions; sadness, on the other hand, in a desire for isolation. This identification exercise facilitates understanding of how these emotions affected your behavior and interaction with your friend, underscoring the importance of emotional literacy in improving emotional management and deepening our understanding of emotional responses.

This approach illustrates the value of emotional literacy, a key concept in the theory of emotional intelligence developed by Salovey and Mayer (1990). The act of recognizing and labeling emotions facilitates their management and enriches our interpretation of emotional responses. Identifying recurrent emotional patterns, like the sequence of anger followed by sadness in conflicts, is a crucial step toward more sophisticated and effective emotional regulation, a central goal in clinical psychology and research in emotional regulation (Gross, 1998), with direct implications for psychological well-being and overall mental health.

Step 2: In-depth Analysis of the Emotional Context

The second step on our ladder towards effective emotional management focuses on the exhaustive analysis of the context and circumstances that gave rise to the previously identified negative emotions. This meticulous analysis is vital for determining the appropriateness of our emotional responses to specific situations, understanding the link between negative emotions, and triggering events, and evaluating the proportionality of our reactions to these events.

Research in the field of emotional psychology, such as that developed by Lazarus (1991), argues that the context in which emotions manifest is fundamental to discerning between adaptive and maladaptive functions. Documenting and reflecting on the circumstances in which these emotions emerge allows us to identify patterns in our emotional responses and their connection to significant experiences, underscoring the importance of understanding the specific triggers of our emotions to achieve refined and effective emotional regulation.

This step is crucial for promoting a broader emotional awareness and the development of more adaptive coping skills. By analyzing the context in which negative emotions arise, we can implement more precise and relevant emotional regulation strategies, which are essential for maintaining optimal mental health and emotional well-being.

Example:

Returning to the previous example of the argument with a friend, this moment focuses on detailing the context in which the event developed. In your journal, you document not only the argument itself but also the events that preceded it and the emotions experienced at those times. You highlight how exhaustion and stress, resulting from a demanding workday, could have exacerbated your reaction during the conflict.

This contextual analysis not only reveals that your anger was a complex response, influenced by previous stress and fatigue, but also allows understanding that the subsequent sadness partly arose from concern about the negative impact on an important relationship.

This reflection process aligns with Gross's (1998) theory of emotional regulation, emphasizing the importance of identifying triggering situations to manage emotions more effectively. Recognizing that the intensity of your anger might have been magnified by your previous emotional state opens the possibility of developing strategies aimed at better stress management and minimizing its negative influence on personal interactions.

This approach, resonant with Lazarus's (1991) theories about the role of our interpretation of events in our emotional responses, proposes that contextualizing emotions within a broader perspective allows us to understand their roots more deeply and promote more efficient and adaptive emotional management.

Step 3: Reflective Analysis of Past Emotional Experiences

This critical step of the therapeutic process highlights the importance of detailed introspection on past experiences marked by negative emotions. Such introspection allows for an in-depth exploration of how these emotions have manifested in various contexts and enables a meticulous evaluation of the proportionality and appropriateness of the emotional responses issued. This analysis is indispensable for understanding the impact that negative emotions have had on previous decisions and behaviors.

The process begins by selecting significant past events, especially those that triggered intense emotions. The intention is to revisit these moments from a critical and honest perspective, aiming to identify and understand the negative emotions experienced.

After identifying these emotions, the next step is to evaluate the appropriateness of the emotional reactions displayed. It analyzes whether the responses were proportional to the specific stimulus or situation and how they influenced subsequent decisions and actions. This examination may reveal patterns of emotional reaction that, although they seemed justifiable at the time, may not hold up under more rigorous analysis.

This step also involves reflection on how these negative emotions have affected interpersonal relationships and self-perception. In situations of anger, for example, it is crucial to examine whether this emotion prompted impulsive behaviors with adverse repercussions in personal or professional realms.

Reflecting on past experiences not only provides clarity on the impact of negative emotions but also promotes transformative learning. By more comprehensively understanding our previous emotional responses, we are in a better position to implement strategies directed towards more efficient emotional management in the future.

This analysis is essential for the development of deep emotional awareness and understanding. Upon completing this exercise, the expectation is to achieve the ability to identify patterns in emotional responses and apply this knowledge to manage emotions more assertively in upcoming situations, which is fundamental for strengthening emotional and mental health.

Example:

Consider the memory of a quarrel with a colleague that provoked an intense feeling of anger. Reflecting on this event involves understanding how this emotion manifested in the context and evaluating the proportionality of your emotional response.

Recalling the incident, you focus on your sensations and immediate reactions. Initially, anger may have felt like the natural response to what was perceived as an injustice. However, deeper introspection may reveal that this anger may have been influenced by a buildup of stress and other concerns unrelated to the specific incident.

This reflection facilitates the recognition that reactions like a raised voice and hurtful comments generated unnecessary tension, leading you to question whether the manifestation of anger was genuinely proportional to the event or was magnified by external circumstances.

Through this introspective exercise, a recurrent pattern is identified: prior stress tends to intensify anger responses. Recognizing this pattern opens the door to specific stress management strategies, such as meditation or yoga practice, to mitigate its impact on future emotional reactions.

This analysis offers renewed clarity on the incident and provides an expanded perspective on how negative emotions have shaped previous behaviors and decisions. Understanding emotional responses and recognizing triggers allows for more effective emotion management in the future, significantly contributing to emotional well-being and the improvement of interpersonal relationships.

Step 4: Analysis of Emotional Proportionality

This segment of the therapeutic process invites a meticulous evaluation of the proportionality of the previously identified negative emotions and their context. It seeks to adopt an objective stance to analyze if the intensity of our emotional response is in harmony with the triggering stimulus.

Evaluating proportionality requires a careful assessment of whether the magnitude of the emotion matches the significance of the provoking event. It is vital to discern whether emotions act as reliable indicators or if, on the contrary, they are being distorted by factors such as preexisting stress, irrational beliefs, or negative thought patterns.

This analysis is inspired by the principles of cognitive therapy, which argues that our emotional reactions are often the product of our thoughts and beliefs about a situation, rather than the situation itself (Beck, 1976). The assessment of proportionality is indispensable for identifying and questioning those distorted thoughts and beliefs that may be causing disproportionate emotional reactions.

This process is key to fostering a broader emotional understanding and the development of more sophisticated emotional regulation techniques. Studies on emotional regulation led by Gross (1998) highlight the importance of judging the relevance of our emotional responses to optimize stress management and promote robust mental health.

By concluding this phase, the ability to distinguish when emotions are proportional to the circumstances and when they may be influenced by mistaken interpretations is enhanced. A more complete understanding of the interaction between emotions and specific events is achieved, as well as effective strategies for their management, contributing to emotional and psychological well-being.

Example:

Consider a recent episode of disagreement with a friend that triggered intense emotions of anger and sadness. Using your journal to reflect on the incident and the emotions it elicited, you focus on the proportionality of your reaction. Upon reviewing the intensity of the anger experienced, you identify that additional elements such as accumulated stress or a night of insufficient rest could have amplified your emotional response.

Reflecting on the sadness that followed the event, you assess whether this was a proportional reaction. You recognize that, although your concern for the friendship was legitimate, the depth of your sadness may have been colored by negative thoughts and unjustified fears about the future of the relationship.

This exercise, aligned with Beck's (1976) cognitive therapy and Gross's (1998) theory of emotional regulation, demonstrates how our interpretations of events influence our emotions. By accepting that your emotions, though understandable, may have been exaggerated, you take a step towards adopting more balanced and adaptive emotional responses.

This reflection provides you with a greater understanding of the nature and proportionality of emotions in conflict contexts, better preparing you to identify and manage your emotions in a way that favors your decision-making and overall emotional and mental well-being.

Step 5: Decoding Trigger Factors

This step is crucial in our journey towards understanding and efficiently managing negative emotions, coming right after the evaluation of emotional proportionality. Its purpose is to precisely unravel the situations, thoughts, or interactions that habitually precipitate intense and sometimes disproportionate emotional responses.

The task involves detailed introspection about the circumstances that give rise to negative emotions, particularly those perceived as inappropriate or exaggerated. This deep analysis should cover both recent and past experiences, greatly benefiting from the use of a personal journal to document and examine these triggers systematically.

It is crucial to identify recurring patterns in the trigger factors, whether they are specific situations (such as interpersonal disputes or pressures in the work environment), thought modalities (for example, catastrophic visions or broad generalizations), or social interactions that consistently unleash negative emotions. This recognition is essential for the development of highly effective emotional regulation techniques.

Based on the principles of emotional psychology and cognitive therapy, studies by figures like Beck (1976) and Gross (1998) highlight the importance of identifying precipitating thoughts and situations. This enables the modification of thought and behavior patterns, significantly improving emotion management.

Upon completing this stage, an accurate identification of the specific triggers of excessive negative emotions is expected, paving the way for more balanced and adaptive emotional responses. This discernment is a pillar for the improvement of emotional intelligence and the enrichment of emotional well-being.

Example:

Imagine you've noticed a tendency to react with disproportionate anger to work stress. This step guides in detecting the specific factors that trigger this anger. It is suggested to keep a comprehensive record for a week of all work instances that incite anger, detailing not just the event itself but also the associated thoughts and emotions. You might discover that your anger intensifies at perceptions of being underestimated by colleagues or when facing pressing deadlines.

Analyzing your notes, a pattern emerges: certain interactions or types of tasks are constant triggers. Additionally, you note that thoughts predicting failure or criticism exacerbate your anger.

This introspective process offers an expanded understanding of your emotional triggers, revealing that anger is not only provoked by the situations per se but also by how you interpret and value these events. This knowledge, supported by Gross's (1998) theory of emotional regulation, emphasizes the importance of identifying and adjusting the situations and thoughts that generate intense emotional reactions.

By completing this step, you will have identified the factors that trigger your negative emotions and will be better equipped to develop emotional regulation strategies. This advancement enhances your ability to face future stressful situations with greater awareness and control, promoting emotional well-being and more assertive emotion management.

Step 6: Exploration of Emotional Functionality

This segment of the exercise invites a deep exploration of the purpose and meaning of negative emotions. Through a reflective analysis of the causes that provoke the appearance of certain emotions in specific contexts, we aim to unveil their intrinsic function. This process benefits from analytical tools like Appendix 5, which provides clarity on the essence and function of various emotions.

The purpose of this step is to recognize that, although negative emotions are often viewed in an adverse light, they play crucial roles in our emotional and psychological existence. Emotions such as sadness, anger, frustration, and fear are essential communication channels that alert us to our needs, establish our boundaries, and shape our interactions with the environment.

This approach is inspired by Lazarus's (1991) theory of emotional functionality, which proposes that all emotions possess an adaptive function, offering us valuable information about how we relate to our environment. For example, anger can indicate an experience of injustice and propel us to take corrective actions, while sadness can promote introspection and the cultivation of empathy.

Similarly, Keltner and Gross (1999) have highlighted that negative emotions play fundamental roles in our adaptation to complex contexts, alerting us to potential dangers and facilitating the adoption of appropriate responses. Understanding the function of these emotions opens the door to more informed emotional management and more effective adaptation to upcoming challenges.

Example:

Consider a recent disagreement with a loved one that unleashed intense emotions of anger and sadness. Using resources like Appendix 5, you reflect on how anger typically emerges in response to perceptions of injustice or violations of personal boundaries. This introspection leads you to question whether the anger was indicative of feeling unfairly treated or misunderstood during the altercation.

Analyzing sadness, you understand that this emotion often manifests in the face of the loss or deterioration of a significant connection. This process allows you to recognize that sadness expressed the value you place on your relationship and the fear of losing that important bond.

This recognition of emotional functionality, rooted in the theories of Lazarus (1991), illuminates how our emotions are adaptive responses to our cognitive evaluations of circumstances. Thus, anger and sadness are not merely negative reactions but emotional signals that reveal fundamental aspects of our values and personal relationships.

Following the insights of Keltner and Gross (1999), this step emphasizes the importance of understanding the functionality of emotions for their effective management. By identifying these emotions as reflections of underlying needs and concerns, they can be used as guides to enrich communication and strengthen relationships in future interactions.

This analysis offers a new perspective on the value and utility of negative emotions. Understanding that anger and sadness are reactions to specific perceptions and valuations within our relationships allows for a more comprehensive and effective management of these emotions in future situations, using these emotions as behavioral guidance tools rather than seeing them as barriers.

Step 7: Strengthening Emotional Regulation through Mindfulness

This crucial segment of the process focuses on strengthening our abilities to regulate negative emotions by adopting mindfulness and somatic awareness practices as fundamental pillars for efficient emotional management. The practice of mindfulness is based on cultivating a conscious and complete presence in the current moment, allowing oneself to observe thoughts, emotions, and physical sensations without emitting critical judgments. This approach is vital for unraveling the nature of negative emotions and their bodily expressions, providing the basis for appropriate and compassionate management. For a detailed guide on mindfulness techniques, consulting Appendix 6 is suggested.

It is highly recommended to integrate mindfulness exercises into the daily routine, including practices such as conscious breathing meditation, mindfulness, and body scanning. During conscious breathing meditation, attention is directed towards the breath flow, perceiving the air's entry and exit from the body and welcoming openly any thoughts or emotions that arise.

Somatic awareness, through body scanning, involves a detailed focus on different parts of the body and the present sensations, which facilitates identifying physical signals linked to negative emotions, such as muscle tension in situations of anxiety.

Research in the field of psychology and neuroscience confirms the benefits of mindfulness in reducing emotional reactivity and strengthening emotional regulation (Kabat-Zinn, 1994; Davidson et al., 2003). By cultivating greater awareness of emotional and physical experiences, a capacity to respond to emotions in a more balanced and reflective manner is developed.

This step is essential for expanding the ability to effectively manage disruptive negative emotions. Upon completion, not only is a richer understanding of emotions and their bodily manifestations acquired, but also a set of practical tools for constructively addressing them. Consistent practice of mindfulness and somatic awareness techniques is key to achieving more robust emotional regulation and a higher state of emotional well-being.

Example:

Consider experiencing significant levels of anxiety in response to certain work challenges. You decide to apply mindfulness and somatic awareness techniques to address this anxiety, maintaining a neutral observation of the emergence of these emotions and their corresponding physical sensations without judgment.

You start with conscious breathing practices each morning, focusing exclusively on your breath and allowing thoughts and emotions to flow freely. When faced with the first signs of anxiety, you perform a body scan to discern in which areas of the body anxiety is physically located, identifying possible tension points such as the chest or shoulders.

In moments of acute stress, you take a moment to reorient yourself towards mindfulness, observing your thoughts and emotions as transient phenomena, without seeking to alter them. This practice helps you perceive anxiety as a passing experience, improving its management.

Over time, you notice a reduction in the intensity and frequency of work-related anxiety. Mindfulness and somatic awareness offer you a new approach to objectively contemplate your emotions, reinforcing your ability to regulate them.

This approach, rooted in mindfulness practice, enhances your competence to effectively manage work-related anxiety. By completing this step, you have not only enriched your emotional understanding but also acquired concrete strategies to face emotional challenges constructively, significantly contributing to your emotional well-being.

Step 8: Integrating Negative Emotions into Decision-Making

In the field of personal development and emotional intelligence, the eighth step stands as a fundamental pillar, encouraging a deep reevaluation of negative emotions. Far from being mere obstacles, this innovative approach invites us to view them as crucial elements in conscious decision-making and in deepening interpersonal relationships. This paradigm shift not only represents an introspective challenge but also a valuable opportunity to uncover and harness the wealth of information these emotions reveal about our true desires, essential needs, and the personal boundaries we must respect. The essence of this transformation lies in recognizing and appreciating our negative emotions, using them as guides towards more authentic decisions aligned with our inner selves.

This process of emotional integration invites us on a journey of self-discovery and reflection, which not only enriches our understanding of ourselves but also enhances our ability to build and maintain deeper and more meaningful interpersonal relationships. The constructive management of our negative emotions equips us to make informed and thoughtful decisions, strengthening our bonds and promoting an environment of empathy and mutual understanding. This focus on negative emotions as vital resources for our personal growth and the improvement of our human connections marks a significant advancement in our emotional development.

This approach is particularly relevant for both mental health professionals and patients, providing a powerful tool for guiding towards a more authentic and fulfilling life. By adopting this perspective, therapists and patients embark on a path of emotional transformation, where each negative emotion becomes a learning opportunity and a step towards well-being. This step forward in therapeutic practice represents significant progress towards a more holistic and empathetic approach, where every aspect of the emotional experience is valued as an essential component of the human journey towards balance and fulfillment.

Example:

Visualize applying this approach in a work context, especially facing a challenging project that arouses feelings of frustration. Instead of letting this emotion trigger hasty or avoidant reactions, it is considered a signal to pause, reflect, and recalibrate the strategy for the project. The first step is to recognize and accept frustration without judgment, understanding that this emotional response signals aspects of the project that require reconsideration or improvement.

Next, a constructive evaluation of the underlying causes of frustration is undertaken. This introspection helps to discern the specific factors of the project that are generating dissatisfaction, whether due to unrealistic expectations, the lack of necessary resources, or insufficient communication with the team. By clarifying the roots of discontent, decisions can be made based on a deep understanding, such as strengthening communication with the team to ensure a shared vision and aligned objectives.

After implementing the relevant modifications, reflection on the effectiveness of these actions is undertaken. This critical review allows determining if the frustration has been mitigated and if substantial progress is observed in the project, making additional adjustments if necessary. This process turns a negative emotion into a driver for personal and professional development, resonating with the principles of emotional intelligence that emphasize the importance of understanding and channeling our emotions productively.

Incorporating this method into the daily routine promotes a state of emotional well-being and contributes to creating a more collaborative and satisfying work environment. This transformative approach demonstrates that, by being aware of the influence of our emotions on decisions and actions, we can use this knowledge to make more considered and effective choices, thereby enriching our personal and professional interactions.

Step 9: Refining Emotional Regulation Strategies

This key step in the process is dedicated to the continuous refinement of emotional regulation strategies, establishing a phase of introspection and vital recalibration for the effective integration of acquired skills and their application in future situations. The essence of this stage lies in conscious reflection and proactive adjustment of the emotional management techniques practiced.

It begins with a detailed review of the effectiveness of the strategies implemented so far. This analysis involves an honest and critical self-assessment, weighing moments of success and situations where expectations were not fully met. This self-observation is essential for mapping the journey taken and understanding the extent of your progress.

Subsequently, specific areas for improvement are identified, leveraging the lessons learned. This may include moments where the management of negative emotions was not optimal or situations in which emotional responses were not proportional or adaptive. Recognizing these aspects marks the beginning of effective evolution.

The next step involves reconfiguring existing strategies. Based on your analysis, modify, or enrich the practices used. If some mindfulness techniques showed limitations under certain pressures, consider introducing or reinforcing other methods, such as deep breathing techniques or guided visualization exercises.

The constant implementation and diligent practice of these recalibrated strategies are fundamental. The refinement of emotional regulation is an ongoing commitment that demands application and consistency. This process is inherently dynamic, adapting and evolving with each lived experience.

A permanent evaluation of your emotions and reactions in a variety of contexts facilitates the monitoring of progress and the introduction of adjustments when pertinent. Feedback from trusted professionals or peers can provide valuable insights for optimizing your emotional management capabilities.

Adaptability and openness to change are indispensable. The willingness to experiment with new strategies or modify existing ones is crucial for effective emotional management. This step represents a transition towards sustained practice and self-development in emotional regulation, strengthening your ability to navigate negative emotions effectively and contributing significantly to your long-term emotional and psychological well-being.

Example:

Imagine that, after diligently applying the techniques from this program, you focus on regulating your negative emotions, especially in work-related stress situations. After implementing various strategies to manage anxiety and frustration at work, it's time to reevaluate and fine-tune the learned techniques to maximize their effectiveness.

Reflect on recent experiences of stress or frustration at work. Think of a specific moment where, despite using deep breathing techniques, anxiety persisted longer than expected. Analyzing this situation, you identify that, although useful, these techniques need to be complemented with guided visualization or cognitive restructuring to address the negative thoughts intensifying your anxiety.

You recognize that certain work contexts require differentiated approaches. In meetings where you feel your value is not adequately recognized, self-affirmation techniques and reiteration of your achievements may be more beneficial to reinforce your confidence and reduce stress.

You decide to integrate positive visualization into your morning routine and commit to actively challenging negative thoughts with evidence of your successes and abilities, reinforcing your self-esteem and fostering self-compassion.

The conscious application of these adjusted strategies in moments of work tension and the evaluation of the results indicate a notable improvement. While the process of reevaluation and strategy adjustment is a continuous cycle requiring patience and dedication, you commit to an uninterrupted practice of self-exploration, adaptation, and improvement, which not only optimizes your management of negative emotions but also enriches your overall emotional and professional well-being.

Step 10: Developing an Action Plan for Emotional Management

Creating a comprehensive action plan is the final pillar on the path to effective emotional management, designed to prepare you for challenging situations and enhance the constructive use of negative emotions in decisions and relationships. This step equips you with a strategic framework that transforms adverse emotions into valuable tools for introspection, personal growth, and improving interpersonal dynamics. The plan could be built considering the following elements:

Preparation for Contingencies: Start by identifying potential scenarios that may trigger adverse emotional responses. Equipping yourself with proven emotional regulation techniques, such as mindfulness meditation, breathing exercises, and cognitive restructuring, allows you to face these moments with serenity and mental clarity, favoring balanced decisions.

Recognition of Emotional Functionality: Adopt a perspective that values negative emotions as essential sources of information about your needs and personal boundaries. This understanding transforms the perception of emotions from obstacles to useful indicators, facilitating a more informed and conscious response.

Emotional Integration into Decision Making: Learn to effectively incorporate your emotional intelligence into the decision-making process. This involves assessing how emotions influence your thoughts and behaviors and applying this knowledge to make more informed decisions, distinguishing between disproportionate emotional influences and rational analysis.

Personalization and Flexibility: Emotional experience is deeply personal, so it's crucial that the plan is adaptable to your circumstances. This means being open to experimenting with various strategies and adjusting based on the effectiveness of tactics in different contexts.

Example:

After a period of self-observation and learning about your emotional patterns, you decide to establish a practical action plan to address future emotional challenges. This blueprint acts as a compass, guiding you through unpredictable situations with a newfound ability to manage your emotions constructively.

For instance, you face a stressful situation at work that would typically trigger an anxiety response. Following your plan, you apply deep breathing techniques upon detecting the first signs of tension, allowing you to address the challenge with greater calm and clarity. Additionally, when experiencing frustration due to a complex project, you pause to reflect on the underlying message of this emotion, identifying needs for additional support or adjustments in your expectations.

This approach also extends to decision-making, where you prioritize a balance between emotions and rational analysis. Before making critical decisions, you carefully evaluate the influence of your current emotions, seeking a balance that considers both your intuition and logical reasoning.

Over time, and through continuous review and adaptation of your plan, you discover that you not only manage your emotions better in adverse situations but also leverage these experiences to enrich your decisions and strengthen your personal and professional relationships.

Commitment to regular review and adaptability of your plan ensures its long-term relevance and effectiveness. By maintaining an open attitude towards learning and change, and periodically evaluating the utility of your strategies, you strengthen your ability to navigate the complex world of emotions. This process not only improves your ability to regulate negative emotions but also amplifies your emotional well-being and your efficacy in decision-making and interpersonal relationships.

Conclusion

Summary and Reflection

This journey has been an exploration towards self-discovery and emotional mastery, combining Emotional Intelligence and Behavioral Therapies to confront emotional disorders. It aimed to develop skills to identify and regulate negative emotions, both appropriate and inappropriate, fostering a deeper emotional and psychological understanding.

The purpose was to highlight the crucial role of our emotions as guides for behavior and decisions, revealing their importance as sources of self-knowledge and understanding of our needs and desires.

It was expected to achieve a new appreciation of emotions for their purpose and functionality, transforming our relationship with them and seeing them as essential tools for personal wisdom and interaction with our surroundings.

Acquiring strategies for emotional regulation is central to this process. This includes learning to moderate emotional intensity to align it with our goals and desires, improving decision-making and interpersonal relationships, increasing emotional resilience, and the ability to enjoy life.

In summary, this journey emphasizes the commitment to a more conscious and authentic life, promoting growth towards a more integrated and compassionate version of ourselves. Continuous practice of these skills enriches our daily experience, turning emotions into key allies for a meaningful and satisfying life. This path prepares us to confidently address the challenges and pleasures of life, seeking sustained mental and emotional well-being.

Step Three

EI in Addressing and Mitigating
Mood Disorders

Introduction to the Topic

Emotional Intelligence encompasses various dimensions: emotional perception, the application of emotions to thinking and decision-making, the understanding of complex emotions, and the ability to regulate emotions effectively (Mayer & Salovey, 1997). Examining these dimensions reveals their significant impact on addressing mood disorders and strengthening mental health.

Emotional perception, as the first dimension, refers to the ability to identify and clearly express our emotions and those of others. This skill is fundamental, allowing for the recognition and proper management of emotional states, and facilitating preventive interventions against negative or challenging emotions.

In terms of the effective use of emotions, this ability allows directing emotions towards enriching thought and optimizing decision-making. In the therapy of mood disorders, such capacity turns emotions, even negative ones, into resources that enhance our cognition and facilitate conflict resolution.

Emotional understanding, on the other hand, involves recognizing the complexity of emotions and their transitions. Understanding how emotions intertwine and evolve is key to anticipating and preparing for mood changes, an essential skill in managing depression, anxiety, and other emotional disorders.

Finally, emotional regulation focuses on the ability to manage emotions in a way that maintains balance and responds adaptively to adverse situations. In the context of emotional disorders, adequate regulation can mitigate the intensity and duration of negative mood states, providing methods to regain control and promote well-being.

Emotional Intelligence is not just a set of emotional and social skills; it is a powerful therapeutic tool. Developing these dimensions can significantly improve individuals' ability to face and overcome mood disorders, achieving a more stable and enduring emotional stability.

Research Evidence

The growing fascination with Emotional Intelligence and its influence in the realm of mental health has spurred a series of research focused on its role within psychological well-being, especially regarding the mitigation of conditions such as stress, anxiety, and depression. Recent studies highlight the importance of EI, particularly emphasizing the pentagonal model proposed by Rafael Bisquerra for its examination (2009).

Brackett and his colleagues (2011) conducted a study that underscores the critical importance of EI in stress management and the prevention of emotional disorders. The findings suggest that individuals with high levels of EI possess a greater ability to handle stressful situations and a lower risk of suffering from mood disorders. This relationship between EI and emotional resilience highlights the preventive value of EI in mental health.

Similarly, Martins, Ramalho, and Morin (2010) performed a meta-analysis identifying EI as a notable predictor of psychological well-being. They found a positive correlation between high levels of EI and a reduction in the prevalence of depression and anxiety symptoms. This comprehensive review of studies asserts that the ability to understand, manage, and effectively express emotions is essential for fostering robust mental health.

Within the therapeutic context, EI-based interventions, particularly those aligned with Bisquerra's pentagonal model, have proven effective in treating emotional disorders. Zeidner, Matthews, and Roberts (2012) argue that such interventions can enhance individuals' ability to manage complex emotions, which, in turn, can contribute to the reduction of anxiety and depression symptoms. Incorporating strategies to improve EI in therapy, such as self-reflection and personal knowledge, is key to the effective management of negative emotional states and mood disorders.

It is imperative to recognize the value of developing EI, especially through this pentagonal model, not only for emotional self-regulation but also as an essential component for achieving optimal mental health. The application of techniques and strategies that strengthen EI in the therapeutic realm offers a holistic approach to treating emotional disorders. Moreover, these practices can significantly improve overall well-being, providing effective tools for managing an emotionally complex and challenging environment.

Instructions

Program for the Cultivation
of Emotional Intelligence

Objective

The purpose of this proposal is to promote the development and strengthening of Emotional Intelligence through four fundamental aspects: recognition, strategic use, deep understanding, and proactive regulation of emotions. A personal diary will act as a key tool, reflecting emotional evolution and facilitating reflection and advancement in emotional skills.

The program proposes a journey of self-discovery through which you will learn to identify and understand your emotions (Step 1), articulating them clearly and building a solid foundation of self-knowledge (Step 2). This process will reveal how your emotions influence decisions and behaviors, highlighting their importance in life experiences (Step 3).

You will progress to differentiate primary from secondary emotions (Step 4), enriching your emotional understanding and improving empathy and social interactions (Step 5). You will also learn to transform negative emotions into drivers of personal and professional growth (Step 6), and to apply emotional regulation techniques, such as mindful breathing and cognitive reappraisal (Step 7), integrating them into your daily life for overall well-being (Step 8).

The program emphasizes the importance of developing emotional independence (Step 9), preparing you to manage your emotions autonomously. It will conclude with the creation of an Emotional Well-being Plan, defining objectives and strategies for the continuous development of your emotional intelligence (Step 10).

By the end, you will have achieved an advanced understanding of your emotions and their influence on your thoughts, actions, and relationships, constituting a significant investment in your personal and professional development. This approach improves your ability to face emotional challenges and reinforces your mental and general well-being.

Step 1: Detection of Emotional Patterns

You will begin your journey with a stage of introspection and emotional logging. The recommended diary will become a kind of confidant, a safe space where you will write down the emotions that accompany you throughout the day. This practice will allow you not only to recognize the range of emotions you experience, whether appropriate or less so, but also to discover recurrent patterns in your emotional responses.

To carry out this exercise most effectively, it is recommended to use a timer and dedicate a few moments every hour to this reflection. Every 60 minutes, take a conscious break of 5 to 10 minutes to meditate on the emotions experienced during that time span. It is essential to pay special attention to the thoughts and physical sensations that accompany these emotions, as the somatic component can reveal hidden dimensions of your emotional experience.

When recording your emotions, accuracy will be your best ally. Transcend vague descriptions like "happy" or "melancholic," and strive to capture the essence of your emotions. Investigate whether what you feel is joyful serenity or exuberant jubilation, reflective sadness, or profound desolation. This meticulousness will provide you with a richer and more nuanced understanding of your emotional universe.

This process of self-inquiry and emotional logging is based on solid scientific principles. According to Gross (2002), the precise discernment of our emotions is the initial pillar toward effective emotional management. Concurrently, studies like those of Barrett

(2006) underscore the importance of advanced "emotional literacy" in promoting robust mental health and preventing mood disorders.

The purpose of this first phase is to cultivate a detailed emotional diary that allows you to unravel patterns and trends in your emotional experience. This self-knowledge is indispensable for evolving towards more refined emotional regulation and enriching your emotional intelligence.

Example:

Imagine you decide to undertake an analysis of your emotional patterns during a typical workweek, motivated by recurrent episodes of challenging emotions. For this, you set alarms to remind you to take 5-to-10-minute breaks every hour, to meditate on your emotions and physical sensations, capturing these reflections in your emotional diary.

Throughout this introspection, you discover that mornings tend to be a period of positive emotions, probably thanks to the optimism and vigor that usually accompany the dawn of a new day. However, you notice that as you progress through the day and find yourself immersed in stressful situations, like tense meetings or high workloads, your mood begins to decline. In your diary, you record an evolution towards more negative emotions such as anxiety, frustration, or melancholy, particularly accentuated during the afternoon hours.

This rigorous tracking reveals a revealing pattern: a tendency to experience negative emotions with greater intensity and frequency in the afternoons. This discovery, previously unnoticed, now emerges as a key element in understanding and managing your emotional world.

Armed with this information, you can start to look for specific interventions, such as including activities that promote relaxation or pleasure during the afternoons in your routine. This could be outdoor walks, meditation sessions, or dedication to a hobby. Additionally, you propose to use emotional regulation techniques at these times, such as the practice of mindful breathing, with the goal of proactively addressing the discouragement that tends to intensify in the afternoons.

This process of self-examination and emotional logging provides a robust foundation for decision-making and the development of strategies for emotional management. By identifying and understanding your emotional patterns, you not only expand your self-knowledge but also acquire practical resources to improve your emotional and psychological well-being.

Step 2: Precise Identification of Emotions

This step demands your full attention and honesty to accurately name each emotion experienced, moving away from vague or generalized descriptions. This activity requires additional effort, as precision in this recognition is key for a detailed understanding of your emotional landscape.

This process invites you to identify not only the emotion itself but also its specific triggers. This means discerning not just the moment when the emotion emerges but also the elements that contribute to its appearance. For example, with anxiety, it is crucial to determine if it originated in a specific work context or from the anticipation of a future event. The detail in this exercise is vital, as a clear understanding is fundamental for effective emotional management and the reduction of emotional disorders.

The task of specifying emotions goes beyond simply labeling feelings; it is a journey towards self-knowledge. The ability to accurately identify our emotions is crucial for their regulation and for healthy interaction with our environment. Gross (1998) has evidenced in his study that the capacity to recognize and name our emotions plays an essential role in our mental health.

By completing this stage, you will have achieved greater emotional awareness, indispensable for the proper management of emotions. This skill will not only allow you to understand your own emotional reactions more clearly but will also improve your ability to effectively communicate your emotions to others, thus strengthening your emotional well-being and the quality of your relationships.

Example:

Imagine that, after a particularly challenging week, you decide to review your emotional diary. You notice that you have frequently used indeterminate terms like "I feel bad" to describe your negative emotions. Delving into this pattern, you commit to being more specific when naming your emotions, using tools like Appendix 4 to guide you.

In one entry, you initially wrote: "I feel bad after the meeting with my boss". Reevaluating this moment, you recognize that this phrase does not accurately reflect your emotional experience. Refining your entry with the help of Appendix 4, you specify: "I feel frustrated and undervalued after my boss dismissed my suggestions during this afternoon's meeting, which made me feel professionally underestimated".

On another day, marked by stress, you had simplified: "I felt bad all day". Revisiting those hours with more attention, you understand that such a generic description does not do justice to the complexity of your emotions. You refine your note: "In the morning, I experienced anxiety before an important presentation. After this, I felt a relief tinged with exhaustion. And in the afternoon, sadness overwhelmed me as I reflected on a friend in difficulty".

This exercise of precisely describing your emotions not only helps you recognize the diversity of your moods but also understand their connection with specific situations in your life. Moving forward in this process, you develop a refined ability to discern and name your emotions, a crucial step to strengthen your emotional awareness and effectively apply emotional regulation techniques. This step is fundamental to completing the exercises that follow in this program.

Step 3: Reflection on Emotional Responses

In this step towards mastering your emotional intelligence, you'll dive into deep reflection on how your emotions affect your decisions and behaviors. This introspection exercise is an opportunity to fine-tune your response mechanisms for future challenges. For this purpose, you'll examine key decisions made recently, whether in the work, personal, or relational spheres. Use your emotional diary as a personal laboratory to break down and analyze these emotional experiences.

Identify the emotions that marked those decisive moments. Remember to be detailed when describing each sensation, whether it's anxiety, happiness, frustration, or confidence. The thoroughness in this step is essential to appreciate the true impact of your emotions on the decisions made.

Evaluate the influence of these emotions on your choices. Ask yourself if they triggered impulsive reactions or, on the contrary, facilitated a calm and deep analysis of the available options. Acknowledge if any emotion played a dominant role and how it affected the outcome.

Then, reflect on the effectiveness of your emotional responses. Consider if the role of your emotions in decision-making was the most appropriate and think about alternatives that could have generated more positive outcomes.

From this analysis, determine how you can fine-tune your emotional responses to face similar situations in the future. Design strategies to manage anxiety more effectively, increase your assertiveness, or prevent frustration from clouding your judgment.

By completing this stage, you will have gained a deeper understanding of how your emotions influence your decisions and behaviors. This self-evaluation facilitates the recognition of emotional patterns susceptible to adjustment and equips you with tools to plan future improvements, strengthening your ability to regulate them efficiently, a crucial aspect for your well-being and success in different aspects of life.

Example:

Consider a recent episode at your job where you had to make a quick decision about an innovative project. During this process, you were influenced by a mix of emotions: anxiety due to the limited time and excitement for the possibility of innovation. Reviewing this experience, you recognize that anxiety hastened your decision without exploring all possible options.

Reflecting on how to act better in future circumstances, you project strategies such as allowing yourself a moment to take deep breaths and calm the anxiety, which could help you consider the alternatives with greater clarity or use it to generate an action plan. Consulting a trusted colleague before deciding could also enrich your perspective.

This self-evaluation exercise proves invaluable for understanding that, although emotions play a determining role in decision-making, it is possible to regulate and leverage them to your benefit. Adjusting your emotional responses not only optimizes your decision-making capacity under pressure but also enhances your emotional intelligence for upcoming challenges.

Step 4: Differentiation and Understanding of Emotions

This crucial moment in the development of your emotional intelligence invites you to classify your emotions into two fundamental categories: primary and secondary. This exercise not only enriches your understanding of how you emotionally interact with your environment but also sharpens your ability to navigate and shape your emotional responses more effectively.

Primary emotions, such as joy, sadness, fear, and anger, are direct and universal responses to external stimuli. These basic and spontaneous emotions are the pillars of your emotional experience. On the other hand, secondary emotions emerge from the combination of primary emotions and are shaped by factors such as cultural context, personal experiences, and your self-concept. Emotions like shame and guilt, which are nourished by fears, sadness, and other basic feelings, exemplify the complexity of secondary emotions.

By undertaking the task of categorizing your emotions, you delve into exploring how different situations and experiences trigger a wide range of emotional reactions. Understanding, for example, that anxiety is a secondary emotion, forged by fear and expectation, provides clarity on its origins and its influence on your behavior.

Annex 3 acts as a compass in this analysis process, outlining the distinctive characteristics of primary and secondary emotions, and is an invaluable tool for deepening your understanding of your emotions and how they manifest in various contexts.

Classifying your emotions not only promotes greater self-awareness but is also fundamental for effectively managing emotional disorders. Understanding the essence of your emotions equips you with more precise strategies for their regulation, especially in moments of tension or uncertainty, which is essential for your emotional and psychological health.

Example:

Imagine a workday marked by a feeling of helplessness after meetings where your contributions seem to go unnoticed. By breaking down this emotion, you discover that it originates from primary emotions like sadness, stemming from not feeling valued, and anxiety, due to the uncertainty of your impact on the team's decisions.

This distinction allows you to understand helplessness as a secondary emotion that reflects significant aspects of your work environment and your self-perception. Sadness might indicate a need to seek ways to gain recognition for your work or to improve how you communicate your ideas. Anxiety might reveal the importance of preparing more diligently for future meetings or fostering collaboration among your colleagues.

By categorizing and analyzing these emotions, you gain a clearer view of their role in your daily life. This step is crucial for the development of your emotional intelligence, as it empowers you to take conscious actions aimed at strengthening your emotional well-being and your ability to effectively address complex situations.

Step 5: Development of Emotional Understanding and Empathy

In this phase of emotional intelligence development, empathy and emotional understanding play a starring role, enhancing your ability to interpret and react to the emotions of those around you. In both work and personal environments, it's crucial to be perceptive to the emotional signals' others communicate, beyond their words. Pay special attention to details such as tone of voice, facial expressions, and body language, as they offer valuable clues about their internal emotional states.

Consider how the detected emotions shape the dynamics of your interactions and communications. If, for example, you identify concern or tension in a colleague, reflect on how this affects their behavior and work relationships. Consider how your own emotional response to these observations could alter the course of the interaction, and how empathy can be the bridge to more effective understanding and communication.

This step also demands the ability to put yourself in others' shoes, striving to understand their emotions from their perspective. This exercise not only strengthens empathy but also deepens your understanding of the complexity of emotions.

Cultivating this competency increases your sensitivity towards others and can enrich your relationships, making them deeper and more satisfying. Empathy and emotional understanding are fundamental for successful social interaction and play a crucial role in your emotional well-being, both personally and professionally.

Example:

Imagine a team meeting at work, a perfect scenario to practice observing and understanding your colleagues' emotions. You notice a colleague, who is normally active and participative, but let's say that on this occasion, they seem distant and quiet.

Instead of overlooking this signal, try to inquire sensitively. After the meeting, you approach this colleague to ask how they are, showing sincere interest in their well-being. Imagine your colleague is going through personal difficulties that make it hard for them to concentrate at work. This conversation provides a broader perspective on their behavior and its effects on the team dynamics.

This exchange teaches you how personal emotions can significantly influence the work environment. Understanding your colleague's situation, you can choose to offer support and understanding instead of responding with judgment or frustration.

This episode highlights the importance of being receptive to others' emotions and acting with compassion. By doing so, you not only improve your relationship with your colleague but also contribute to creating a more empathetic and supportive work climate. You understand that paying attention and responding with empathy to others' emotions can significantly strengthen communication and relationships. By fostering these social skills, you can become a more insightful observer and a more effective communicator, benefiting your interactions in a variety of contexts.

Step 6: Transformation of Negative Emotions into Drivers of Growth

In this step, we address the capability to refocus negative emotions, not as obstacles but as catalysts for personal and professional growth. Recognizing these emotions as inherent elements of the human condition rather than deficiencies facilitates their conversion into valuable tools for advancement and improvement.

Consider a sense of frustration due to a lack of recognition in the workplace. This feeling can be the starting point for profound self-evaluation and the redesign of your professional trajectory, indicating the opportunity to explore new horizons or to acquire additional skills.

It is crucial to reflect on the impact of these emotions on your decisions and behaviors. Does frustration paralyze you, or does it propel you to act? Channeling this negative emotional energy towards motivation for change, through the definition of clear and achievable goals, is key to overcoming these challenges.

Understanding the underlying meaning of negative emotions is essential. Often, they reflect unmet needs or fundamental personal values, whose attention can increase both emotional well-being and professional performance. Adopting a reflective and self-compassionate approach, which welcomes emotions without judgment and considers personal growth as the fruit of faced challenges, guides toward self-awareness and development.

This approach urges viewing negative emotions not as impediments but as opportunities for learning and evolution, turning adversities into valuable experiences and fostering emotional and intellectual progress.

Example:

In response to a feeling of frustration due to unrecognized work, transform this emotion into a stimulus for positive action. First, record in your diary the intention to turn this negative emotion into a driving force for your growth. To do this, you must focus your attention on defining personal goals that reflect your progress and achievements, such as expanding your knowledge in your area of specialty, participating in additional training courses, or taking on projects that represent a greater challenge.

This initiative marks a path toward self-development, independent of external recognition. By pursuing these objectives, you not only expand your skills but also strengthen your self-esteem and confidence, crucial elements for your emotional well-being. Additionally, by documenting this journey, you can monitor your progress and observe how these changes positively influence your mood and self-perception. This continuous evaluation allows you to fine-tune your strategies and better align them with your fundamental goals and values. This approach illustrates the power of turning frustration into a window towards self-drive, taking an active role in improving your emotional and professional well-being, rather than considering it a negative emotion.

Step 7: Strengthening Emotional Regulation

This step focuses on refining effective techniques for emotional regulation, indispensable skills for achieving emotional stability and promoting overall well-being. Emotional regulation encompasses the ability to manage and direct our emotions constructively.

Begin this process by integrating conscious breathing practices into your daily routine. This simple yet transformative method facilitates mental calmness and attenuates negative emotions. Dedicate a few minutes each day to deep and slow breathing, focusing entirely on your breath. This exercise promotes concentration on the here and now, thus minimizing reactivity to disturbing emotions (Appendix 6).

Cognitive reappraisal, which involves reinterpreting situations that generate adverse emotions, is another valuable technique. When facing setbacks in the workplace, seek to redefine the scenario from a more constructive perspective. Question whether there is a more positive interpretation of the situation or specific actions you can take to improve the outlook.

Meditation, incorporated as a daily habit, is also a cornerstone in cultivating self-awareness and emotional management. Dedicating a few minutes each day to meditation can deepen your understanding and management of emotions. This exercise does not need to be prolonged; brief periods of practice are sufficient to refine your emotional regulation.

It is vital to understand that emotional regulation does not mean repressing our emotions but deeply comprehending and managing them in a way that they become beneficial. With constant practice, you will acquire advanced skills in emotional management, preparing you to face challenges with greater calmness and balance.

Example:

Facing a particularly intense day at work, an environment that causes you stress, you decide to apply the emotional regulation techniques you have been refining. Upon noticing emerging frustration, you briefly step away to practice conscious breathing. With closed eyes, you focus on your breath until you notice a reduction in tension with each inhalation and exhalation cycle.

Subsequently, you use cognitive reappraisal to reflect on the challenge, seeking other ways to interpret the situation. This change in perspective allows you to see obstacles as opportunities to demonstrate your competence and learning ability.

At the end of the day, you also dedicate time to meditate in a serene place, even at home, focusing on your breath for ten minutes. This moment of introspection allows you to observe your thoughts and emotions from a non-critical stance, facilitating the recognition of your emotional patterns.

Applying these strategies in real situations significantly improves your ability to control unfavorable emotions. Instead of being dominated by them, you have practical tools for their proper management, favoring more conscious decisions and maintaining emotional balance. These emotional regulation practices become an essential component of your approach to managing stress and enhancing your well-being.

Step 8: Applying Emotional Intelligence in Daily Life

This step invites you to deeply reflect on the effective implementation of the emotional competencies acquired in everyday life, aiming to enhance your emotional well-being through meaningful actions.

Identify key areas of your life–personal, work, and social–where emotions play a critical role, such as interactions with family members, conflict management at work, or maintaining healthy friendships. Evaluate how emotions influence these spheres and how you can apply your expanded emotional awareness and regulation techniques to optimize these dynamics.

In the personal realm, for example, explore ways to communicate your emotions more clearly with loved ones. For this, you might write down your emotions in your journal, assess them, and seek the best way to express them.

In the professional field, apply your emotional intelligence to effectively address work stress and challenges. Cognitive reappraisal is a recommended technique to transform your perception of professional challenges into opportunities for personal and professional growth. Remember to observe reality from different viewpoints and discard any that affect your tranquility. Not everything is black or white; life is full of nuances.

In the social domain, always promote an empathetic attitude and active listening, which not only improves your understanding of others but also deepens your emotional connections. If you promote empathy, even if sometimes it is not returned, you are more likely to cultivate healthy relationships; "do good without looking at whom" is a universal rule.

Set specific goals to integrate these emotional skills into your daily life, such as allocating moments of the day for emotional introspection or using emotional regulation techniques in stressful situations, as described in Appendix 6. The conscious incorporation of emotional intelligence skills into your daily life not only optimizes your emotional management but also contributes to superior well-being and quality of life. This stage is fundamental for living in a more integrated, conscious, and harmonious way with your emotions.

Example:

After exploring the previous steps, focus your effort on the daily application of these emotional competencies. This involves recognizing how your emotions impact your decisions and behaviors in various aspects of your life and formulating strategies to manage them productively.

In personal situations that typically generate frustration or anger, you now manage to identify these emotions from the outset. You decide to take a moment to breathe deeply and reflect on the origin of your frustration, which facilitates a calmer and more measured reaction that improves communication and avoids misunderstandings. It's always important to take your time.

In the workplace, facing challenging projects that would previously trigger anxiety, you apply cognitive reappraisal, perceiving the challenge as an opportunity for your development. This approach alleviates anxiety and enhances your efficiency and creativity. Obstacles are opportunities, and anxiety is the brain's way of saying, "we need to make a plan".

Socially, you dedicate yourself to practicing empathy and active listening, which allows you to better understand your friends in difficult situations and strengthen those bonds. When you are an empathetic person, you create a friendly environment with the people around you.

Set daily goals to maintain these practices, such as periods of emotional self-examination or mindfulness exercises. These consistent actions strengthen your conscious connection with your emotions and improve your quality of life. The conscious implementation of emotional intelligence enriches your well-being in all areas of life, demonstrating that the practice of emotional skills is key to achieving a balanced and satisfying existence.

Step 9: Strengthening Emotional Autonomy

In this key stage of emotional development, the focus is on cultivating emotional autonomy, a fundamental capacity to independently manage your emotions, reducing the influence of external factors. This process is crucial for fostering confidence in your own emotional abilities.

Begin this journey by evaluating past situations where your emotions were notably influenced by the environment or other people. Recognize those moments when your emotional state was more affected by external circumstances than by your true internal feelings. Reflect on these experiences, identifying how external influences may have directed your decisions or behaviors in ways that didn't reflect your authentic self.

Next, dedicate efforts to increase your emotional awareness. Take the necessary time to distinguish between your genuine emotions and those shaped by external influences. In new situations, ask yourself whether the feelings you're experiencing are truly yours or are being affected by the environment.

Develop strategies that allow you to remain true to your real emotions. You can resort to techniques such as deep breathing, meditation, or simply taking a moment to step back and clarify your emotions. These practices will be greatly helpful in maintaining calm and objectivity during periods of emotional turbulence.

Also, reinforce your self-confidence. Value your ability to effectively manage your emotions and affirm your feelings, regardless of external reactions. The use of positive affirmations can be a useful tool to solidify your emotional autonomy.

Finally, implement these skills in your daily life. In the face of emotional challenges, apply your emotional regulation techniques, staying true to your own emotions. With practice and consistency, your capacity for autonomous self-management of your emotions will be notably enhanced, benefiting your overall well-being and resilience in the face of life's challenges.

Example:

Imagine facing a challenging project at work, a situation that previously might have led you to absorb the team's stress and anxiety. Now, with a firm commitment to emotional autonomy, you approach the setback from a renewed perspective.

Noticing the team's tension, you take a moment to connect with your own emotions, asking yourself: "What do I truly feel about this project delay? Are these feelings originating in me or am I reflecting the emotions of the environment?".

Through the practice of conscious breathing, you manage to center yourself and recognize that, despite the setback, you identify opportunities for growth and improvement. This acknowledgment allows you to adopt a more balanced and proactive stance.

During the team meeting, instead of succumbing to collective frustration, you present your perspective with calmness and clarity, pointing out challenges and proposing viable solutions. Your attitude helps to moderate the atmosphere and foster constructive dialogue.

This exercise in emotional autonomy demonstrates your capacity to remain loyal to your authentic emotions, even in the face of adversity. You feel satisfaction for having managed the situation effectively, preserving your emotional integrity and contributing positively to the team.

This achievement reinforces your confidence and ability to direct your emotions independently. As these practices become habitual, your emotional self-efficacy is strengthened, preparing you to face future challenges with greater assurance and effectiveness.

Step 10: Designing a Comprehensive Emotional Well-Being Plan

The culmination of strengthening your emotional intelligence is realized in the creation of a personalized emotional well-being plan, a roadmap designed to sustain and expand the progress achieved in your emotional development. This plan symbolizes your commitment to continuous emotional growth, ensuring sustained improvement in your emotional well-being.

This crucial step demands deep and reflective introspection about your emotional journey, recognizing both significant advancements and areas that still require attention and improvement. Analyze the emotional competencies you have mastered and those that need to be strengthened or understood more deeply.

Begin by setting clear and realistic goals for your emotional evolution, from strengthening your emotional regulation capacity in the face of stress to increasing empathy in your interpersonal relationships. Define specific goals, ensuring they are measurable, achievable, relevant, and time bound.

Develop concrete strategies to achieve these goals. Identify specific actions that will reinforce your emotional autonomy or deepen your understanding of others' emotions. Decide which emotional regulation practices or mindfulness exercises you will integrate into your daily routine and select additional resources such as readings, courses, or workshops that can support your process.

Incorporate into your plan a system for self-assessment and periodic review. Schedule regular reviews to assess your progress, adjust your goals and strategies as necessary, and celebrate the achievements reached. Continuous review is vital to maintain your motivation and adapt to changes in your life circumstances and emotional needs.

Remember that the path to emotional mastery is a continuous journey. Embracing constant learning and growth is key to moving toward an optimal state of emotional well-being. Each step forward reinforces your ability to handle the complexities of emotional life, enriching your existence. Your Emotional Well-being Plan becomes your personal guide to a richer, more conscious, and emotionally balanced life.

Example:

With the emotional knowledge and skills acquired, proceed to the drafting of your Emotional Well-being Plan. This document will be your compass in the continuous refinement of your emotional health and psychological well-being. To do this, reflect on your achievements and challenges. Distinguish the moments when you effectively managed challenging emotions and those when you could have improved your reaction. These reflections will form the basis of your future objectives.

Set concrete goals for your emotional growth. For example, if managing anxiety in decisive moments is an area for improvement, set a goal to develop skills to manage anxiety under pressure. Specify actions to achieve this goal, such as adopting advanced relaxation techniques, stretching, deep breathing, or even taking time to engage in an activity that allows you to clear your mind.

Draft a detailed action plan. If your goal is to increase empathy in your relationships, plan to read related articles. Set realistic deadlines for each goal and determine how and when you will evaluate your progress. For instance, you might propose reading a personal development article every morning.

Include a strategy for regularly reviewing and adjusting your objectives. Decide how often you will evaluate your progress and how you will modify your plan according to changes in your life. If techniques are not working, you can always seek alternatives.

Consider this plan as a pact with yourself to nurture your emotional well-being. Keep a journal of your experiences and learnings and celebrate every victory on this path. This Emotional Well-being Plan is just the beginning of an endless journey of growth and learning towards an emotionally enriched and balanced life.

Conclusion

Summary and Reflection

This introspective exercise, inspired by Rafael Bisquerra's pentagonal model, has led to a deeper understanding of your emotional intelligence. You have moved towards new levels of self-awareness, learning to recognize, interpret, and effectively manage your emotions.

Throughout this process, from identifying emotional patterns to creating an Emotional Well-being Plan, you have developed crucial skills for emotional self-regulation, strengthening your autonomy, social competence, and overall well-being. You have progressed in emotional mastery, improving the accuracy of identifying and classifying emotions, and understanding how they influence your decisions and relationships.

Self-assessment and the adoption of emotional regulation strategies have highlighted the importance of emotions in your behavior and interactions with others, enhancing empathy and personal relationships. Improving your emotional autonomy has been key, increasing your ability to manage emotions independently and minimize external influence.

The Emotional Well-being Plan represents your commitment to sustained emotional growth, serving as a guide for evolution in the face of future challenges.

This journey has enriched your life, integrating emotional skills into your daily living for a more complete and balanced existence. These advancements are essential for managing emotional disorders, demonstrating a deep commitment to your mental health and well-being.

Step Four

Self-Compassion and Self-Care

Introduction to the Topic

Self-compassion, as defined by Kristin Neff (2003), includes being kind to ourselves, recognizing our shared humanity, and practicing mindfulness. This concept, key in positive psychology, encourages us to treat ourselves with the same kindness we would offer a loved one in difficult times, distinguishing itself from self-esteem by focusing on empathy and internal understanding rather than external comparisons.

On the other hand, self-care consists of intentional practices to promote overall well-being, such as eating healthily, staying active, getting enough rest, and effectively managing stress. These actions are fundamental to maintaining optimal physical and mental well-being.

Combining self-compassion with self-care is presented as an effective strategy for improving emotional well-being, nourishing both our mental and physical health.

Research Evidence

Research in psychology supports the benefits of self-compassion for mental health. Neff (2003) found that self-compassionate people experience fewer negative thoughts and lower levels of anxiety and depression. Self-compassion promotes emotional resilience, allowing individuals to effectively face adversity.

Regarding self-care, studies indicate its crucial role in developing resilience and reducing stress. Activities such as exercise and meditation positively impact emotional well-being and mental health.

The research underscores the importance of self-compassion and self-care as tools to improve quality of life, highlighting their practical usefulness for managing stress, anxiety, depression, and fostering a resilient and positive attitude towards life.

Instructions

Practicing Self-Compassion and Fostering Resilience

Objective

This exercise aims to promote self-compassion and self-care as essential tools for well-being and effective emotional management. Focusing on the practical application of strategies such as cognitive restructuring and emotional regulation, it proposes a compassionate approach towards oneself and intentional actions to maintain comprehensive well-being.

Self-compassion involves treating ourselves with kindness and understanding in the face of difficulties, recognizing that mistakes and challenges are natural aspects of life. Self-care, in turn, encompasses all those deliberate practices to care for our physical and mental well-being, fundamental for a healthy balance.

Incorporating these practices into daily routine not only improves short-term well-being but also reinforces long-term mental health. Adopting self-compassion and self-care develops resources to face challenges resiliently, offering a significant improvement in quality of life and the ability to overcome adversities.

This holistic approach to mental health promotes a more balanced life, placing self-care and self-compassion as foundations for sustained emotional well-being and enriched inner strength. Integrating these practices marks a step towards profound transformation and lasting emotional well-being.

Step 1: Recognition and Acceptance of Emotions

Beginning the journey towards self-compassion and self-care starts with the ability to recognize and accept our emotions. This crucial first step lays the groundwork for profound self-awareness, marking the onset of a significant personal transformation. Understanding that emotions are a natural and healthy part of our existence establishes the foundation for positive and lasting change in our lives.

Dedicate 10 to 15 minutes daily in a serene, distraction-free space to connect with your internal emotional world. During these moments of introspection, allow your emotions to surface freely, observing them without judgment and accepting them as they are. This act of recognition and acceptance is a cornerstone of self-compassion; by validating our emotions, we start treating ourselves with more kindness and understanding, essential ingredients for self-care.

Utilizing a personal journal proves invaluable in this process. Writing offers a powerful means to process and express our emotions, facilitating greater clarity and reflection on our feelings and thoughts. Recording our emotional experiences helps us understand and analyze our emotions in more detail, providing perspective and insight into our emotional state.

As you delve deeper into this practice, you will gain a more intimate understanding of your emotions, identifying triggers and comprehending the roots of your emotional reactions. Your journal becomes a mirror of your emotional and personal growth, allowing you to observe patterns, celebrate progress, and recognize areas still in need of development.

Example:

Imagine facing a work challenge that didn't meet your expectations, generating feelings of frustration and disappointment. During a moment of calm, specifically identify these emotions: "I feel frustrated and disappointed with the project's outcome". Subsequently, contextualize these emotions, recognizing them as natural responses to the challenge and criticism.

Instead of suppressing or criticizing these emotions, allow yourself to fully experience them, adopting a stance of acceptance: "It's entirely human to feel frustration when things don't go as planned. It's a normal response to perceived failures". By documenting these reflections in your journal, you begin to view your emotions in a more compassionate and constructive light.

This exercise not only allows you to better understand your emotions and reactions to adversities but also transforms your internal dialogue into a more empathetic and understanding one. Accepting your negative emotions as integral parts of the human experience, rather than viewing them as flaws, marks the beginning of your path towards enhanced emotional resilience and self-compassion.

Step 2: Identification and Transformation of Self-Criticism

The path towards effective self-compassion and self-care involves confronting and transforming our self-criticisms. Once we have recognized and accepted our emotions, the next step is to pay attention to the criticisms we direct at ourselves, particularly in moments of stress or in situations perceived as failures. These self-criticisms, often severe and disproportionate, can deeply undermine our emotional and mental well-being.

It is essential to note these self-criticisms in a personal journal, documenting the judgments and negative self-valuations. Subsequently, it is important to subject these thoughts to critical scrutiny: Are these self-criticisms fair or accurate? In what way do they truly contribute to your growth or well-being? Questioning and reevaluating these internal judgments allows us to adopt a more compassionate and constructive perspective.

This step is crucial for diminishing the negative impact of self-criticism and facilitating the development of a kinder internal dialogue and a healthier relationship with oneself. By identifying, challenging, and reconfiguring our self-criticisms, we begin the process of dismantling harmful thought patterns, favoring deeper self-acceptance, and lasting emotional well-being.

Transforming our self-criticisms into positive reflections is an invaluable resource for strengthening our relationship with ourselves, promoting a more compassionate treatment towards our experiences and emotions. This step is crucial on our journey towards self-compassion and self-care, allowing us to foster a more benevolent and understanding attitude towards our own thoughts and feelings.

Example:

When self-criticisms arise from situations like a work project that did not meet expectations, it is vital to address them to foster self-compassion. During this step, you focus on the criticisms you make of yourself, such as "I should have done much better; I'm a failure at my job" or "I always make mistakes when I'm under pressure".

By recording these self-criticisms in your journal, you begin a valuable introspection. You question the truthfulness of these statements: "Do I really always fail under pressure or is this perception a distortion of specific experiences?". Furthermore, you reflect on their utility: "Do these self-critical judgments help me improve, or do they simply increase my stress and deteriorate my self-esteem?".

This process is essential for modifying your negative internal dialogue. Recognizing that these self-criticisms may be exaggerated or unfounded, you begin to adopt a more constructive and empathetic view, replacing constant criticism with a more realistic and nuanced understanding of your capabilities and limitations.

You understand that mistakes, or not meeting certain expectations on some occasions, do not define your professional competence or your value as a person. These situations become opportunities for learning and personal and professional development. By embracing this approach, not only do you reduce self-imposed pressure, but you also set yourself on a path towards a more robust self-esteem and improved emotional well-being. This reflective and constructive process is vital for your personal development and strengthens your relationship with yourself.

Step 3: Cultivating a Compassionate Internal Dialogue

Cultivating a compassionate internal dialogue is essential on the journey towards self-compassion, representing a transformative shift in how we relate to ourselves. This step transcends self-criticism and harsh judgments, embracing instead a treatment full of understanding, encouragement, and empathy, as we would with a dear friend in difficult circumstances. It's about a profound transformation of our personal narrative, where the severe and critical internal voice gives way to an internal presence that is kind, encouraging, and supportive. This change not only enriches emotional well-being but also reinforces the ability to face adversities with strength and balance.

By adopting a more compassionate dialogue with oneself, a healthier and more positive relationship towards our being is fostered, creating a mental environment that nurtures personal growth and emotional adaptability. Self-compassion equips us to handle challenges with grace and firmness, emphasizing self-care and compassion towards oneself as pillars of optimal emotional balance. This approach lays the foundation for sustained personal development, allowing us to approach life's obstacles with renewed confidence and emotional stability.

Example:

Facing a professional challenge, such as a project that didn't achieve the expected results, it's crucial to transform initial self-criticisms of "I am a failure" or "I always make mistakes" into a more kind and uplifting internal dialogue. Imagine offering to yourself the same understanding and support that you would give to a friend in your situation. Recognizing that a setback does not determine your professional competence and that every setback is an opportunity for growth is key.

In this process of reconfiguration towards self-compassion, use your journal to reformulate those self-imposed judgments with positive and motivating messages. Validate that, although disappointment with the project is understandable, it does not define you as a professional. Adopt affirmations like "Every experience is a lesson; every challenge strengthens me" or "My skills and talents are valuable beyond this moment".

This compassionate internal dialogue is vital for reorienting your perception, strengthening your self-esteem and confidence in yourself. By embracing a kinder and more understanding attitude towards yourself, you mitigate negative stress and promote uninterrupted personal growth and a fuller life. With diligent practice, this approach will transform into your natural response to difficulties, cultivating resilience and a positive outlook on future challenges.

Step 4: Promoting Present Moment Awareness

Integrating mindfulness is essential on the path toward self-compassion and in-depth self-care. This approach invites a full experience of the present moment, distancing ourselves from past ruminations or future anxieties. By focusing on observing our thoughts, emotions, and physical sensations at the present without judgment, we facilitate a space of acceptance and understanding.

Cultivating mindfulness allows us to embrace our internal experiences as they are, key to reducing the tendency to dwell on past disappointments or worry excessively about what is to come. Practicing mindfulness interrupts the flow of recurrent negative thoughts, opening the door to a fresher and more balanced perception of circumstances.

Regular mindfulness practice solidifies the ability to be fully immersed in the now, enriching awareness of daily experiences and improving our interaction with them. As presence in the "here and now" strengthens, new ways of relating to thoughts and emotions are explored, leading to a calmer and more centered existence.

The ability to remain fully present has a beneficial impact on emotional and mental well-being, fostering inner peace and deeper self-knowledge. Mindfulness emerges as a powerful tool for stress management, reinforcement of emotional resilience, and promotion of a more harmonious and conscious living.

Example:

Implementing mindfulness practices is crucial for healthily and compassionately addressing challenging thoughts and emotions, especially in stressful situations or disappointment, such as a setback at work (Appendix 6).

Imagine deciding to dedicate time to mindfulness practice after facing self-criticism for a work project that didn't meet your expectations. Find a quiet space where you feel comfortable, and if you wish, close your eyes. Focus your attention on your breathing, observing the natural flow of air entering and exiting your body. When your mind wanders to the project or to personal criticisms, gently redirect your attention back to your breathing.

Gradually, expand your awareness to the sensations in your body, noting any areas of tension or discomfort, without trying to change these sensations, simply allowing yourself to feel what your body is experiencing at that moment.

Later, direct your focus to ambient sounds, the sensation of air on your skin, and other present stimuli, anchoring yourself in the current moment, thereby reducing the weight of negative thoughts associated with the past or future.

Upon concluding your mindfulness practice, you will notice that your emotional state regarding the work situation has undergone a significant change. You feel more serene and focused, and the intensity of your self-critical thoughts has noticeably decreased. This renewed perspective enables you to approach the situation in a more constructive manner, less prone to rumination.

Consistent practice of mindfulness proves to be an effective strategy for enhancing overall well-being, strengthening your capacity to face future challenges with calm and emotional balance.

Step 5: Designing a Comprehensive Personal Care Plan

Creating a personalized personal care plan is the fifth essential step on the path to deep self-compassion and self-care practice. Built on the learnings from previous steps, this plan is a key strategy for effective stress management and handling challenging emotions.

For this plan to be truly effective and resonant, it must be highly personal, reflecting your preferences, routine, and specific needs. It should encompass a range of activities designed to promote your physical, emotional, and mental well-being. Consider including physical exercises tailored to your preference (such as yoga, walking, or specific workouts), relaxation practices (through meditation, mindfulness, or breathing techniques), and hobbies that bring you joy and personal satisfaction (such as reading, gardening, or artistic activities).

It is crucial that your plan covers fundamental aspects for your overall health, such as maintaining balanced nutrition, ensuring good sleep quality, and reserving moments to disconnect from technology and alleviate daily stress. Additionally, enrich your plan with activities that foster social connections and emotional support, like enjoying quality time with loved ones or participating in communities with common interests.

Regularly review and adjust your personal care plan to keep it relevant and useful in the face of changes in your life and needs. Consistency in applying your plan, along with the flexibility to adapt it, are essential. The goal of this plan is to improve your overall well-being and quality of life in an integrated manner.

Committing to your personal care plan lays the groundwork for effective life challenges management, fostering lasting well-being and greater life fulfillment.

Example:

Developing a personal care plan after recognizing negative emotions and patterns of self-criticism linked to work challenges is vital to strengthen your resilience and emotional management capacity. This plan, designed to nourish your physical, emotional, and mental well-being, includes specific activities to reduce stress and increase personal contentment.

An essential component of your plan could be integrating a running routine at the end of the workday, benefiting both your physical health, and providing a space for introspection and tension release. Adding stretching practices in the mornings prepares your body and mind for the day's challenges with a positive attitude.

Incorporating moments to disconnect from work concerns through hobbies like gardening, painting, or reading, dedicating time each weekend to these activities, is equally important. These hobbies offer a valuable respite from daily stress and significantly contribute to your sense of accomplishment and happiness.

Implementing this personal care plan brings tangible benefits, such as an increase in energy and serenity, facilitating more efficient stress management. The selected activities become key tools for healthily addressing future stressful situations.

This holistic approach to self-care not only improves your current well-being but also establishes a solid foundation for the ongoing care of your emotional and physical health in the long term. By committing to these practices, you reinforce your ability to overcome adversity, ensuring enduring well-being and strengthened emotional resilience.

Step 6: Fostering Gratitude for Emotional Transformation

Gratitude emerges as an essential pillar in the process of self-compassion and emotional well-being, transcending mere feeling to become a deliberate and transformative practice. This act deeply enriches your perception of life, enhancing your emotional strength and resilience.

To weave gratitude into the fabric of your daily life, set aside a few moments each day, ideally at dawn or dusk, to reflect on what ignites your gratitude. From the small daily joys to the fundamentals of your existence, such as health and meaningful relationships, the goal is to nurture a conscious sense of appreciation for the gifts in your life.

An effective strategy to embrace gratitude is to maintain a gratitude journal. Write down three things that inspire gratitude in you every day. This simple yet profoundly impactful practice shifts your focus toward the positive, offering a counterbalance to negative or self-critical inclinations.

With dedication to this practice, you will experience a transformation in your life perspective, moving toward a balanced appreciation of your experiences, valuing both the joys and the challenges. This approach promotes a significant increase in well-being and personal satisfaction.

Gratitude plays a crucial role in the foundation of your resilience. In moments of tension or adversity, consciously evoking the positive aspects of your life offers a comforting and balanced perspective. Adopting this positive approach reveals itself as a powerful tool for navigating difficulties with a spirit of optimism and hope.

In summary, the practice of gratitude stands as a vital component in self-care and the cultivation of self-compassion. It not only beautifies your day-to-day but also sets the stage for facing the future with a strengthened and positive attitude. Regularly incorporating gratitude into your life strengthens your emotional resilience, paving the way toward a more fulfilling and rewarding existence.

Example:

After a day of work full of challenges, you choose to focus on gratitude instead of frustrations. In a quiet corner of your home, you take a moment to ponder the positive aspects of the day. The following statements serve as reference:

You remember a moment at work where your effort was recognized, despite the obstacles: "I am grateful for my ability to successfully navigate challenges", you meditate.

Reflect on a friendly conversation with a colleague: "I appreciate the presence of colleagues who brighten my day", you think.

Value the comfort and security of your home, a sanctuary at the end of the day: "I am grateful for having a cozy and safe place", you consider.

Express gratitude for your health and vitality: "I feel grateful for my physical well-being that allows me to face each day", you reflect.

Finally, think about the small pleasures that enriched your day: "I am grateful for these moments that beautify my routine", you conclude.

This ritual of gratitude shifts your focus from tensions to a state of recognition and joy. Gratitude becomes an essential tool for cultivating a balanced and positive outlook on life, reinforcing your daily enjoyment and resilience.

Step 7: Strengthening Emotional Resilience

Resilience, our ability to recover and adapt in the face of adversity, is an indispensable component in the journey towards self-care and self-compassion. This step invites a conscious and deliberate practice of strategies that cultivate our inner strength in life's challenges.

Beginning by reflecting on the obstacles you have already overcome is enlightening, allowing you to identify the strategies and attitudes that contributed to your overcoming them. These past moments serve as powerful reminders of your ability to navigate difficulties, reinforcing your confidence in facing future challenges.

It is also crucial to recognize and value the resources available, both internal and external. Internally, qualities such as tenacity and optimism are pillars of support; externally, the emotional support network and activities that nourish your well-being are fundamental.

Adopting a growth mindset transforms the perception of challenges, seeing them not as barriers but as valuable opportunities for learning and personal enrichment. This perspective fosters an attitude of openness towards the development of new skills and the exploration of creative solutions to adversity.

Physical well-being is the foundation upon which emotional resilience is built. Healthy practices such as exercise, balanced nutrition, and restorative sleep are essential to maintaining a mind and body prepared to manage stress and approach life with positivity.

Flexibility and adaptability are essential qualities for enduring resilience. Being open to adjusting plans and strategies in the face of changing circumstances ensures an effective response capacity to challenges.

This comprehensive approach to emotional resilience lays the groundwork for more effective management of difficult situations, promoting sustained emotional well-being and enriching your life experience.

Example:

Facing a work project that did not meet expectations presents an invaluable opportunity to strengthen your resilience. Although it may be an initial source of frustration, this experience acts as a catalyst for personal and professional growth.

Analyze the lessons learned and how they can be applied to future projects. Despite the outcome, you have gained insights and skills that enrich your professional repertoire. Also recognize the resources that helped you manage the situation, from the support of colleagues to personal decompression activities. These constitute valuable tools for future adverse circumstances.

Remember previous situations where you demonstrated resilience, reflecting on overcoming those challenges and what they taught you. These experiences are tangible evidence of your capacity to adapt and move forward. It is important to develop a proactive plan to continue strengthening your resilience, setting goals that challenge you, seeking opportunities to acquire new competencies, or dedicating time to activities that promote your overall well-being.

Transforming a challenge into a platform for growth and emotional resilience paves the way to face future difficulties with greater assurance, fostering a richer and more satisfying life.

Step 8: Practicing Self-Compassion in Difficult Times

Cultivating self-compassion during adverse moments is crucial for healthy emotional management, allowing for more harmonious recovery and better adaptation to stress and anxiety. This process starts by recognizing and accepting negative emotions as part of a shared human experience, rather than signs of weakness or failure.

To begin, it is crucial to identify and embrace the emotions that arise in challenging circumstances. For example, in the face of work pressure, openly admit your feelings: "I accept that I am feeling stressed and anxious because of my workload". This honest acknowledgment is the first step towards addressing these emotions with understanding and care.

Next, try to view the situation from a compassion perspective, asking yourself how you would treat a friend in similar conditions and applying that same kindness towards yourself. This shift in focus softens self-criticism, promoting a more benevolent treatment of yourself.

Incorporating mindfulness practices, such as conscious breathing, helps to anchor you in the present and calm the mind, reducing the intensity of disturbing emotions and clarifying thought.

Moreover, reformulate self-critical thoughts with positive affirmations of self-compassion. Instead of punishing yourself for the circumstances, strengthen yourself with reminders of your effort and capacity to overcome: "I am doing the best I can" or "It's human to feel overwhelmed from time to time".

Finally, reflecting on the learnings from these situations and how they can serve to strengthen your resilience in the future is essential. Consider: "What can I learn from this? How can I apply these lessons to face future challenges more effectively?".

The constant practice of self-compassion in difficult moments not only improves immediate emotional well-being but also equips you with valuable tools to face future adversities with greater serenity and confidence.

Example:

When facing a period of intense work pressure, with an accumulation of tasks and tight deadlines, self-criticism can easily surface. At this point, self-compassion becomes an invaluable resource.

Recognizing your emotions without judgment is the first step: "I am experiencing stress and anxiety due to my workload". This act of acceptance is crucial for addressing these feelings from a place of understanding.

Adopting a compassionate attitude, asking yourself how you would treat yourself if you were your best friend, can transform your relationship with the situation: "I am doing everything I can under these circumstances". This compassionate internal dialogue is key to mitigating self-criticism.

Deep breathing and mindfulness can provide immediate relief, helping to calm the mind and decrease anxiety. Positive affirmations encourage self-compassion: "I have the strength to overcome these challenges", focusing attention on your capabilities and progress rather than perceptions of failure. Reflecting on the experience after overcoming it reveals valuable lessons for increasing resilience to future challenges.

This approach not only relieves present stress and anxiety but also provides effective strategies for long-term emotional management, establishing a solid pillar for future emotional and mental well-being.

Step 9: Implementing Healthy Boundaries

Implementing healthy boundaries is an essential strategy for preserving both emotional and physical well-being, acting as vital defenses to protect your needs and personal space. These boundaries are crucial for optimizing your energy and cultivating relationships based on respect and balance.

Begin by identifying areas in your life where you feel your boundaries have been compromised, whether in the workplace, personal relationships, or during your leisure time. Reflect on instances where you feel your needs and well-being have been neglected, such as being overburdened with work or unreasonable demands on your time by others.

After recognizing these situations, think about the boundaries that would be beneficial for you to establish. For example, in the work context, setting a boundary could translate into refusing additional tasks or negotiating more realistic deadlines.

Clear and assertive communication is key to establishing effective boundaries. Express yourself in a respectful and firm manner, practicing beforehand, if necessary, to improve your confidence and clarity in your message.

Remember, setting boundaries is a form of self-care that safeguards your mental and physical health and enriches your interactions with others. Maintain flexibility, adapting your boundaries as your circumstances and personal needs change.

Adopting healthy boundaries reduces stress and burnout, enhancing your ability to fully enjoy life and face challenges with strengthened resilience. Establishing and maintaining these boundaries is fundamental for cultivating a healthy balance both with oneself and with others.

Example:

Facing excessive work demands, defining healthy boundaries is key to your overall well-being and performance. Visualize a work situation where the constant load of additional tasks generates tension. Recognizing this dynamic is the initial step to demarcate clear boundaries.

Evaluate how many additional tasks you can take on without compromising your well-being, deciding, for example, to accept only one extra project per week.

Communicate your boundaries to colleagues and superiors assertively and respectfully, articulating your stance clearly, such as: "To ensure the quality of my work and maintain my well-being, I will limit the number of additional tasks I can take on".

Stay firm in the face of resistance, remembering that establishing boundaries is an essential act of self-care.

Reflect on how you felt when setting and communicating these boundaries, likely noticing a sense of relief and greater control over your work environment.

Consistent practice in setting boundaries significantly contributes to better management of work-related stress, strengthens your emotional resilience, and improves work dynamics. This process is not only crucial for your personal and professional development but also prepares you to face future challenges with more confidence and serenity.

Step 10: Reflection and Progress in Self-Compassion

At this critical juncture, it's essential to dedicate time to reflecting on and evaluating the impact that consistent practice of self-compassion has had on your emotional and mental well-being. This introspective exercise is vital for appreciating the progress made and discerning areas for continued growth.

Start by assessing your emotional and mental state prior to embarking on this journey of self-compassion. Recall the emotional challenges you faced, your self-perception, and your feelings towards yourself and others. Analyze what your levels of stress, anxiety, or frustration were like to have a clear notion of your starting point.

Review the path taken through the different steps focused on reinforcing self-compassion and self-care. Reflect on integrating mindfulness practices, cultivating a compassionate internal dialogue, valuing gratitude, reinforcing resilience, and how you've implemented these elements in your daily life.

Evaluate how these practices have transformed your day-to-day life. Ask yourself if you've noticed a change in your attitude towards yourself and the challenges you face. Consider specific situations where you applied these techniques and the outcomes achieved.

Also, examine the impact on your interpersonal relationships. Determine if you've experienced an increase in your capacity for empathy and understanding towards others and if you feel that your bonds have strengthened.

Document these reflections and observations in your personal journal. This record will not only serve as a testimony of your growth but also as a guide for your future evolution. Set short and long-term goals based on these reflections and develop a plan to integrate self-compassion even more into your existence.

This step of evaluation and contemplation marks the beginning of an ongoing journey of self-discovery and personal growth. Self-compassion is not a destination but a path to a fuller and more balanced life, and each step forward brings you closer to greater well-being and happiness.

Example:

You started this journey towards self-compassion with the goal of improving your relationship with yourself and others. Throughout this time, you have developed strategies to better manage difficult emotions, learned to be kinder and more understanding towards yourself, and strengthened your personal bonds through greater empathy.

On a quiet afternoon, reflect on how this journey has changed your perception and handling of adverse situations. How has practicing mindfulness or establishing healthy boundaries influenced your emotional well-being? How has your internal dialogue evolved in the face of stress?

Consider changes in the dynamics of your relationships. Do you notice greater openness and connection with those around you? How have these changes impacted your overall well-being?

Write down your thoughts and feelings in the journal. This act of documentation is a celebration of your progress and a renewed commitment to your continuous growth. Set new objectives that reflect your learning and desires for the future. This process of reflection and evaluation is a valuable opportunity to recognize your strength and resilience.

Conclusion

Summary and Reflection

This journey towards self-compassion and self-care has marked a profound path of self-discovery and personal development, fostering a more loving and harmonious relationship with oneself. You have learned to see emotions as essential indicators of your well-being, overcoming self-criticism, and adopting a more compassionate internal dialogue.

This shift towards loving self-care represents a significant evolution in your personal narrative, encouraging greater resilience and emotional well-being. Mindfulness and a personal care plan have become pillars of this process, focusing on the present and promoting a renewed commitment to your happiness and health.

The integration of self-compassion and self-care into your daily routine has had a positive impact on your overall well-being, reaffirming your worth and acting as a constant reminder of the importance of self-love.

This path transcends the performance of specific activities, becoming an essential change in how you live and relate to yourself, with self-compassion and self-care emerging as fundamental elements of a conscious and satisfying existence.

The journey of self-compassion is ongoing, offering new opportunities each day to practice kindness towards oneself, facing challenges with tools and a strengthened perspective, and establishing self-compassion as the foundation of your personal growth and emotional balance.

Step Five

Developing Social Skills

Introduction to the Topic

The enhancement of social skills and assertiveness is key for healthy interpersonal interaction and the effective management of mood disorders. These skills include the ability to communicate effectively, understand and share emotions (empathy), accurately interpret non-verbal communication, and collaborate with others. They are fundamental for building and maintaining meaningful relationships, resolving conflicts, and navigating social complexities.

Assertiveness, understood as the ability to express our thoughts, feelings, and needs honestly and respectfully, is vital for affirming our rights while respecting those of others. This competency is essential for self-respect, self-efficacy, and plays a crucial role in the prevention and management of depression and anxiety, avoiding resentment and feelings of helplessness.

Enhancing these social skills and assertiveness can significantly improve interpersonal relationships, personal satisfaction, and reduce stress and anxiety in social situations. They are especially crucial for effective self-expression and conflict management, positively impacting mental health.

In the context of mood disorders, improving these skills can contribute to raising self-esteem, reducing isolation, and strengthening the sense of control in social interactions, besides being fundamental for establishing and maintaining solid social support, key in recovery.

In summary, the development of social skills and assertiveness are essential for emotional well-being, offering lasting benefits in various aspects of life and contributing to a more effective management of mood disorders.

Research Evidence

Research highlights the importance of social skills for mental health. Deficiencies in these skills can increase the risk of disorders such as depression and anxiety, often leading to social isolation and relational difficulties that increase stress.

Assertiveness is crucial for clear and respectful communication of our thoughts and feelings. Studies show that assertiveness training can improve self-esteem and decrease anxiety. A lack of assertiveness can lead to low self-esteem and resentment, while an excess of it can provoke conflicts.

Cognitive Behavioral Therapy, recognized for its effectiveness in treating mood disorders, emphasizes the development of social skills and assertiveness as key components. These skills can increase self-esteem and facilitate the management of depression and anxiety.

Strengthening social skills and assertiveness is vital for mental health, improving interpersonal relationships, minimizing social stress, and fostering a sense of self-efficacy and control, all essential for our emotional well-being.

Instructions

Developing Social Skills:
A Path to Interpersonal Well-being

Objective

The enrichment of social skills and assertiveness stands as a fundamental pillar in promoting effective interpersonal communication and emotional well-being. This path is designed to provide individuals with practical tools and essential knowledge to improve their daily interactions, deepen their relationships, and strengthen their mental health.

The starting point for this journey of personal growth is careful introspection about current social competencies and levels of assertiveness, establishing a foundation upon which to build. Next, a series of strategies and exercises focused on improving effective communication are proposed, emphasizing the importance of expressing oneself clearly and practicing active listening to foster meaningful connections.

Emphasis is placed on cultivating empathy and social intelligence as key elements to understanding and resonating with the emotions of others, facilitating the constructive resolution of conflicts. Assertiveness is addressed as the ability to openly express thoughts, feelings, and needs, maintaining a balance that respects both one's own limits and those of others.

The impact of these skills transcends the personal sphere, showing significant benefits such as decreased stress and anxiety, increased self-esteem, and the promotion of a sense of personal competence and autonomy. Additionally, their application extends to the professional realm, optimizing adaptability and the management of various social and work situations.

This comprehensive approach to the development of social skills and assertiveness invites the reader to embark on a process of self-exploration and continuous improvement. Upon completing this journey, the individual is expected to be better equipped to establish and nurture healthy and rewarding interpersonal relationships, making a substantial difference in their quality of life and overall well-being.

Step 1: Reflection and Improvement of Social Skills

Detailed reflection on our social skills stands as the initial pillar towards the improvement and development of these essential capabilities, both in personal and professional realms. This introspective process not only lays the groundwork for comprehensive growth but also promotes a deeper understanding of how our interactions impact the various environments we navigate, from casual conversations to critical professional situations like work meetings.

It's crucial to understand that social skills transcend mere communication ability; they encompass a wide range of learned behaviors and reactions that determine the quality of our interaction with the world. These skills include respecting cultural and social norms, the ability to express ourselves effectively, and forging meaningful connections with those around us. Through conscientious self-evaluation, we can examine our efficacy in communication, both verbal and non-verbal, assessing whether our body language and tone of voice align with our intentions and if we manage to convey our thoughts and emotions in a clear and considerate manner.

This introspection also involves reviewing our capacity for listening and empathizing, allowing us to gauge whether we truly understand and value others' perspectives and feelings, and if our responses demonstrate understanding and empathy. The ability to communicate our own thoughts and emotions constructively is crucial to avoid misunderstandings or conflicts, thus maintaining healthy and productive interpersonal relationships.

Additionally, conflict management emerges as a vital component of social competencies self-assessment. Reflecting on our approach to disagreements helps us discern whether we promote constructive solutions or tend to evade or exacerbate conflicts. The ability to effectively resolve disputes reflects our social competence and emotional maturity.

Therefore, self-assessment should not be seen as a one-time task but as an ongoing process that facilitates monitoring our progress and identifying areas that require additional attention. This constant reflection is crucial for our personal and professional development. Strengthening our social skills not only improves our daily interactions but also increases our ability to handle mood disorders. By interacting more effectively, we reduce our isolation, strengthen our support network, and increase our emotional resilience, which is vital for our overall well-being.

Example:

Taking as a point of reflection a recent experience in a social or work situation in which you actively participated allows you to deepen the self-evaluation and strengthening of your social competencies and assertiveness. Imagine a work meeting focused on an important issue, which presents an ideal opportunity to review your behavior and contributions.

You should begin by evaluating your participation and ability to listen actively: Were you truly attentive to others' expressions? Active listening involves capturing context and underlying emotions, beyond the words.

Next, it's vital to analyze how you articulated your ideas. Assertiveness is based on expressing our thoughts clearly and respectfully, seeking a balance that avoids imposing our opinions or undermining others'.

It's also important to reflect on your management of disagreements or tensions. Did you approach these moments with an open and solution-oriented attitude, or did you tend to avoid conflict or react defensively? Effective disagreement management involves negotiation skills and openness to considering different perspectives.

Evaluating whether you managed to adapt your communicative style to various people and situations is essential, recognizing that each social interaction demands a particular approach, adjusted to the group dynamics and context.

Finally, you must contemplate your emotions during and after the interaction, pondering any aspects you would like to address differently in the future. This thorough analysis provides a clear perspective on your strengths and areas for improvement in social competencies.

This process of constant self-evaluation and reflection is indispensable for the development and reinforcement of social competencies and assertiveness, enhancing your ability to interact effectively and satisfyingly in various social and professional contexts. This opens doors to new growth opportunities, adaptation, and ensures more fruitful and enriching interactions.

Step 2: Strengthening Assertiveness for Emotional Well-Being

Perfecting assertiveness, an indispensable social skill, stands at the core of this pivotal stage. This ability empowers us to articulate our thoughts, emotions, and needs in a transparent, candid, and considerate manner, simultaneously ensuring respect for the rights of others. Assertiveness, distinguished by its balance, diverges from both passivity, which involves renouncing our own needs, and aggressiveness, which seeks to impose those needs without consideration for others.

This process aims to facilitate the identification and reformulation of non-assertive communication patterns. Adopting assertive behavior can positively revolutionize the quality of our interactions and relationships, serving as a cornerstone in the treatment of emotional disorders by promoting self-esteem, reducing stress, and optimizing the management of interpersonal relationships.

Self-awareness is presented as the first step toward mastering assertiveness. It's essential for introspection about our own thoughts and feelings to clearly identify what we wish to communicate. Taking time to recognize our needs, desires, and emotions is fundamental; this degree of self-awareness forms the basis for expressing our thoughts and feelings directly and openly.

The adoption of assertive language plays a crucial role in this process. It's recommended to use expressions that begin with "I feel" or "I believe", avoiding accusations or generalizations that could be interpreted as confrontational or defensive. This mode of expression allows us to share our perspective personally and honestly, without delegitimizing the opinions or feelings of others, favoring a more constructive and effective interaction.

Assertiveness concerns not only the way we express our own ideas and emotions but also how we listen and respond to others. Active listening is a fundamental component of assertiveness, involving full attention to others' words, as well as the emotions and motivations that underlie them. Active listening fosters mutual understanding and respect for different perspectives.

Understanding and respecting personal boundaries, both our own and those of others, is essential for effective communication. Establishing clear boundaries helps us define our comfort spaces and what we are willing to accept, promoting harmonious and healthy relationships, and reducing misunderstandings and conflicts.

The proper management of emotions, especially frustration and anger, is a critical aspect of assertiveness. Being assertive doesn't imply the absence of intense emotions, but the capability to express them constructively. Developing strategies to control emotions in moments of tension allows us to maintain assertive communication, even in adverse situations.

Enriching assertiveness in our lives is a continuous process, nourished by practice and reflection. Its application is particularly valuable in managing emotional disorders, offering an essential tool for expressing ourselves healthily. This can lead to a significant reduction in anxiety and an improvement in overall mental health.

By adopting assertiveness, we choose a path of mutual respect, both for ourselves and for others, essential for a fulfilling and balanced personal and professional life. Beyond improving our relationships, assertiveness contributes to our overall well-being, enabling us to express our needs and feelings effectively and healthily.

Example:

Imagine a situation, whether in a work or personal context, where you feel your opinions or needs are not being properly considered. Faced with this common challenge, instead of opting for silence, which might generate resentment, or an aggressive response, which could escalate the conflict, choose an assertive approach. You might say something like: "I understand and value your viewpoint. However, from my perspective, I feel that my opinion isn't being fully considered in this discussion. It would be beneficial to explore this further to understand your points and share mine, looking for common ground". This approach exemplifies assertive communication.

By using language that begins with "I feel" or "from my perspective", you share your thoughts and emotions in a personal and direct way, avoiding confrontations. This reduces the likelihood of the other person feeling attacked and more open to considering your viewpoint.

Recognizing and respecting the other's perspective through active listening not only shows respect for their ideas but also promotes an environment of mutual understanding, where both parties feel heard and valued.   Establishing and respecting your own boundaries during the conversation defines what you need and expect healthily and constructively, avoiding unnecessary misunderstandings and conflicts and promoting equitable and respectful interactions.

Properly managing your emotions in these situations, maintaining calmness, and expressing your feelings constructively not only improves the quality of the interaction but also sets a positive model for how to approach disagreements healthily.

Practicing assertiveness in situations like the one described not only improves your ability to communicate effectively but also invests in your emotional well-being and the quality of your relationships, defending your needs and opinions respectfully for yourself and others, which is fundamental for achieving a fulfilling personal and professional life.

Step 3: Optimizing Active Listening for Mental Health

Active listening emerges as an essential communicative skill, not only for strengthening healthy interpersonal relationships but also as an invaluable resource in managing and supporting individuals with mood disorders. This step is oriented towards improving our ability to listen actively and empathetically, which involves a much deeper commitment than merely hearing words; it's a practice that requires full attention, a profound understanding of the message, and a considered and appropriate response.

Perfecting active listening demands a deep understanding and constant practice. It transcends the superficial processing of words to immerse oneself in the totality of the communicative experience, capturing not just the explicit message but also the emotions and intentions that accompany it. This competence is vital for fostering a deeper understanding and connection with others, fundamental elements for enriching interpersonal relationships and effectively managing emotional disorders.

The use of eye contact emerges as a powerful strategy to demonstrate attention and respect during conversation. Maintaining direct gaze, adapting to relevant cultural norms, signals genuine interest in the speaker, reinforcing the connection and fostering an environment of trust and sincerity. However, it's crucial to be aware of cultural variations related to eye contact, as its interpretation can vary considerably across different cultures.

Patience and respect are pillars of active listening, implying the avoidance of interrupting the other while expressing their ideas. Interrupting can suggest that we consider our perspectives more relevant or reveal a disinterest in the speaker's message. Instead, it is advisable to let the speaker finish their thoughts and pause before responding, ensuring they have completed their message.

It's fundamental to be attentive to the emotions underlying the words. Effective communication goes beyond verbal content; aspects such as emotions, tone of voice, and body language are crucial for grasping the essence of the message. Recognizing and validating the speaker's emotions can significantly enhance mutual understanding and empathy in the dialogue.

To confirm understanding, it is helpful to paraphrase or summarize what has been heard, using our own words. This not only demonstrates that we have been attentive but also allows us to verify that we have correctly understood the message, avoiding potential misunderstandings.

Asking relevant and thoughtful questions shows genuine interest and commitment to the conversation. Such questions, aimed at clarifying or deepening the speaker's message, enrich the understanding and can lead to a more profound and meaningful exchange, opening paths to new levels of comprehension.

The practice of active listening acquires special relevance in the field of support for people with mood disorders, as it promotes greater understanding and empathy towards their experiences and feelings.

This skill is key to creating an essential support environment for recovery and emotional well-being. By developing and refining our active listening ability, we enrich not just our communication but also our interpersonal relationships and emotional intelligence. This personal development benefits our daily interactions and our ability to provide emotional support and mutual understanding, both in personal and professional contexts.

Example:

Imagine you're conversing with a friend or colleague going through a challenging situation. This circumstance requires your complete attention and empathy, highlighting the importance of active listening as a key tool for providing appropriate support.

During your friend or colleague's narrative, strive to be fully present. Attentive and respectful eye contact conveys sincere interest in their story. Gestures like nodding or slightly leaning forward can reinforce that you are following the conversation, always respecting the cultural and personal norms of the speaker.

Avoid distractions or preparing your response while the other person speaks. Focusing your attention on understanding both the words and the underlying emotions and feelings is key. Once they have finished speaking, take a moment to reflect before responding. Paraphrasing or summarizing what was heard demonstrates that you have been attentive and facilitates clarification of any unclear points. You might express, for example, "It seems like you're feeling very overwhelmed by this situation. Is there anything specific you think could relieve you?".

Asking open-ended questions that encourage further exploration of their feelings or thoughts can enrich the conversation. Questions like "How has this personally affected you?" or "What do you think you need at this moment?" can foster a more enriching dialogue and provide more meaningful support.

This approach focused on active listening not only will strengthen your relationship but also will allow you to offer more effective and empathetic support. By practicing these listening skills, you improve not just your communicative competence but also become a more understanding and supportive ally, capable of aiding that can make a significant difference during times of adversity.

Step 4: Effective Articulation of Needs and Emotions

The ability to articulate our needs and emotions in a clear, precise, and respectful manner is a fundamental pillar in establishing healthy and effective interpersonal relationships. This skill is particularly valuable in the context of managing emotional disorders, as open and sincere communication is essential to prevent misunderstandings, reduce stress, and foster deep mutual understanding.

The first step toward effective expression involves dedicating time to self-reflection to identify and understand our own needs and emotions. This introspection exercise allows us to genuinely recognize what we experience and need in different situations, laying the groundwork for authentic communication of our feelings and desires.

When it comes to expressing our needs and emotions, it's crucial to be direct and respectful. Avoiding the issue or using vague language can lead to incorrect interpretations. Clarity and precision in our communication ensure that others understand our message unequivocally, which is of utmost importance in emotionally significant or delicate interactions.

The use of first-person statements, like "I feel" or "I need", allows us to discuss our emotions and needs in a way that personalizes the expression without assigning blame or provoking defensive reactions in others. For example, instead of saying "You make me feel ignored", it's preferable to say, "I feel ignored when my messages don't receive a response". This approach places the conversation in the realm of our own experiences and perceptions, avoiding direct pointing or criticisms of others.

Similarly, it's vital to be considerate and respectful of others' needs while communicating our own. Effective communication requires reciprocity; just as we wish our needs to be respected, we must show the same respect for the needs of others. This promotes an environment of empathy and mutual understanding, essential for maintaining constructive and healthy relationships.

Even in moments of high emotional charge, it's important to strive to maintain composure and express ourselves clearly. Intense emotions can lead to misunderstandings if not handled properly. Therefore, maintaining a calm tone of voice and choosing our words carefully are key strategies to ensure effective communication of our messages.

The ability to effectively express our needs and emotions plays a crucial role in the proper management of mood disorders. By communicating openly and effectively about what we feel and need, we facilitate an environment conducive to support and mutual understanding, fundamental pillars for our emotional and mental well-being. This competency not only strengthens our interpersonal relationships but also empowers us to take an active role in managing our emotional health, leading to a more harmonious and satisfying life.

Example:

Consider a situation where you feel overwhelmed by demands at your workplace, a common scenario in today's work environment. Constant pressure can negatively affect both your emotional and physical well-being. In such circumstances, it's crucial to communicate your needs effectively to your supervisor, not just for your own well-being but also to maintain optimal performance.

Instead of suppressing these feelings, which could increase stress and have a negative impact on your health and work performance, it's advisable to express your needs in a clear and direct manner. Approaching your supervisor and calmly and precisely communicating your current feelings and needs is a beneficial strategy.

You could say: "I've been reflecting on my overall well-being and work performance, and I've realized that the current workload has left me feeling quite overwhelmed. I believe that taking a brief break, even just a few days, would be extremely helpful. It would allow me to recharge and come back with a renewed capacity to focus and be productive". This mode of communication is effective because it's direct, honest, and facilitates your supervisor understanding your situation from your own perspective.

By using first-person statements, you take responsibility for your emotions and thoughts without attributing the cause to another person or external circumstance. This reduces the likelihood of your supervisor feeling attacked or becoming defensive, opening the door to a more empathetic and productive conversation.

It's important to be open to your supervisor's response and willing to discuss possible solutions or compromises, such as planning how your workload will be managed during your absence or exploring alternatives to alleviate your workload.

Mastering the clear and respectful expression of needs and emotions is essential not just in the workplace but in all aspects of life. It enables you to advocate for your well-being and personal needs while maintaining healthy and productive professional relationships. By communicating in this manner, you take active steps to care for your mental and emotional health, an essential component for a balanced and fulfilling life.

Step 5: Advanced Strategies for Conflict Management and Negotiation

Effective conflict management and negotiation skills are crucial elements for cultivating healthy interpersonal relationships and promoting emotional and mental well-being. These skills become even more important in the context of emotional disorders, where emotions can be particularly intense, and relationships face additional challenges. Developing the ability to address conflicts assertively and constructively is essential to prevent the deterioration of significant bonds and maintain a healthy emotional balance.

A key competency in conflict management is the ability to practice active listening and show genuine empathy. Listening with the purpose of fully understanding, rather than simply waiting for a turn to respond, allows us to capture not only the verbal content of the other person's message but also their emotions and underlying motivations. This depth of understanding can be key to defusing tensions and finding common ground.

Focusing solely on differences can exacerbate conflicts. Conversely, identifying and concentrating on shared interests or common goals facilitates the creation of solutions that benefit all parties involved. Establishing a basis of mutual interests can be a solid starting point for building constructive and lasting agreements.

Clarity and assertiveness in communication are indispensable. When expressing your perspective, it's crucial to do so in an understandable manner and without resorting to aggression. Using personal statements, such as "I feel" or "I believe", instead of direct accusations, promotes an open dialogue and reduces the likelihood of defensive responses.

Maintaining emotional control and calm during a conflict is essential. Reacting to provocations or hurtful comments only serves to intensify the conflict. A serene and objective stance allows for clearer reflection and a more effective response.

The willingness to compromise and flexibility are also vital for successful negotiation. Often, reaching a satisfactory solution for all parties requires adaptability and the exploration of intermediate options. Far from being a sign of weakness, compromise demonstrates a genuine commitment to resolving the conflict and the well-being of the relationship.

The development of these skills benefits both personal and professional spheres. Learning to resolve conflicts constructively and negotiate effectively can decrease stress and significantly improve interpersonal relationships, contributing to a more satisfying and harmonious work environment. In managing emotional disorders, these skills offer adaptive strategies for facing stressful situations healthily, which is crucial for a balanced and rewarding life.

Example:

Imagine a disagreement with a colleague at work, a common situation that requires delicate handling to preserve a positive work environment. Approaching this situation with an open mind and a constructive attitude is key to an effective resolution.

Start the conversation from a place of respect and clarity, for example: "I've been thinking about our project and noticed we have different viewpoints. I'm interested in understanding your perspective and finding a way for us to work together that benefits us both." This approach shows a willingness for dialogue and resolution.

Practice active listening, paying attention not only to words but also to emotions and body language. Showing empathy and validating their feelings can ease tensions and open the door to effective communication. Empathetic questions like "Can you explain more about your approach?" can facilitate mutual understanding.

When expressing your needs and concerns, do so clearly and without making accusations. For example, replace "Your method is incorrect" with "I have some concerns with this approach due to X and Y. Could we consider these alternatives?".

The search for common interests and openness to compromise are crucial. Identify shared goals and propose solutions that satisfy both.

Show flexibility and willingness to work together, which is fundamental for effectively resolving the conflict.

Concluding by thanking the effort to reach an agreement reinforces the working relationship and lays the groundwork for future collaborations. Proper conflict management not only improves relationships within the work setting but also contributes to a more harmonious and productive work climate. Developing negotiation and conflict resolution skills is invaluable, providing tools for adaptively and healthily managing stress, essential for overall emotional and mental well-being. By addressing conflicts constructively, you invest in personal and professional development, enriching all aspects of life.

Step 6: Implementing Healthy Boundaries   for Emotional Well-being

Implementing healthy boundaries is indispensable for emotional health and the development of enriching interpersonal relationships. This practice is especially relevant in managing emotional disorders, as it acts as a protective barrier against emotional wear and tear, preserving personal autonomy and self-respect. The ability to establish appropriate boundaries in various areas of life is crucial for safeguarding an individual's overall well-being.

Healthy boundaries set clear parameters on what is considered acceptable behavior towards oneself, playing a vital role in protecting emotional, physical, and mental well-being. Moreover, they are essential for fostering strong self-esteem and mutually respectful and equitable relationships. A boundary can manifest in various ways, from setting clear expectations on mutual respect to defining indispensable personal spaces for self-care.

The process for defining effective boundaries begins with introspection about personal values, needs, and priorities. This internal exploration involves a conscious assessment of personal experiences, emotions, and the aspects most valued in relationships and daily life.

Once the boundaries have been identified, the challenge lies in communicating them explicitly and assertively. Expressing these boundaries should be done using clear and respectful language. In situations of unsolicited criticism, for example, it's appropriate to say, "I appreciate your viewpoint, but I prefer not to discuss my personal decisions unless I ask for your opinion". This form of communication demonstrates firmness and respect simultaneously.

Learning to refuse, when necessary, especially for those with a tendency to please others, is a fundamental aspect of establishing boundaries. Saying "no" to requests that compromise personal well-being is an essential act of self-care.

Being vigilant about situations where established boundaries are tested is crucial. In face of transgressions to these boundaries, it's important to react assertively, reaffirming the established boundaries or taking steps to protect your space and emotional well-being.

Consistency in maintaining established boundaries is fundamental. Inconsistent boundaries can create confusion and weaken respect for personal needs. Consistency in applying boundaries sends a clear and firm message about personal expectations.

Establishing boundaries is not just an act of self-care and self-respect; it also educates others on how one wishes to be treated, improving quality of life, and laying the foundation for respectful and balanced relationships. For those facing emotional disorders, well-defined boundaries provide a sense of control and stability, contributing significantly to overall well-being. Mastering the skill of setting and maintaining healthy boundaries creates a safer and more harmonious environment both for oneself and those around us.

Example:

Suppose you're dealing with a situation where a friend or family member constantly asks for favors, draining your time and energy. This dynamic can negatively impact your well-being, indicating the need to establish a clear boundary.

Decide how and when to address this situation, choosing an appropriate time for both parties. Begin the conversation with respect and determination, explaining, "I want to talk about something important to me. I value our relationship and my willingness to help, but the frequency of your requests is affecting my personal time and energy".

Specify your boundary clearly: "I'd like to establish a balance on how much I can help you". By communicating your boundary in language that reflects your needs without assigning blame, you facilitate mutual understanding and respect.

By defining this boundary, you promote a relationship based on mutual respect. Often, the other party is not fully aware of the impact of their actions. Clear communication of your needs offers the opportunity to modify behaviors.

Remember, establishing healthy boundaries is an essential component of self-care and self-respect. If your boundaries are ignored, be consistent and reaffirm them as needed. This demonstrates your commitment to your own well-being and lays the groundwork for healthier and more balanced relationships. Mastering the practice of setting and communicating clear boundaries is vital for emotional health and fostering satisfying interpersonal relationships.

Step 7: Developing Empathy and Understanding Others' Perspectives

Fostering empathy and the ability to understand others' perspectives is crucial for building strong interpersonal relationships and improving assertive communication. Empathy, understood as the ability to feel and share another person's emotional experiences, is essential for adopting someone else's viewpoint and understanding situations from a different perspective. This approach is invaluable in managing interpersonal relationships and in preventing and handling emotional disorders.

To cultivate empathy, it is recommended to start with introspection about your recent interactions, whether daily conversations, work meetings, or family exchanges. Identify moments when you truly tried to understand the other person's viewpoint, considering how they felt and what factors might have influenced their actions or reactions.

Active listening plays a crucial role in practicing empathy. It involves paying full attention to what the other person is saying without getting distracted by thinking about your next response. Practice listening without interrupting and ask questions that deepen your understanding of the other, asking yourself: "How does this person feel?" or "What is the motive or need behind their words or actions?".

It's crucial to recognize and validate others' feelings. This does not necessarily mean agreeing with them but accepting that their emotions are legitimate from their perspective. Show understanding and respect for their feelings, even if they differ from yours.

Putting yourself in the other person's shoes is also fundamental. Try to visualize how you would feel in their situation, considering their life experiences and personal circumstances. This exercise is especially useful in situations of conflict or misunderstanding, where understanding the other can be key to finding harmonious and satisfactory solutions.

Developing empathy is a continuous process. By integrating these practices into your daily life, not only will you improve your relationships, but you will also become a more understanding, assertive, and emotionally intelligent person. Empathy is vital for effectively navigating emotional and social challenges.

Example:

Imagine a work scenario where a colleague disagrees with your approach on a project, creating a tense situation. Instead of responding defensively, adopt an empathetic attitude to better understand their position.

First, control any impulsive reaction, remembering the value of empathy in the work environment. Try to understand the emotions and motivations of your colleague. Reflect on the pressures or experiences that may be influencing their attitude. Could there be a misunderstanding at play?

With these considerations, approach the topic seeking open and constructive dialogue. Communicate your interest in understanding their concerns about the project, saying something like: "I want to understand your concerns about the project. Could you explain them to me?". During this conversation, practice active listening, showing genuine interest and avoiding hasty judgments. Validate their points and ask for clarification when necessary. This approach promotes greater understanding and facilitates a constructive resolution beneficial to both.

Afterward, take a moment to reflect on this experience. Note what you learned about your colleague's perspective and how this new understanding influenced your handling of the conflict. Evaluate how empathy and the appreciation of different viewpoints can be beneficial in future situations, both professional and personal.

This empathetic exercise is key to developing social skills and assertiveness, effectively contributing to handling complex situations and strengthening a collaborative and respectful work environment. The constant practice of empathy is essential for creating a positive and productive work atmosphere.

Step 8: Strengthening Team Problem-Solving Skills

Mastering effective techniques for team problem-solving is crucial for the development of advanced social skills and increasing assertiveness capacity, especially in scenarios that demand collaboration and teamwork. This process involves adopting strategies that promote group unity and a conflict resolution beneficial for all involved.

An essential task is self-assessment of your role within teams. Reflect on your tendency to lead or follow and consider how your behavior influences group dynamics. Document your collaboration experiences, whether in work, social, or community contexts, and analyze how you interact with others.

Active listening is a pillar in this context. It involves paying full attention to the interventions of others, understanding not only the verbal message but also the emotional and contextual subtext. In your next group activities, practice listening without interrupting and make questions that deepen your understanding of the topic. This not only helps to recognize different perspectives but also fosters an atmosphere of cooperation and mutual respect.

Promoting and valuing the diversity of ideas is another crucial aspect. Contribute with your proposals and be open to the ideas of others. Understand that the plurality of viewpoints enriches the problem-solving process, leading to innovative and effective solutions.

Develop and apply negotiation and mediation skills. In the face of discrepancies, look for areas of agreement and suggest alternatives that contemplate the interests of all participants. The goal is to find a balance between defending your positions and being flexible to adapt to collective needs.

Reflect on how these practices impact your participation in the team. Evaluate what learnings you have obtained and what areas you can perfect. Have you noticed changes in the receptiveness of others towards your ideas? Do you feel more integrated and productive in collective work?

This approach not only improves your interpersonal relationships and professional performance but also prepares you to effectively tackle complex challenges, being crucial for maintaining good emotional health and managing mood disorders adequately.

Example:

Imagine you are involved in a team project at your workplace that presents significant challenges. This situation represents an optimal opportunity to practice and perfect your collective problem-solving skills.

During meetings, exercise active listening, showing genuine interest in your colleagues' contributions. When presenting your ideas, do so clearly and assertively, inviting constructive feedback.

In case of differences, use your negotiation and mediation skills to find solutions that harmonize different viewpoints, always with the shared goal in mind.

For example, in a disagreement about the project's direction, instead of imposing a vision, look for ways to integrate different strategies to develop a unified plan.

After each work session, take a moment to reflect on your contribution and how it influenced the group. Use a journal to record your observations, what you learned, and how you can optimize your collaboration in future instances.

This reflective process will allow you to recognize both your strengths and areas susceptible to improvement, enhancing your effectiveness in collaborative contexts and contributing to the strengthening of your emotional well-being and your ability to face challenges.

Step 9: Enrichment of Non-Verbal Communication

Mastery of non-verbal communication is indispensable for enhancing social skills and assertiveness, playing a crucial role in how messages are perceived and interpreted. Non-verbal communication, which includes gestures, postures, facial expressions, and tone of voice variations, complements, and often reinforces verbal content, either facilitating or hindering message understanding.

To improve this form of communication, it is essential to begin with self-assessment in various contexts, from everyday interactions to formal situations such as work meetings. Analyze your body language, paying attention to your posture, gestures, and facial expressions. Reflect: Is your posture receptive, encouraging interaction, or rather closed, suggesting resistance? Do your gestures underscore and enrich your message, providing clarity and conviction?

Eye contact, a key component of effective communication, conveys interest, confidence, and sincerity. An adequate balance in eye contact can strengthen the connection with the interlocutor, while an excess or deficiency in this can create misunderstandings. Practice maintaining appropriate eye contact, adjusting your gaze according to the context and observing the response in your interlocutors.

Voice tone modulation, reflecting emotions coherent with the message, complements verbal communication. A varied and expressive tone captures attention and reinforces the message, while a monotone or inappropriately emotional tone can distort the intention. Experiment with different tones and observe which most effectively supports your communication.

Self-observation using mirrors or recordings can be a valuable tool for adjusting and improving your non-verbal communication. This personal reflection allows you to identify areas for improvement and reinforce those practices that are effective.

Observing individuals with outstanding social skills can provide role models. Notice how they effectively use their non-verbal communication and consider integrating similar techniques into your interactions.

By perfecting your non-verbal communication, you become more aware of your own expression and more receptive to the non-verbal cues of others. This heightened awareness facilitates more assertive and empathetic responses, leading to deeper and more satisfying interactions. This continuous improvement process is essential for personal and professional growth, significantly enhancing the quality of interpersonal relationships and emotion management.

Example:

Imagine you are preparing for an important presentation at work, an ideal opportunity to apply the non-verbal communication skills you have been perfecting.

Before the presentation, focus on adopting an open and confident posture, avoiding crossing arms or legs, which could be interpreted as a lack of openness or defensiveness. Establish eye contact with the audience, modulating your gaze to maintain a connection without becoming overwhelming.

During your speech, use gestures to emphasize key points, ensuring they complement your message without distracting. Modify your tone of voice to maintain interest and demonstrate passion for the topic you're presenting.
Observe the reactions of your audience to adapt your presentation in real-time. If you detect signs of disconnection, consider pausing to clarify a concept or inviting questions.

When responding to queries, demonstrate that you're actively listening through your body language, leaning slightly towards the speaker, and nodding to indicate understanding. At the conclusion, an upright posture and confident farewell will leave a positive and lasting impression.

This approach demonstrates how conscious and well-executed non-verbal communication can transform your interactions, boosting your self-confidence in social and professional environments. The effective use of these techniques enhances the ability to relate to others and manage complex emotions, being a powerful tool for emotional well-being and assertiveness.

Step 10: Reflection and Continuous Adjustment for Personal Growth

The final stage in the development of social skills and assertiveness consists of a process of reflection and continuous adjustment, essential for the effective integration of these skills into various life situations. This cycle of self-evaluation and improvement is particularly crucial for those facing emotional disorders, as it allows the adaptation of the learned techniques to different contexts, thus enhancing their effectiveness and contributing to emotional well-being.

The process of constant reflection enables deep introspection, facilitating the identification of successful strategies and those that require modifications. This practice of continuous self-analysis not only fosters growth in emotional management and effective interactions with others but also adapts to the constantly changing social dynamics.

The use of a personal journal emerges as a powerful tool for personal development. Recording both social and emotional experiences allow for the detection of patterns, celebration of achievements, and recognition of areas needing attention. This record promotes detailed reflection on interactions in different scenarios, driving self-awareness and continuous improvement.

Analyzing specific situations where social skills were applied facilitates understanding of others' reactions and the outcomes obtained, offering valuable insights for adjusting future interactions and learning from each experience.

Seeking feedback from trusted individuals complements the development process, providing external observations and constructive suggestions on communication and conflict resolution, fundamental for refining social skills.

Setting clear and achievable goals for the strengthening of social skills guides the path to progress, focusing efforts on specific areas of development.

The daily practice of skills in real-life situations solidifies learning. Every social interaction becomes an opportunity to exercise and perfect the acquired skills, adjusting the approach as needed. This constant exercise not only reinforces existing skills but also provides the confidence to effectively handle a wider range of social situations.

This cycle of reflection and adjustment not only drives personal and professional growth but is also essential for emotional health. By reviewing and continually improving social skills, the ability to effectively manage emotional disorders is enhanced, and the skill to successfully face life's challenges is strengthened, cultivating healthier relationships and a more emotionally balanced and fulfilling existence.

Example:

Imagine a recent interaction with a coworker that presented a communicative challenge. This encounter is a valuable opportunity to apply a reflective approach and perfect your social skills, vital for the effective management of emotional disorders.

Reflect on how you approached the conversation. Evaluate whether you applied active listening and truly understood your coworker's point of view. If you identify areas for improvement, consider how you can strengthen this skill in future interactions.

Analyze your way of communicating needs and boundaries. If your message was not as clear as desired, think of ways to express your thoughts more effectively. Practicing assertive statements in a safe environment can be beneficial.

Review how you maintained calm in the face of disagreement. If you had difficulty managing your emotions, propose incorporating relaxation techniques into your routine, improving your response in tense situations.

Use this experience to identify strengths and areas for improvement. Set specific goals, such as practicing mindfulness techniques before challenging conversations, to strengthen your emotional management and assertiveness.

By reflecting and adjusting your approach in social interactions, you not only improve your interpersonal skills but also your ability to handle stressful or emotional situations effectively, essential for those facing emotional disorders. Through continuous review and conscious application of learned strategies, you advance towards the strengthening of healthier and satisfying relationships, both professionally and personally.

Conclusion

Summary and Reflection

The journey towards enhancing social skills is a continuous voyage, essential for overall well-being and the proactive management of emotional disorders. Through meticulously outlined steps, we have guided the reader on a path of self-discovery and growth, significantly impacting all dimensions of their existence.

This journey begins with self-assessment, a crucial step that invites deep introspection to recognize both strengths and areas for improvement in social interaction. Moving forward on this path, the reader delves into the art of communicating thoughts, emotions, and needs in a clear and assertive manner, indispensable skills for fostering healthy relationships and managing emotions effectively. Active listening and the cultivation of empathy are presented as the backbone of this process, allowing not only to understand others but also to connect with them on deeper levels.

As this journey unfolds, the importance of effectively expressing needs and feelings is emphasized, a practice essential for self-care and the preservation of self-respect. Addressing conflicts and effective negotiation emerge as key competencies to enrich interpersonal relationships and reduce stress and anxiety. Similarly, the value of establishing healthy boundaries, a crucial act of self-affirmation to safeguard emotional and physical well-being and foster interactions based on balance and mutual respect, is highlighted.

The process of reflection and constant adjustment is revealed as a stage of perpetual growth. This step involves the review and adaptation of social skills to various environments and situations, maintaining a fresh and adaptable perspective. This phase ensures that the developed competencies are effectively integrated into daily life, bringing tangible benefits to emotional health.

The development of social skills is, in essence, an expedition towards a greater understanding of oneself and the environment. By integrating these skills into everyday life, not only is the capacity for interaction and communication enhanced, but also the competence to face emotional and social challenges confidently and effectively is strengthened. This journey, marked by continuous learning and self-improvement, not only enriches interpersonal relationships but also expands the understanding of life, equipping the individual with valuable tools to navigate the world with greater security, understanding, and empathy.

Step Six

Introduction to Rational Emotive Behavior Therapy

Introduction to the Topic

Rational Emotive Behavior Therapy (REBT), founded by Albert Ellis in 1957, stands as a fundamental pillar within cognitive therapies, noted for its focus on the intimate relationship between thoughts, emotions, and behaviors. This revolutionary therapeutic modality proposes that it is not events themselves that disturb people, but the irrational beliefs and thoughts these events trigger.

Centering on Ellis's "ABC" model (Activating event, Belief, and Consequence), REBT educates individuals to identify, question, and modify their irrational beliefs in favor of more logical and adaptive ones. This approach aims not only to transform dysfunctional thought patterns but also to promote healthy behaviors and emotions through deep cognitive restructuring.

The therapeutic process of REBT is dynamic and participatory, beginning with the identification of the patient's irrational beliefs, followed by a critical questioning of these beliefs, and concluding with the adoption of new, more rational, and beneficial perspectives. This approach promotes unconditional self-acceptance and increased tolerance towards others and life's adversities, essential elements for achieving sustainable emotional well-being.

The integration of REBT with principles of Emotional Intelligence amplifies its effectiveness, significantly improving individuals' ability to recognize and regulate their emotions. The synergy between the ability to modify irrational thoughts and the competence to manage emotions enriches the therapeutic process, providing patients with valuable tools to face emotional and cognitive challenges with greater resilience.

REBT has proven to be an effective methodology across a wide range of contexts and issues, successfully adapting to individual, group, and self-help formats. The incorporation of Emotional Intelligence strategies not only reinforces REBT but also provides a solid foundation for the prevention and treatment of emotional disorders, highlighting its relevance in promoting optimal mental health.

The combination of REBT with Emotional Intelligence represents a comprehensive therapeutic strategy, capable of equipping individuals with the necessary cognitive and emotional skills to navigate life more effectively and satisfactorily. This holistic approach strengthens people's emotional well-being, facilitating a more balanced and fulfilling life.

Research Evidence

The effectiveness of Rational Emotive Behavior Therapy in treating mood disorders has been widely supported by scientific research. Studies like the one by David et al. (2008) have shown that REBT is particularly effective in reducing symptoms of anxiety and depression, offering patients valuable tools to manage their emotions in a healthier and more adaptive way.

Additionally, a meta-analysis conducted by Engels et al. (1993) confirmed the utility of REBT in managing a variety of emotional and psychological challenges, highlighting its capacity to significantly improve the quality of life of affected individuals. This empirical support underscores the versatility and efficacy of REBT as a robust psychotherapeutic intervention.

MacInnes (2003) delved into the benefits of REBT, emphasizing its role in minimizing emotional distress and promoting greater emotional adaptability in people with mental health disorders. This adaptability is essential for improving patients' ability to cope with mood fluctuations and daily life challenges.

Research conducted in academic settings, like the study by Gonzales et al. (2004), revealed that the implementation of REBT among university students not only improves their academic performance but also reduces their anxiety levels. This finding demonstrates the applicability of REBT beyond the clinical realm, proving its utility in enhancing emotional well-being and performance in various areas of life.

Beyond addressing symptoms, REBT focuses on transforming the patient's life philosophy, emphasizing long-term well-being and self-realization. Through questioning and reformulating irrational beliefs, REBT guides individuals towards a more rational and fulfilling existence.

The integration of REBT with Emotional Intelligence opens new perspectives in the field of psychotherapy. Although research on this synergy is in its early stages, the combination of these disciplines is anticipated to enhance patients' ability to identify irrational beliefs and manage emotions effectively, complementing and enriching the therapeutic process of REBT.

In conclusion, scientific evidence firmly supports REBT as an effective strategy for managing emotional disorders, and its integration with Emotional Intelligence promises to further expand its efficacy. As research on this integration deepens, the foundations for its application in clinical practice will be strengthened, aiming not only for symptom remission but also for fostering an emotionally rich and satisfying life.

Instructions

Identification of Irrational Beliefs:
Albert Ellis's ABC Method

Objective

This exercise is inspired by the ABC method of Rational Emotive Behavior Therapy, an innovative proposal conceived by Albert Ellis. Its essential purpose lies in facilitating the identification and transformation of those irrational beliefs that undermine emotional well-being. Through a meticulously designed structure, this approach allows unraveling how assumptions and limiting beliefs are the genesis of disturbing emotions and counterproductive behaviors, opening the door to a renewed understanding of the interaction between thoughts, emotions, and actions.

The itinerary of this method begins with the Preparation of the Environment, establishing a space that invites introspection and deep personal analysis. Next, the Identification of the Event (A) phase proposes recognizing a specific incident that has triggered emotional turmoil, preparing the ground for a more detailed scrutiny of the underlying beliefs. In the Analysis of Beliefs (B), a critical exploration of thoughts and assumptions linked to the event in question is promoted.

The Evaluation of the Consequences (C) stage invites deep reflection on how these beliefs affect the individual's emotional state and behavior. The Debate of Irrational Beliefs introduces a moment of confrontation, urging to question their validity and usefulness. Moving towards the Creation of New Beliefs, the articulation of alternative perspectives that are more rational and constructive is encouraged.

In the Visualization of New Consequences phase, imagining the positive impact these new beliefs can have on behavior and emotions is encouraged. Practice and Repetition stand as fundamental pillars to cement these changes, promoting their effective incorporation into the individual's daily life. Through the Progress Diary, continuous monitoring of the application and effectiveness of these new beliefs is facilitated. Finally, Reflection and Continuous Adjustment ensure a constant process of self-evaluation, allowing for the recalibration of strategies as necessary.

This method transcends the mere improvement of resilience and adaptability, inviting a journey of self-exploration and personal growth that underpins more effective emotional management and enduring emotional well-being. It represents a journey towards self-realization, promoting an existence marked by robust emotional health and a balanced and enriching life perspective. This methodological enrichment is not only a valuable tool for mental health professionals but also stands as a beacon of hope and direction for those in search of a more fulfilling emotional life.

Step 1: Environment Preparation

In the journey towards understanding and reconfiguring our irrational beliefs, Albert Ellis's ABC method initially invites us to create optimal conditions for introspection and self-analysis. This first step is fundamental to ensure a process of deep and effective reflection. Choosing a space that harmonizes with our needs for concentration and tranquility is essential. Imagine a place that, beyond being merely a physical area, becomes a personal sanctuary of serenity and self-knowledge.

The creation of this environment must be intentional, selecting a corner that is free from interruptions and resonates with a sense of inner peace. This could be a private study, a dedicated space in your home for meditation, or even an outdoor place that inspires calm. Personalizing this environment is key: consider adjusting the lighting to be soft and welcoming, and incorporate elements that promote a state of meditative concentration, such as soft instrumental music or ambient sounds of nature.

It is essential to equip this space with the necessary tools for your introspective journey, with a personal diary of special relevance. This notebook will become the repository of your thoughts, emotions, and the revelations that arise during the process. Documenting your journey facilitates a conscious tracking of your evolution and becomes an invaluable source of self-knowledge.

Environment Preparation transcends the physical to delve into mental preparation. As you enter this dedicated space, do so with a focused and clear intention towards your emotional and mental development. This act of commitment to yourself sets the tone for a meaningful exploration of your beliefs and emotions, laying the foundation for profound transformation. This first step is not only the beginning of a process of change but also a declaration of your readiness to embark on a journey of growth and self-awareness. This carefully curated environment thus becomes the ideal setting for introspective work, providing the support and tranquility necessary for a reflective and constructive analysis of your inner world.

Step 2: Identification of an Event (A)

The second step in your introspective journey involves focusing your attention on selecting a specific event that has triggered a significant emotional response in you. This event could be recent or from the past; the essential part is that you choose one that continues to influence your current emotional state. Use the personal journal you prepared in Step 1 as a key tool in this exercise.

When you recall the event, encourage yourself to describe it in your journal with as much accuracy and detail as possible. Focus on specific and observable aspects of the occurrence, avoiding, for the moment, including personal interpretations, emotions, or beliefs. Precisely describe the place and moment of the event, the people involved, the actions taken, and any other concrete and relevant element.

At this stage, it is crucial to focus exclusively on the facts. Your description should be objective, as if you were an external witness narrating the events without issuing judgments or personal analyses. This approach will provide you with a clearer and more accurate perspective of the event, preventing your current emotions or beliefs from distorting the reality of what happened.

The accurate identification of the Event (A) is fundamental, as it lays the groundwork for the detailed and reflective analysis you will carry out in the subsequent steps. By recording this event in your journal, you are creating a crucial reference point for understanding how your beliefs and emotions interact and influence your emotional well-being.

Once you have completed this step, you will have identified a significant event that will act as a starting point for exploring and modifying those irrational beliefs that might be affecting your mood and behavior. This process constitutes a vital step on your path towards a deeper understanding and more effective management of your emotions.

Example:

Imagine that for several years, you have worked at your company with tireless dedication and commitment. You have placed special emphasis on demonstrating your professional competence and your capacity to assume increasing responsibilities. Recently, a vacancy was announced to lead a major project. Believing that this position would be the natural advancement in your career, you meticulously prepared for the application.

With great enthusiasm and dedication, you invested time in developing innovative and cutting-edge proposals, clearly showing your interest and aptitude for assuming this new role. Finally, the day of the meeting where the project leader would be announced arrived. Sitting in the conference room, you were filled with expectations and confidence. However, completely unexpectedly, your superior announced that a colleague, who had recently joined the company and had less experience, had been chosen to lead the project. You found yourself maintaining composure, while internally dealing with your emotions, watching your colleagues congratulate the new leader.

This scenario is a clear example of an Event (A) that could trigger a significant emotional response. By describing it in detail in your journal, you focus on the concrete and observable facts: the existence of the vacancy, your exhaustive preparation for the application, the anticipation before the meeting, and the unexpected announcement of the project leader's selection. This objective and detailed description provides you with a solid foundation for the subsequent analysis of the beliefs and emotions associated with this event, as you advance in the following steps of the ABC model.

Step 3: Analysis of Beliefs (B)

Once you have meticulously identified and described the event in your journal, it's time to tackle the next critical step: the analysis of beliefs and thoughts that emerged in response to that event. This process is key to understanding how your personal interpretations of the occurrence impact your emotions and behaviors.

In this phase, deeply reflect on your internal dialogue that occurred after the event. It is vital to pay special attention to the underlying beliefs, particularly those characterized by statements like "should", "must", or "need to". These terms are often indicative of absolutist or irrational thought patterns. For example, you might have thought: "I deserved to be chosen for that position" or "It's unbearable for me not to be recognized at my job".

It's essential to examine these beliefs under the categories established by Albert Ellis in his ABC model. These categories include rigid demands (beliefs that certain things "must" or "have to" be a specific way), catastrophizing (exaggerating the negative consequences of an event), low frustration tolerance (the belief that you can't handle certain situations), and global labeling (negatively labeling a person or yourself based on a single situation). These types of beliefs are commonly irrational and can lead to disproportionate negative emotional responses.

To facilitate a more thorough analysis, we encourage you to consult Appendix 7, which offers a detailed guide for identifying and classifying these irrational beliefs. By becoming aware of these beliefs and understanding how they distort your perception of events, you'll be better equipped to confront and mitigate mood disorders. This step represents a significant advancement toward a more robust and balanced emotional and mental health.

Example:

Imagine that, upon reviewing your internal dialogue after not being chosen to lead the project, you encounter phrases like: "I should have been the person chosen to lead the project; it's unfair that it wasn't me", "My dedication and effort deserve to be recognized", "Validation from my boss is essential to affirm my professionalism and worth". These phrases are indicative of irrational thoughts that can be harmful to your emotional well-being.

These statements reveal the presence of rigid demands and a tendency to catastrophize the situation, which can intensify feelings of anxiety, frustration, or personal devaluation. For example, the belief that you "should" have been chosen suggests the existence of an inflexible norm that, when unmet, provokes feelings of injustice and anger. Similarly, the need to obtain external recognition and validation can lead to an unhealthy dependency on others' approval, undermining your self-esteem and emotional autonomy.

Faced with these beliefs, it is crucial not to accept them as absolute truths but rather to challenge them and seek more rational and adaptive perspectives. For example, you could reframe the thought "I should have been chosen" to something like "I would have liked to be chosen, but I recognize that there are other factors that could have influenced the decision". This approach allows you to honor your desires without imposing inflexible expectations on circumstances beyond your control.

Likewise, instead of relying on your boss's validation to affirm your professional worth, you can focus on positive self-evaluation, recognizing your skills and personal achievements. This contributes to building a more robust and autonomous self-esteem, less dependent on external factors.

The process of questioning and reformulating your irrational beliefs is fundamental to the development of greater emotional health and mental well-being. Learning to identify and modify these beliefs empowers you to face challenges more effectively, reducing emotional distress and promoting a healthier and more adaptive response to adversities.

Step 4: Evaluating the Consequences (C)

After identifying and examining your beliefs, the next step is to discern how these influences your emotions and behaviors. Take a moment to deeply reflect on the feelings that emerged due to these beliefs and the actions you adopted in response. This step involves a thorough analysis of the cause-effect relationship between your internal convictions and your emotional and behavioral reactions.

Imagine, for example, the emotions triggered by the belief that "you should have been selected to lead the project". Did you feel frustration, sadness, anger, or disappointment? It's crucial to observe how these emotions affected your subsequent behavior. Did you become distant in work meetings, show hostility towards your colleagues, or did your productivity decrease? Recognizing that each emotion and action is a direct consequence of your beliefs is key to understanding the dynamics between thought and behavior.

This step offers you the opportunity to clearly see how your interpretations of events impact your emotional well-being and your interactions with others. By exploring these consequences, you can identify response patterns that may be harmful or ineffective. Such awareness is crucial for initiating change in those thought and behavior patterns that do not favor your well-being.

Additionally, as you reflect on these consequences, it's important to identify any further thoughts that arose because of your emotions. For example, the frustration of not being chosen could have generated thoughts of insecurity or doubts about your professional competence. By being aware of these chain reactions, you gain the ability to challenge and modify negative or irrational thought patterns.

In summary, evaluating the consequences is a crucial step in understanding how your beliefs affect both your emotional state and your actions. Developing a deeper understanding of these dynamics equips you with the necessary tools to initiate positive changes in your thinking and acting, leading to more effective management of mood disorders and an overall increase in your emotional well-being.

Example:

Upon hearing your boss's decision, you were overwhelmed by a sense of bodily heaviness. Feelings of betrayal and belittlement emerged, translating into a mix of frustration, anger, and resentment, not only towards your superior but also towards the newly appointed project leader. This set of emotions had a direct and tangible effect on your work behavior in the following days.

You began to act distant and reserved, with a notable decrease in your usual motivation. Your active participation in meetings drastically reduced, and every time you saw the new project leader, your feelings of resentment intensified. Even daily tasks, which you previously performed with ease, became emotional challenges difficult to face.

This emotional response triggered a series of behavioral reactions. For example, you likely actively avoided opportunities for collaboration or effective communication, potentially affecting not only your job performance but also your relationships with colleagues and superiors. This behavioral change could have created a tenser and more disconnected work environment, both for you and those around you.

It's essential to document these emotional and behavioral consequences in your journal. By doing so, you'll initiate a process of self-awareness, where you can clearly observe how your beliefs about the situation influenced your emotions and, consequently, how these emotions impacted your behavior. This act of recognition represents a crucial step in the process of questioning and modifying irrational beliefs and in the search for more constructive and healthy strategies to manage your emotional and behavioral responses in similar future situations. This exercise of introspection and recording not only favors a better personal understanding but also lays the groundwork for more resilient and adaptive emotional development.

Step 5: Debating Irrational Beliefs

At this critical point in your introspective process, your task is to question and challenge the irrational beliefs you have identified, using a critical and constructive reflection approach. Begin this internal debate by asking yourself: Is there really evidence that supports these beliefs? Are these beliefs beneficial or harmful to my emotional well-being and the achievement of my goals? (Appendix 8).

Analyze each belief in detail. Assess its truth and rationality. For example, in response to the belief "I should have been selected for that position", ask yourself: Is this a realistic expectation? Could there have been factors outside my control that influenced the decision? This type of questioning will help you determine whether you are maintaining a belief based on objective facts or unfounded assumptions.

Reflect also on the impact of these beliefs on your mood and behavior. Consider whether they are contributing to your progress or plunging you into a cycle of negative emotions. The goal is to identify and recognize thought patterns that are not only irrational but also counterproductive to your development.

When challenging these beliefs, strive to develop more rational and flexible alternatives. Instead of clinging to the idea that you "should" have obtained the position, explore the possibility that this situation may represent an opportunity for personal and professional growth, perhaps venturing into new areas or strengthening existing skills.

This step is fundamental to transforming your internal dialogue into one that is healthier and more constructive. By concluding this phase, you will have taken a significant step towards modifying limiting thought patterns and adopting a more positive and realistic perspective towards the situations you face. This approach not only improves your emotional well-being but also enhances your adaptability and resilience to future challenges.

Example:

In this example, proceed to challenge the previously identified belief: "I should have been the one to lead the project; it's unfair that I wasn't selected". Begin this process by questioning the authenticity and logic of such a statement. Ask yourself: Are there universal rules that determine who should be selected for a promotion? Is this expectation based on objective facts, or does it originate from a personal assumption?

To address these questions, consider reviewing your company's promotion policies. Analyze whether your interpretation of these policies aligns with reality or if there are elements you may not have considered. This analysis will help you discern whether your belief represents a realistic expectation or if it is more of a projection of your own desires and ambitions.

Additionally, perform an objective evaluation of the skills and competencies of the colleague who was promoted. Reflect on whether their professional profile meets the project's requirements in a way that perhaps yours does not. This approach will provide a more balanced and less biased view of your boss's decision.

It's also crucial to adopt a more flexible and open-minded attitude. Recognize that the work environment is influenced by a variety of factors and that promotion decisions do not always match our personal expectations. By accepting this reality, you can transform your initial belief and view the situation from a more objective and emotionally detached perspective.

This critical questioning exercise is essential for dismantling irrational beliefs and fostering a more rational and adaptive approach in your professional life. By completing this step, you will have made significant progress in mitigating the negative impacts that such irrational beliefs can have on your emotional well-being, paving the way for a healthier and more constructive attitude in your work environment.

Step 6: Creating New Beliefs

Once you have confronted and questioned your irrational beliefs, the next step is to formulate new statements or beliefs that are more rational, realistic, and beneficial. This process involves a conscious restructuring of your thoughts to align with an objective and equitable assessment of the situation.

Begin by reflecting on how you can reinterpret the event or circumstance in a way that emphasizes the positive aspects, or the lessons learned. For example, instead of clinging to the idea that "I should have been the one to lead the project; it's unfair that I wasn't", consider adopting a new, more adaptive belief such as "Although I wasn't chosen to lead this project, this situation represents an opportunity to learn and progress professionally in the future".

It's important that this new belief is authentic and realistic for you, reflecting a more nuanced understanding of the situation. Recognize that there are multiple factors that influence professional decisions and not all situations will unfold according to your personal expectations.

Moreover, try to formulate your new beliefs in a way that promotes self-compassion and personal development. Instead of focusing on what was not achieved, direct your energy towards how you can use this experience to strengthen your skills and better prepare for future opportunities.

The purpose of this step is to replace limiting and negative beliefs with healthier ones more conducive to your emotional well-being and professional growth. By completing this step, you will have established a set of constructive new beliefs, which will serve as valuable tools for effectively addressing similar situations in the future with a more optimistic and positive perspective.

Example:

By replacing the absolutist belief "I SHOULD have been the chosen one to lead the project" with a more nuanced one like "I WOULD HAVE LIKED to be the chosen one to lead the project", you initiate a substantial change in your perception of the situation. This new statement allows you to recognize your personal preference without presenting it as an unavoidable demand. It's important to understand that, although you would have preferred to lead the project, your professional development does not depend solely on this achievement. There is a range of opportunities and pathways through which you can shine and evolve in your career.

Begins by expanding your perspective to appreciate the wide range of possibilities available for standing out and progressing professionally. With this new understanding, you will not only benefit in terms of mood but also be able to redirect your energy towards identifying and seizing new challenges. Additionally, this attitude will allow you to adopt a more open and collaborative role in the current project, benefiting both your individual performance and your relationships with colleagues.

Adopt the view that every situation, even those that initially seem adverse, represents an opportunity to enrich your experience and hone your skills. Maintain an optimistic approach, considering that every experience, big or small, constitutes an essential part of your growth and development, both professionally and personally. This attitude not only prevents unnecessary conflicts at work but also contributes to fostering a more harmonious and productive work environment.

This process of formulating new, more constructive, and flexible beliefs will prepare you to handle similar situations in the future with greater adaptability and resilience, which in turn will improve your emotional well-being and your ability to face professional challenges more effectively and healthily.

Step 7: Visualizing New Consequences

In this step, you must use your imagination to anticipate what your emotional reactions and behaviors might be if you integrated these new, more adaptive, and realistic beliefs into your life. The purpose of this visualization is to help you understand the beneficial impact that a change in your thinking can have on your emotional well-being and behavior in similar future situations.

To carry out this practice, find a calm moment to reflect. Visualize scenarios like the one you previously described, but now react from the perspective of your new beliefs. For example, if you find yourself in a situation where you are not selected for a specific role or task again, imagine how you would react, remembering that each experience, whether achieved or not, contributes to your professional development. Reflect on how this new belief could influence your emotional state, reducing feelings of frustration and fostering attitudes of acceptance and motivation to continue advancing.

Focus on the positive emotions that could emerge from adopting this renewed perspective. You might feel calmer, motivated, or even inspired to explore new opportunities. Visualize also how this positive attitude can improve your interactions with colleagues and supervisors, and the possible positive impact on your work performance.

This visualization exercise not only allows you to foresee healthier and more adaptive emotional and behavioral reactions to future challenges but also helps to internalize and reinforce these new rational beliefs. By regularly practicing this visualization technique, you are mentally preparing to face challenges in a more constructive and positive way, which will positively affect your emotional well-being and the overall quality of your life.

Example:

Imagine you are in an upcoming project meeting in which you were not designated as the leader. With your renewed mindset, visualize yourself participating actively and enthusiastically, not from a stance of resentment but with a spirit of openness and collaboration. Instead of perceiving yourself as excluded, recognize this situation as an opportunity to make a significant contribution. Visualize how your constructive participation and enthusiasm can positively transform the team dynamics and elevate your own mood.

In this scenario, visualize how by sharing your ideas and working cooperatively, you experience a sense of satisfaction and achievement, understanding that there are multiple ways to progress in your professional career. This positive and proactive attitude not only improves your emotional well-being but can also catch the attention of your superiors and colleagues. Contemplate how your contribution to the project could open doors to future opportunities, highlighting you as a versatile and collaborative professional.

Additionally, imagine the impact of this new perspective on your work relationships. By interacting with your colleagues, including the new project leader, from a position of collaboration and not competition, you will strengthen your professional bonds. This can lead to a more harmonious and productive work environment, where you feel valued and recognized as an integral part of the team.

This visualization exercise is a powerful tool to internalize your new belief and mentally prepare to apply it in real situations. By practicing this visualization regularly, you will strengthen your ability to face similar challenges in the future in a more positive and constructive way, benefiting not only your emotional well-being but also your professional development. This approach will allow you to tackle future situations with greater self-confidence and an open attitude, which is essential for continuous and successful growth in your career path.

Step 8: Practice and Repetition

The effective integration of these new rational and constructive beliefs into your daily life is achieved through constant and conscious practice. This process involves regularly applying these beliefs across various situations, both in your professional and personal life, thus reinforcing their internalization and their positive impact on your emotional well-being.

Begin by being aware of key words in your internal dialogue that signal absolutist or irrational thought patterns, such as "should", "must", or "need". While these expressions might seem trivial, they are powerful indicators of how you interpret and respond to situations.

In moments when you would normally experience a negative emotional reaction, become aware of these terms, and reflect. Instead of thinking about what "should" be, ask yourself if you simply "would like" it to be that way. This subtle change in language and perception can have a notable impact on how you view and handle circumstances.

Record improvements in your emotional state and in your behaviors because of applying these changes. Observing how you feel and act in situations where you previously would have reacted differently is essential. This constant monitoring will allow you to recognize and appreciate the benefits of adopting a more rational and constructive approach to your life.

Finally, commit to the regular and reflective practice of these new beliefs. It is important to remember that sustained change in thought and behavior patterns requires time, effort, and persistence. Repeating this process will strengthen your ability to effectively manage your emotions and lead a more balanced and satisfying life. Keep a record of your progress and challenges in your personal journal and use it as a support tool for your ongoing development in emotional management. Over time, these new beliefs and practices will become an integral part of your approach to life, allowing you to face challenges with greater confidence and resilience.

Example:

Imagine that each morning, upon waking, you take a moment to reaffirm your new belief: "I would like to be recognized at work, but my professional worth does not depend solely on a promotion or a specific project". Visualize yourself facing the day with this mindset, preparing for any work situation with a calm and objective perspective.

Throughout the day, keep a self-observation journal. In situations where you previously would have felt undervalued, such as in meetings where your contributions are not acknowledged as expected, note your emotional reactions and how the new belief helps you handle the situation more positively and constructively.

At the end of the day, take some time to review your journal. Reflect on the application of the new belief in different contexts and evaluate whether you felt calmer and in control. This exercise will allow you to identify moments when you might have reverted to old thought patterns and offers the opportunity to consider how you might approach these situations differently in the future.

With each passing week, make time to review your journal and celebrate progress, no matter how small. Recognize that each step forward is an advancement on your path to emotional well-being.

Gradually, begin to apply this belief in other areas of your life, such as in your personal life, where you also seek recognition and validation. Discover how this new way of thinking helps you feel more fulfilled and less dependent on external approval.

This process of practice and repetition becomes an essential component of your daily routine. Over time, you will notice how this change in your way of thinking not only improves your emotional well-being but also enables you to face challenges with greater ease and effectiveness. Through this consistent and reflective approach, you transform into a more resilient and balanced individual, capable of handling life's ups and downs with greater strength and a positive outlook.

Step 9: Progress Journal

Now that you have begun to integrate new rational and constructive beliefs into your life, it is essential to keep a detailed record of these changes and their impact. I encourage you to maintain a Progress Journal. This journal will become an invaluable tool for documenting your experiences, reflections, and adjustments as you progress toward more effective emotional management.

Take a moment each day to write in this journal. It can be in the morning, setting your intentions for the day, or at night, reflecting on the day's events. Start by recording specific situations where you applied your new beliefs. Detail the context, how you replaced an irrational belief with a rational one, and your feelings about it.

For example, if you encountered a situation at work where you would normally have felt undervalued, describe how you modified that perception to a more balanced one and what actions you took as a result. Note your response to colleagues' comments and how you felt at the end of the day by adopting this new belief.

Moreover, document how these new beliefs affect your emotions and behaviors. Observe if there is a decrease in stress or anxiety levels. Record any improvement in your interpersonal relationships or work performance. Use this journal also to identify areas for improvement. If you notice that in certain situations you revert to old thought patterns, jot it down. Reflect on the reasons for this regression and what you could do differently in the future.

The purpose of this journal is not to judge yourself but to provide a means to observe your progress and learn from your experiences. Over time, you will see how much you have advanced in adopting healthier beliefs and how this has positively benefited your life. This record will become valuable evidence of your evolution toward better emotional health and increased well-being, demonstrating the power of a reflective and conscious approach to your personal and professional development.

Example:

"Today, as I walked through the glass doors of the meeting room, I faced an unexpected challenge. During the presentation of my most recent proposal, my boss publicly expressed his doubts. Normally, this would have triggered a mix of resentment and discouragement in me. In the past, I tended to interpret these situations as a direct attack on my professional competence, and my boss's criticisms resonated in my head as a disturbing echo: 'I should be recognized and valued, it's unfair that I'm not'. However, today I experienced things differently.

With the intention of transforming my old beliefs, I had mentally prepared myself for situations like this. 'I would like my boss to value my idea, but his disagreement does not define my worth', I reminded myself, seeking to adopt a more balanced and constructive perspective. When receiving the critique, instead of sinking into disappointment, I took a deep breath and chose to approach the situation with an open mind, asking my boss how I could improve my proposal.

The emotional response I experienced was enlightening. Although I initially felt a wave of anxiety and frustration, by actively applying my new beliefs, I found myself progressively calmer and in control. My behavior also reflected this change: instead of being withdrawn or defensive, I actively participated and was receptive to constructive suggestions. This adjustment in my attitude not only allowed me to remain calm and focused but also reinforced my sense of security and valuation within the team.

Reflecting on this episode in my Progress Journal, I realize that this new approach not only improves my emotional well-being but also strengthens my professional skills and work relationships. I understand the importance of maintaining a positive and open attitude to feedback, even in the face of an initial reaction of feeling rejected or underestimated. This experience has taught me that every situation, no matter how difficult, represents an opportunity for growth and learning. As I continue to document my experiences and reflections, I am determined to keep applying these new beliefs, thus strengthening my ability to handle emotionally complex situations, and contributing to my personal and professional development".

Step 10: Reflection and Continuous Adjustment

Reaching this critical point in the exercise, it's important to dedicate yourself to reflection and continuous adjustment of the strategies you've been implementing to manage your emotions and moods. This continuous evaluation process is crucial to ensure that your approach remains relevant and effective over time. Periodic review of your practices will allow you to identify which aspects are working effectively and which need to be modified to better suit your changing needs and situations.

Set aside time each week to review your Progress Journal. There, you'll find a detailed record of your experiences and reflections, crucial for assessing the impact of your new mindset and practices on your overall well-being. Ask yourself key questions: Are your new beliefs contributing to improved mood? How are these beliefs influencing your daily behavior and interactions with others? Is there any belief or practice that needs to be reviewed or replaced with something more effective?

Don't be afraid to experiment with adjustments to your approach. If you find that a belief or thought pattern remains challenging, consider exploring it from a new perspective or seeking additional support, such as reading relevant material, participating in support groups, or consulting with a mental health professional.

In addition to evaluating your beliefs and behaviors, reflect on the overall impact of this process on your emotional and mental health. Ask yourself: Do you feel more equipped to face emotional challenges? Have you noticed improvements in your quality of life and interpersonal relationships? These reflections will help you keep a clear focus on your goal of improving your emotional well-being.

Finally, remember to be patient and compassionate with yourself on this journey of self-discovery and growth. Developing emotional intelligence and effectively managing mood disorders is an ongoing process that demands time, practice, and commitment. Each step you take on this path represents progress towards a deeper understanding and more effective management of your emotions, which in turn will lead to a more fulfilling and satisfying life. Keep in mind that every small change and adjustment you make is an important step towards your emotional well-being and personal and professional growth.

Example:

Imagine that, after several weeks of practicing the steps of Albert Ellis's ABC model, you decide to take time to assess the progress made so far. You sit in a quiet place with your Progress Journal, ready to reflect on your journey of self-discovery and emotional improvement.

You start by reviewing the entries in your journal, where you detailed specific situations, the irrational beliefs you identified, the new beliefs you developed to replace them, and the impact of these changes on your emotions and behaviors. You notice, for example, an entry where you described a work situation where you initially felt undervalued. Then, you realize how adopting new beliefs, such as "I have the potential to grow and seize new opportunities", has allowed you to face similar situations with greater confidence and a more proactive attitude.

Reflect on the effect this change in perception has had on your overall well-being. You might realize that you now feel less anxious about work challenges and more willing to collaborate on projects, even when you're not in a leadership role. You may have noticed a reduction in your stress levels and an improvement in your sleep quality.

Next, you consider if there are areas that still require improvement. Are there situations where old irrational beliefs still emerge? How could you adjust your approach to address these areas more effectively? Perhaps you decide to seek additional resources, like books on personal development, or consider discussing your challenges with a therapist or support group.

As you conclude your reflection session, you feel inspired by the progress you've made and have a clear idea of the next steps to take. You recognize that the path to emotional improvement is an ongoing process and commit to continue evaluating and adjusting your approach. With each review, you become more skilled at managing your emotions and building a more robust and sustainable emotional well-being. This ongoing process of self-evaluation and adjustment allows you to face future challenges with greater skill and confidence, reinforcing your personal and professional growth.

Conclusion

Summary and Reflection

At the conclusion of our exploration of Albert Ellis's ABC Method, it's time to reflect on the progress made. This journey has been a profound quest for self-knowledge and understanding of our emotional reactions to life's situations. We have fostered introspection and improved our emotional management.

We began by identifying disturbing events and carefully analyzing the underlying beliefs, challenging those irrational ideas that compromise our emotional well-being. We recognized how our emotions often stem from our personal interpretations, rather than from the events themselves.

Questioning the validity of irrational beliefs has guided us towards a more objective perspective, adjusting our beliefs towards a healthier and more balanced approach. We implemented practical strategies such as visualization to consolidate these changes, improving our emotional and behavioral response.

This journey has transformed our perception and response to experiences, allowing us to neutralize disruptive thoughts and establish a foundation of rational beliefs that promote well-being. It's a time to appreciate these achievements, seeing them as steps towards a more harmonious life.

This commitment to personal improvement, seeking inner peace and life coping skills, underscores our dedication to growth. This effort brings us closer to a more fulfilling and satisfied life, marking a significant advance in our personal development.

Step Seven

Introduction to Cognitive Behavioral Therapy

Introduction to the Topic

Cognitive Behavioral Therapy (CBT) is a comprehensive and effective psychotherapeutic approach within the field of mental health. Beck (1964) demonstrated its utility in understanding and modifying thought and behavior patterns that contribute to emotional and psychological disorders. Since its development in the 1960s, CBT has been based on the premise that cognitions, including thoughts, beliefs, and attitudes, significantly influence our emotions and behaviors, as well as our mental health.

Characterized by being brief and focused on current problems and the present, CBT has proven its effectiveness through empirical research, especially in the treatment of mood disorders, such as depression and anxiety (Hofmann, Asmundson & Beck, 2013). CBT emphasizes identifying and restructuring negative automatic thoughts, maladaptive core beliefs, and distorted cognitive schemas (Beck, Rush, Shaw & Emery, 1979).

Therapeutic collaboration is essential in CBT, where therapist and patient work together to explore and challenge underlying beliefs, with the goal of constructing a more adaptive narrative (Beck et al., 1979). Techniques such as gradual exposure, skill practice, and problem-solving enable patients to modify dysfunctional behaviors, improving their quality of life (Hofmann & Smits, 2008).

Integrating Emotional Intelligence into CBT can enhance its benefits (Salovey & Mayer, 1990). EI improves the understanding and management of one's own and others' emotions, facilitating emotional regulation and empathy (Mayer, Roberts & Barsade, 2008), valuable aspects in CBT for identifying problematic emotions and cognitions (Mayer & Salovey, 1997).

For example, emotional self-awareness allows recognizing automatic thought patterns and assessing their accuracy and utility. Emotional regulation equips patients with strategies to manage intense emotions, reducing vulnerability to cognitive distortions and enhancing the ability to cope with challenges. Empathy and social competence facilitate the construction of healthier relationships and the establishment of support networks, reducing the isolation often found in mood disorders (Mayer et al., 2008).

Additionally, CBT enriched with EI can be especially effective in group settings, where patients practice EI skills socially, learning from others and providing mutual feedback and support. This approach not only fosters individual change but also promotes a therapeutic environment of collective learning and growth (Durlak et al., 2011).

In summary, CBT is a robust approach for treating mood disorders, and its enrichment with EI can result in a more comprehensive treatment. This combination offers patients enduring tools for emotional regulation and behavioral adaptation, improving their ability to handle present and future difficulties (Greenberg, 2006).

Research Evidence

The efficacy of Cognitive Behavioral Therapy in treating mood disorders has been extensively documented, including major depression, generalized anxiety disorder, panic disorder, social phobia, and post-traumatic stress disorder, among others. CBT provides practical tools for patients to improve their mood and behavior in daily life (Hofmann, Asnaani, Vonk, Sawyer & Fang, 2012).

Backed by empirical evidence, CBT focuses on systematic research. Hofmann et al. (2012) in their meta-analysis, highlighted the sustained long-term effectiveness of CBT for various mental health conditions, providing not only symptomatic relief but also promoting coping skills that enhance the quality of life and overall functionality of the patient.

The integration of Emotional Intelligence into CBT represents an innovation that adds an additional dimension to the treatment of mood disorders. By focusing on thought and behavior, CBT benefits from the inclusion of EI, possibly resulting in a deeper understanding of the interaction between emotions, thoughts, and behaviors (Zeidner, Matthews & Roberts, 2009).

Incorporating EI skills, such as mindfulness, emotional awareness, and empathy, within the CBT framework can enhance individuals' ability to recognize and regulate their emotions more effectively. EI facilitates the challenge to negative thought patterns and develops a more balanced and adaptive perspective of experiences (Salovey, Bedell, Detweiler & Mayer, 1999).

In conclusion, CBT is confirmed as an effective approach for mood disorders, and its enrichment through the integration of EI could constitute a more holistic and effective treatment for emotional and psychological well-being (Brackett, Rivers & Salovey, 2011). Future research will provide a more solid basis for this combined practice, anticipated with interest in the field of mental health.

Instructions

Identification and Restructuring
of Cognitive Distortions

Objective

This exercise, based on Cognitive Behavioral Therapy, focuses on cognitive restructuring. Its purpose is to guide you in identifying automatic thoughts and questioning the cognitive distortions that affect your perception of reality, causing negative emotions and unwanted behaviors.

Through this process, you will learn to recognize and modify harmful or unproductive thoughts with more balanced and rational ones. This cognitive change aims not only to reduce emotional tension but also to promote overall well-being. This technique is an effective tool for developing skills in emotional self-management and behavioral modification.

During this exercise, which ranges from preparing a conducive environment for reflection to the continuous evaluation and adjustment of your progress, you will increase your resilience and your ability to address future challenges safely and effectively. This process will provide you with a framework for introspection and practical strategies to implement positive and lasting changes in your daily life.

The goal is to achieve a deep understanding of oneself, which will contribute to improving your quality of life and enriching your interpersonal relationships. With this approach, the aim is not only to mitigate symptoms or address specific problems but also to promote personal growth and constant improvement in all areas of your existence.

Step 1: Setting the Environment

To effectively start the process of identification and restructuring of cognitive distortions, the first essential step is the creation of a conducive environment. This space should be a sanctuary of calm and concentration, free from interruptions and distractions. It is ideal to select a place in your home, such as a study or a quiet corner, that promotes introspection and in-depth analysis. This environment should be welcoming and stimulating for your inner work, facilitating your full immersion in the reflection and self-examination process.

Within this space, it is vital to have your personal journal at hand. This journal will become a faithful companion throughout your journey, providing a safe space to record thoughts, observations, and any revealing perceptions that arise during the exercise. A journal is more than just a notebook; it becomes a powerful tool for documenting your progress, reflecting on your experiences, and keeping a concrete record of your emotional and cognitive evolution.

When preparing your environment, it is also important to consider elements that enhance your concentration and well-being. This may include adequate lighting, a comfortable chair, and possibly personal items that inspire you, such as a plant, a piece of art, or soft background music, if this contributes to your focus. The goal is to create a personal sanctuary where you feel safe, comfortable, and fully prepared to undertake significant and transformative work.

This prepared setting acts as a catalyst for the process of self-analysis and personal growth. By dedicating a physical and mental space for your development, you establish a solid foundation for the introspective work you will perform. This is an essential step to effectively address and reframe cognitive distortions, paving the way for greater self-awareness and emotional well-being.

Step 2: Identification of Emotions

In this crucial step of your therapeutic process, dedicate yourself to introspection to identify and name the emotions you are experiencing. This phase is essential for establishing the relationship between your feelings and the specific situations that trigger them. Start by asking yourself: "What emotions am I currently feeling?" and "How do these emotions physically manifest in my body?". It is vital to observe each emotion and associated bodily sensation without judgment or trying to alter them. Simply accept them as they emerge in your awareness.

Note down in your personal journal all the emotions you identify, including details such as their intensity, duration, and associated thoughts. This record not only promotes a deeper understanding of your emotional state but is also key to recognizing patterns and recurring emotional triggers.

If you find it challenging to name or understand your emotions, it might be helpful to consult Appendix 3, which provides a detailed guide on emotions and their characteristics. This resource will help you differentiate between similar emotions and better understand the complexity of your emotional experience. You are also invited to consult Appendix 9.

The accurate identification of your emotions is a crucial step in the process of restructuring cognitive distortions. By clearly understanding what you feel and why, you will be better equipped to analyze how your thoughts and beliefs impact your emotional state and behavior. This level of self-knowledge is fundamental in Cognitive Behavioral Therapy and lays the groundwork for the following steps of your treatment.

This process of emotion identification allows you not only to recognize and better understand your emotional reactions but also prepares you for the next step of exploring and challenging the beliefs and thoughts behind these emotions. By doing so, you pave the way toward a greater understanding of yourself and the development of healthier strategies for managing your emotional responses, vital for your growth and emotional well-being.

Example:

Imagine you recently faced a challenge at work: a project in which you invested considerable time and effort was unexpectedly canceled. This is an opportune moment to reflect on your emotions. You identify feeling "frustrated and disappointed". However, it's crucial to delve beyond the mere identification of these emotions. Notice how these emotions manifest in your body: you may experience a sense of tightness in your chest and notable tension in your shoulders.

For a more detailed analysis, quantifying these sensations might be useful. You could assign a score from one to five to the intensity of your physical and emotional discomfort. In your personal journal, record these emotions and physical sensations with a numerical value. For example: "I experience a tightness in my chest that I would rate as a 4 in intensity, and the tension in my shoulders is a 3".

Furthermore, reflect on the degree of comfort or discomfort these sensations generate. Ask yourself: "How pleasant or unpleasant do I find these physical and emotional sensations?" and assign a similar score. This will help you gain a clearer understanding of how these emotions impact your overall well-being. For example, you might say, "The frustration I experience is quite unpleasant, I would rate it a 4 in terms of unpleasantness".

Recording these observations is an essential step in the process of identification and restructuring of cognitive distortions. By documenting these experiences, you establish a clear link between the felt emotions and physical reactions. This exercise is crucial for beginning to understand how your thoughts and emotions are interconnected and how they affect your mood and behavior. This level of self-awareness is vital for addressing and modifying thought patterns that may be contributing to negative emotional responses, which in turn is an important step on your journey towards better emotional management and greater well-being.

Step 3: Recording Automatic Thoughts

In this phase of the exercise, it is essential that you dedicate time to identifying and recording the automatic thoughts that emerge in your mind. These thoughts are spontaneous and immediate reactions to specific situations, especially those that trigger intense emotions. They often arise so quickly and subtly that they go unnoticed, yet they have a significant impact on our emotional state and behavioral reactions.

To implement this step, whenever you face a situation that provokes an emotional response, pause to observe the thoughts that arise in your mind. These thoughts may be brief or fleeting, but it is essential to capture them as they manifest. They can be judgments, assumptions, predictions, or any other type of spontaneous thought.

Write these thoughts down in your personal journal as faithfully as possible. It is crucial that you record them exactly as you experience them, without attempting to alter them or judge them for their apparent insignificance or discomforting nature. Even those thoughts that may seem minor or trivial can provide valuable insights into your thought patterns.

For example, if after a work meeting you feel particularly anxious, pay attention, and note down the thoughts that cross your mind. They might be reflections such as: "Surely my presentation wasn't good enough" or "They probably think I'm not suitable for the project". These automatic thoughts reflect your underlying beliefs and are fundamental to understanding how your emotions and behaviors are formed.

This step is vital in the process of identifying and restructuring cognitive distortions. By becoming aware of these automatic thoughts, you begin the process of understanding how your perceptions and beliefs affect your emotional and behavioral experience. This meticulous record is the preamble to the following steps of analyzing and modifying these automatic responses, allowing you to address them in a more conscious and systematic manner. Through this exercise, you are equipping yourself with the necessary tools to unravel and transform the beliefs that limit your emotional well-being, thus moving towards a greater understanding and management of your emotions and reactions.

Example:

In relation to a recent argument, you had with a loved one, it is crucial that you take time to reflect and document the automatic thoughts that arose during or after that interaction. These thoughts, which are spontaneous reactions to the emotions experienced, can provide deep insight into your habitual thought patterns.   For example, after the disagreement, you might have thoughts like: "I always fail to make myself understood", "I feel undervalued by others", or "I always end up being the one to blame in these situations". These thoughts are indicative of underlying beliefs that might be driving your negative emotions and your way of reacting to the situation.

It is essential that you record these thoughts honestly and in detail in your personal journal. Try to capture the exact essence of each thought, maintaining its original form and emotional charge. Accuracy in this record is key to a full understanding of your internal mental processes.

Besides noting these thoughts, reflect on your physical and emotional sensations at that moment. Did you experience tension in any part of your body? Did you feel any physical sensation like heat or cold? What was the intensity level of your emotion? By correlating these thoughts with physical and emotional responses, you will gain a more comprehensive view of how certain situations trigger specific thought patterns and emotional reactions.

This step is a crucial element in the process of identifying and restructuring cognitive distortions. By recognizing and understanding these automatic thoughts and their influence on your mood and behavior, you prepare to analyze and modify these responses in the following stages of the exercise. This knowledge better equips you to address and alleviate mood disorders using Cognitive Behavioral Therapy techniques, thus advancing towards better emotional management and greater well-being. This detailed record of automatic thoughts is an essential step towards awareness and changing thought patterns that may be limiting your happiness and effectiveness in personal relationships and other areas of your life.

Step 4: Identifying Cognitive Distortions

In this crucial step of the exercise, you focus on confronting and unraveling the cognitive distortions that have infiltrated your automatic thoughts. These distortions are erroneous thought patterns that distort your perception of reality, often in illogical or exaggerated ways, and are a common source of negative emotions and behaviors. Your task in this introspection process is to meticulously examine the thoughts you previously recorded, looking for patterns that indicate a distorted perception of reality.

One of these patterns is personalization, where one may attribute the responsibility for situations entirely outside of their control to themselves. For example, if you think a slight disagreement with a friend is entirely your fault, you are personalizing the situation. A common related pattern is dichotomous thinking, also known as all-or-nothing thinking. In this case, situations are seen in absolute terms: something is either completely good or completely bad, with no room for nuances or shades of gray. This type of thinking often leads to extreme and unrealistic conclusions about oneself and others.

Another important pattern is overgeneralization, where a single negative event is taken as an endless pattern of failure and disappointment. For example, if after a bad day at work you conclude that you're always incompetent, you're overgeneralizing from a single instance. There's also mental filtering, which involves focusing only on the negative aspects of a situation, ignoring the positive or neutral ones. This leads to an unbalanced view of events and reinforces feelings of hopelessness and negativity.

Finally, catastrophizing is a distortion where the worst possible scenario is anticipated, often without a realistic basis. This tendency to imagine the worst case unnecessarily increases anxiety and stress. Your goal in this step is to identify and mark these patterns in your personal journal, next to the automatic thoughts you've recorded. Identifying these is the first step towards dismantling these distortions and replacing them with more balanced and realistic thoughts.

You are recommended to consult Annex 10 for more detailed information on cognitive distortions. Appendix 2, on the other hand, is a scale that can help you have an estimate of what distortions may be present in you.

Example:

Continuing with the process of introspection and analysis that we've started; we now focus on the recent disagreement situation to carefully examine the recorded thoughts. By doing so, you will begin to identify thought patterns that might be distorting your perception of reality.

Take, for example, the statement "I believe I never manage to make myself understood". This thought may reveal a clear tendency towards overgeneralization. Here, the use of the word "never" indicates how a specific and possibly isolated event has been extrapolated to encompass all possible communication situations. This type of absolute thinking, although common, can significantly affect your mental and emotional state, leading you to a biased and negatively distorted view of your communication abilities.

Another possible reflection that may have arisen in your mind during this exercise is "I am responsible for all misunderstandings". This statement suggests personalization, where you irrationally assume all the blame, without considering other factors or circumstances that may have contributed to the misunderstanding. The use of an absolute term like "all" is a clear indicator of a distorted and absolutist perception of the situation.

These examples of automatic thoughts and the associated cognitive distortions are fundamental to understanding how we interpret and react to everyday situations. By becoming aware of these distortions and actively working on recognizing and questioning them, you will start to notice a reduction in the negative influence they exert on your emotional well-being. This step is vital for laying the groundwork for restructuring these thoughts, which we will address in the following steps of this exercise. This process will lead you to a more realistic and balanced view of your interactions and self, marking significant progress on your path towards better emotional management and greater self-awareness.

Step 5: Challenging Automatic Thoughts

At this critical point in the exercise, with automatic thoughts identified and cognitive distortions recognized, we move on to a crucial stage: challenging these thoughts. This step is essential because it involves an active and conscious questioning of the validity and utility of the ideas and perceptions that automatically arise in your mind.

To begin this process, adopt an attitude of deep inquiry, akin to that of a detective in search of the truth. Use the Socratic method (Appendix 8), a technique that involves asking reflective and profound questions, to analyze each thought. Question each idea by challenging its truthfulness and functionality. Faced with a thought like "I never manage to make myself understood", ask yourself: Are there concrete proofs that support this claim? Can you remember situations in which you indeed succeeded in making yourself understood? This type of questions will help you determine if your thoughts are based on reality or if they are mere generalizations or exaggerations.

Also, reflect on the usefulness of these thoughts. Evaluate whether they contribute to your personal goals or well-being. Are there more logical or constructive ways to interpret the situation? For example, instead of believing that you are entirely responsible for a misunderstanding, you could consider that communication is a two-way process influenced by external factors as well.

This process is crucial to reduce the negative impact that cognitive distortions have on your emotional well-being. By questioning and reevaluating these thoughts, you will start to notice a decrease in the influence they exert on your mood and behavior. This step prepares you for the next one, where you will focus on the active restructuring of these thoughts, transforming them into ideas that are more rational and beneficial for your emotional and mental health. This procedure not only improves your emotional well-being but also provides you with effective tools for more healthily managing everyday situations and emotional challenges, marking significant progress on your path to self-awareness and personal improvement.

Example:

Continuing with the scenario of the previously mentioned disagreement, we now delve into a crucial phase: applying critical analysis to the identified automatic thoughts. This process is vital for transforming the way you interpret and react to emotionally charged situations.

In this situation, where you feel frustrated and disappointed after a disagreement, start by questioning the truthfulness and utility of your immediate thoughts. For example, a common thought might be: "I never manage to make myself understood in arguments". In response to this thought, pose critical questions like: "Is it really true that I never manage to communicate effectively, or are there occasions where my communication has been successful?". Look for concrete examples of past situations where you managed to express yourself clearly and were understood, thus challenging the idea that it is an excessive generalization.

Another thought that might arise is: "I am always to blame in disagreements". In the face of this statement, reflect deeply: "What evidence do I have that contradicts the notion that I am always responsible in disagreements?". By questioning this idea, start to recognize moments when the disagreement was not entirely your fault or situations where responsibility was shared.

Additionally, examine the functionality of these thoughts. Ask yourself: "What benefit do I gain from feeling this way?". Evaluate whether this thought contributes to your well-being or plunges you into a cycle of negativity and despair. This type of reflections is key to determining if these thoughts are truly useful or if they simply perpetuate negative emotions and behaviors.

This exercise of introspection and questioning is fundamental for challenging and, over time, modifying the cognitive distortions that influence your perception and reaction to difficult situations. By conducting this analysis, you begin to move towards a more balanced and objective perspective of circumstances, thus setting the groundwork for thought restructuring that will be explored in the following stages of the exercise. This process is an essential step on your path to a better understanding and management of your emotions, allowing you to tackle life's challenging situations with a healthier and more constructive mindset.

Step 6: Thought Restructuring

In this phase of the process, the focus shifts towards transforming distorted automatic thoughts into ones that are more balanced and realistic. This restructuring step is essential for changing how you interpret and react to situations that commonly generate stress or anxiety for you.

After identifying and questioning your automatic thoughts, the next step is to develop more rational and balanced alternatives. These new thoughts should be based on an objective and nuanced assessment of the situation, rather than relying on assumptions or excessive generalizations.

For example, if your automatic thought was "I never manage to make myself understood in arguments", a possible restructuring could be: "Although I sometimes find it difficult to communicate in arguments, there are occasions when I manage to express my views effectively". This new perspective acknowledges both the challenges and successes in communication, providing a more balanced approach.

Similarly, in response to a thought like "I am always to blame in disagreements", you could reframe it to: "While in some situations I may contribute to the disagreement, I am not always solely responsible, and there are times when responsibility is shared". This more nuanced approach allows you to recognize the complexity of human interactions and reduces the tendency for excessive personalization.

The key to this step is to challenge limiting thought patterns and replace them with others that reflect a more realistic and nuanced understanding of your experiences. By recording and reflecting on these alternative thoughts, you begin to question and change the internal narrative that has been fueling negative emotions and behaviors.

This process of cognitive restructuring is not a one-time act but a continuous practice of self-observation and adjustment. Over time and with constant practice, these new thought patterns will take root and become more natural and automatic, making it easier for you to handle challenging situations more effectively and with a greater sense of control and well-being. This gradual transformation of your thoughts will contribute to improving your emotional and mental health, allowing you to approach life with a constructive and positive perspective.

Example:

Continuing with the thought restructuring process, we address the automatic thought "I believe I never manage to make myself understood" and consider its reformulation. Instead of focusing on absolute and negative terms, it's essential to adopt a more balanced and realistic perspective. A possible restructuring of this thought could be: "Although on some occasions I have difficulties in communicating, there are many times when I have managed to express my ideas clearly and have been understood. Today's disagreement does not define my communicative ability. Moreover, if I really need to improve my communication, I can see it as an opportunity for development rather than an insurmountable personal failure".

This approach allows us to recognize that, while the recent incident was a challenge, it is not a complete reflection of our communicative abilities. By acknowledging past successes in communication, we reinforce the idea that we can express ourselves effectively. Furthermore, by considering the possibility of improvement, we focus on personal growth rather than destructive self-criticism. This type of thinking helps us handle similar situations in the future with more confidence and less stress.

By adopting this renewed perspective, we begin to see setbacks as opportunities to learn and grow, rather than as evidence of incapacity. This positive and proactive approach not only improves our mood but also increases our resilience in the face of future communication challenges. Recording these restructured thoughts in a personal journal helps internalize and reinforce this new, more constructive, and realistic thought pattern. Through this continuous exercise, the ability to change the internal narrative is strengthened, which has a transformative effect on how we perceive and respond to life's situations, promoting a more solid and lasting emotional well-being.

Step 7: Analysis of Core Beliefs

The seventh step of this exercise represents a profound and revealing process: the analysis of your core beliefs. These beliefs form the foundation upon which your thought structure is built and have a profound influence on how you view the world, perceive yourself, and interact with others. These beliefs, often formed in childhood or early stages of life, can remain unexamined for many years, even decades.

To begin this analysis, reflect on the automatic thoughts you have identified in previous steps. Ask yourself: "What beliefs about myself, others, and the world support these thoughts?". For example, if a recurring thought is "I never do anything right", it may be rooted in a core belief of inadequacy or failure.

After identifying these core beliefs, it is crucial to evaluate their impact on your life. Consider whether they are realistic, whether they contribute to your growth and advancement, or if they keep you trapped in negative thought and behavior patterns. Often, core beliefs are exaggerated and absolutist, like "I must always be perfect" or "I am not good enough", and can lead to emotions such as anxiety, sadness, or anger.

Once you have identified these core beliefs, reflect on whether they are beneficial for you or if they need to be adjusted. This adjustment does not necessarily mean a radical change in your way of thinking but rather a modification of these beliefs to make them more nuanced and realistic. For example, instead of clinging to the thought "I never do anything right", you could adapt it to "Although sometimes I make mistakes, there are many occasions where I have succeeded".

This process of analyzing and adjusting core beliefs is crucial in CBT, as it offers a healthier and more realistic foundation for your thoughts and behaviors. By confronting and modifying these deeply ingrained beliefs, you will begin to experience significant changes in your emotional state and your reaction to everyday situations. This step is not only an advance towards better emotional health but also represents a fundamental shift in self-perception and worldview, leading to a more fulfilling and satisfying life.

Example:

Consider the belief that arose from the previously mentioned argument: "If I can't make others understand me, that indicates my insufficiency in communication". This belief suggests that your worth and competence are measured exclusively by how others perceive and understand your messages, which can generate constant feelings of failure and inadequacy.

To address this core belief, it is essential to recognize that communication is a two-way process, and its success does not depend solely on you. Additionally, the ability to communicate effectively does not define your overall worth as a person. This acknowledgment is the first step towards restructuring your belief in a more balanced and realistic manner.

A healthier and more constructive alternative to this belief might be: "Although I value effective communication and strive to be clear, I am aware that misunderstandings can sometimes arise. These moments are opportunities to learn and improve; they do not define my total worth as a person or communicator". This new perspective allows you to value effort and continual improvement without harshly judging yourself for every interaction that doesn't go as expected.

By transforming this core belief, you promote a more compassionate and realistic view of yourself, relieving the pressure to be "perfect" in every interaction. Additionally, this restructuring encourages a learning and growth mindset, rather than a self-punishment approach for communication errors or misunderstandings.

This process of reviewing and adjusting core beliefs is essential for changing how you interpret and respond to life's situations. By adopting more realistic and less critical beliefs, you begin to experience an increase in your emotional well-being and an improvement in your quality of life. This approach not only allows you to face communication challenges with more confidence and resilience but also helps you develop healthier and more satisfying relationships, both personally and professionally.

Step 8: Development of Positive Affirmations

The next step on your path towards better emotional and cognitive management involves the development of positive affirmations. This step is essential for consolidating the cognitive changes you have been implementing. Positive affirmations are statements that reflect constructive and realistic aspects about yourself and your surroundings, encouraging the strengthening of a more balanced and optimistic mindset.

To start this process, reflect on the new beliefs and thoughts you have developed in previous steps. Consider the positive aspects of these renewed thoughts. How can you transform them into affirmations that strengthen your self-esteem and confidence? It's crucial that these affirmations are realistic and based on concrete facts or your potential for personal and professional growth.

Craft affirmations that align with your goal of improving communication and emotional management. An affirmation could be: "I am capable of clearly communicating my ideas and am open to learning and improving constantly." This statement not only acknowledges your current ability but also emphasizes your willingness for growth and continual learning.

Another possible affirmation is: "I accept that I don't always have control over others' reactions, but I can manage my own responses in a positive and constructive manner". This affirmation reminds you that while you cannot control all situations, you have the power to manage your own reactions effectively and healthily.

Integrate these affirmations into your daily routine. Spending a few minutes each morning to repeat them or turning to them during moments of doubt or insecurity can be very helpful. You might write them down in your journal, place them on sticky notes in frequently seen locations, or even say them out loud in front of a mirror.

The power of positive affirmations lies in their ability to progressively restructure your internal dialogue towards a more positive and empowering perspective. As you internalize them, you will notice a significant change in your self-awareness and confidence. This change will empower you to face life's challenges with a more balanced, resilient, and optimistic mindset, leading to a better quality of life and healthier, more satisfying relationships.

Example:

After working on restructuring your thoughts and beliefs, it's time to strengthen this cognitive change by developing positive affirmations. These affirmations are powerful statements that serve to consolidate and reinforce changes in your way of thinking, contributing to a more balanced and optimistic view of yourself and your surroundings.

Consider the situation where you felt frustrated for not being understood in a discussion. From this experience, you can create positive affirmations that reflect your ability to communicate effectively and your willingness to improve. For example, you could affirm: "Although I don't always manage to make myself understood, I recognize that I am a good communicator and am actively working to improve my skills in this area". This affirmation not only shows a positive focus but also a proactive attitude towards learning and continuous development.

Another valuable affirmation could be: "I understand that differences of opinion are a natural part of human interactions, and I am learning to manage them with serenity and clarity". This statement reminds you that disagreements are not inherently negative and that you can handle them constructively.

Integrate these affirmations into your daily routine. You might recite them during your morning reflection time, write them in your journal, or repeat them mentally in situations of stress or uncertainty. These affirmations act as mental anchors, reaffirming your strengths and your ability to face and overcome challenges.

As you continue practicing these affirmations, you will notice a change in your internal dialogue, becoming more positive and affirmative. This change will provide you with greater confidence and control when facing difficult situations. The purpose of these affirmations is to reinforce the cognitive changes you have been working on, propelling you to build a more resilient and optimistic mindset. This process is an important step towards improving your emotional and mental well-being, allowing you to approach life with a new, more positive, and confident perspective.

Step 9: Behavioral Change Strategies

The ninth step of this exercise focuses on implementing behavioral change strategies, a key phase to actualize in your daily behavior the new cognitive perspectives you've developed. The aim is to identify and modify those action patterns that have been feeding your negative automatic thoughts.

Begin by evaluating current behaviors you wish to change. Reflect on specific actions you took when feeling frustrated or misunderstood during the previously mentioned discussion. Identify those behaviors that might have contributed to a negative outcome or that didn't accurately reflect your true intentions or feelings.

Once these behaviors are identified, develop an action plan with concrete steps. For example, if you tend to react impulsively in disagreement situations, an effective strategy could be to implement a reflective pause before responding. This pause would give you time to process your thoughts and emotions, allowing you to react in a more measured and considerate manner.

Practicing assertive communication is another valuable strategy. If you tend to downplay your viewpoints or avoid expressing your opinion to evade conflicts, make it a point to share your thoughts clearly and respectfully in future conversations. This behavioral change will reinforce your new belief that you have the right and ability to express yourself effectively.

Consider also adopting relaxation or mindfulness techniques to better manage intense emotions in moments of stress. These practices can be crucial for maintaining calm and clarity in challenging situations, promoting more balanced and rational responses.

Document these changes in your behavior in your personal journal. Record situations where you've applied these new strategies and reflect on the outcomes. This tracking will allow you to observe concrete progress in your self-improvement process and adjust when necessary. It's important to remember that behavioral change is a gradual process that requires practice and patience. Over time, these new behaviors will naturally integrate into your response repertoire, aiding you in facing future challenges in a healthier and more effective way. This step is essential not only for improving your emotional well-being but also for fostering healthier and more satisfying relationships in all areas of your life.

Example:

In this step, focused on implementing behavioral change strategies, propose applying concrete actions and behaviors that reflect and reinforce the new cognitive perspective developed in previous steps. The goal is to modify those behaviors that have been feeding negative automatic thoughts and affecting your emotional well-being.

Visualize a situation where you feel misunderstood during a conversation. Instead of reacting impulsively or withdrawing, commit to improving your communication skills. An effective strategy is the practice of active listening. This involves fully paying attention to your interlocutor, without interruptions, and demonstrating understanding. A useful technique for this is paraphrasing what was heard, thus confirming your understanding.

Another important aspect is developing the skill to express your opinions assertively. Assertiveness involves clear and direct communication, respecting both your rights and those of others. It's beneficial to prepare in advance what you want to communicate, especially in potentially difficult situations.

Additionally, it's valuable to request feedback on how your communication is perceived. Inquire with your interlocutors if they understood your points of view and if there are aspects you could have expressed more clearly. This step demonstrates an open attitude to learning and improves the quality of interaction.

Establishing the practice of asking for clarifications is also crucial. If you have doubts about the other's message or suspect possible misunderstandings, do not hesitate to request more information. This attitude can prevent communication issues and strengthen interpersonal relationships.

Finally, record in your personal journal the progress you make with these strategies. Reflect on how these tactics are influencing your emotional well-being and relationships. This continuous self-assessment will allow you to adjust and effectively improve your communication skills. This conscientious attention to improving your communication skills will not only contribute to your personal and professional development but also significantly enhance your daily interactions, leading to more enriching and satisfying relationships.

Step 10: Progress Evaluation and Adjustment

Continuous evaluation and adjustment are essential in your cognitive and behavioral transformation process. It's important to regularly dedicate 10 to 15 minutes to reflect on the impact that changes in your thinking and behavior are having on your emotions and daily life. These moments of introspection are crucial for assessing the progress made and identifying areas that still require improvement.

During these reflection sessions, ask yourself key questions such as: "How have changes in my thinking influenced my emotions and actions?", "Have I noticed improvements in my emotional well-being or interpersonal relationships?", "Are there thought or behavior patterns that I need to continue addressing?". Recording these observations in your personal journal provides invaluable insight into your change and personal development process.

Moreover, be willing to adjust your strategies based on your observations. If you discover that certain negative thoughts persist, consider exploring new cognitive restructuring techniques or focusing more on core beliefs. Likewise, if you identify behaviors that remain challenging, explore new behavioral change strategies, or seek alternative approaches to handle these situations.

This stage is also an opportunity to recognize and celebrate your achievements. Appreciate the efforts made and the progress achieved, no matter how small. Every step forward is a significant advance on your path to better mental health and emotional well-being.

Lastly, maintain an open and flexible attitude toward the change process. Personal development is a continuous journey with always room for growth and improvement. Your dedication to self-evaluation and constant adjustment ensures continuous evolution towards a more enriching and satisfying life. This commitment to personal growth will not only help you face future challenges more effectively but will also enrich all aspects of your life, providing greater clarity, confidence, and peace of mind on your journey towards self-awareness and self-actualization.

Example:

At the end of each week, take a moment to reflect on occasions when you have practiced your newly improved communication skills.

Examine specific situations where you applied these techniques and assess whether you achieved a reduction in misunderstandings or an increase in the clarity of your interactions. Ask yourself questions like: "How did I feel expressing my thoughts more effectively? Did I notice any change in how others reacted when I communicated my ideas clearly?".

Record these experiences in your journal, describing both the successes and challenges you faced. This practice is crucial for identifying patterns and areas where your communication can still improve. For example, if you notice that you still have difficulties in certain contexts, consider additional strategies to strengthen your communication skills. These could include participating in workshops or seminars, seeking constructive feedback from colleagues, friends, or family, or even consulting with a communication professional or therapist.

Recognizing and celebrating your progress is important, but so is being honest with yourself about aspects that require more attention and work. Maintain a constant learning attitude and be willing to adapt your strategies as needed. For example, if you find that certain techniques are not as effective as expected, be proactive in exploring alternatives or adjusting your current method.

The goal is continuous progress, not perfection. Acknowledging and valuing even small achievements is vital to staying motivated and committed to your change process. At the same time, being open to feedback and considering professional advice, when necessary, can offer you valuable additional resources for your personal and professional growth. This balanced and reflective approach will enable you to evolve in your communication ability and overall emotional well-being, paving the way for more effective and satisfying relationships both personally and professionally.

Conclusion

Summary and Reflection

Concluding this process based on Cognitive Behavioral Therapy, we have made notable progress in self-awareness and emotional self-regulation by identifying and modifying thought patterns that affected our well-being.

The exercise began with the identification of emotions and their physical expressions, avoiding judgment. This analysis clarified the automatic thoughts and their impact on our perception, subjecting them to critical examination to assess their validity.

During this journey, cognitive distortions such as overgeneralization and dichotomous thinking were addressed and reformulated, adjusting interpretations towards a more realistic view. Fundamental beliefs were also reviewed to align them with authentic and positive personal development.

Behavioral strategies were implemented, improving communication, and clarifying interactions, reinforcing personal evolution, and the quality of relationships. Continuous reflection has allowed for the evaluation of the effectiveness of these changes, improving understanding and connection with the environment.

This path of cognitive and behavioral transformation has not only enriched individual life but has also strengthened skills to interact more effectively, marking the step towards more complete and satisfying well-being.

Step Eight

"Cognitive Emotional Behavioral Therapy": A New Proposal

Introduction to the Topic

Cognitive Emotive Behavioral Therapy (CEBT) emerges as an experimental proposal in the field of psychotherapy, merging aspects of Cognitive Behavioral Therapy, Rational Emotive Behavioral Therapy, and the principles of Emotional Intelligence. This theoretical and practical integration provides a renewed and expanded approach for the treatment of stress, anxiety, and depression.

CEBT is based on the premise that cognitive processes have a decisive influence on emotional regulation and behavior, a concept shared by both CBT and REBT (Beck, 1976; Ellis, 1957). This approach is distinguished by its emphasis on cognitive restructuring, enriched with an expanded understanding of emotions and their impact on internal well-being and the ability to regulate emotions (Greenberger & Padesky, 1995). CEBT promotes a holistic intervention that, through the integration of EI, enhances patients' abilities to identify, understand, and effectively express their emotions, complementing cognitive restructuring (Goleman, 1995).

This innovative approach underscores the importance of unconditional self-acceptance and compassion towards oneself and others, crucial aspects for optimal mental health (Ellis, 2005). Additionally, CEBT emphasizes the development of empathy as a resource to enrich interpersonal understanding and sensitivity towards others' emotional states, which, in turn, strengthens interpersonal relationships and social support. It also provides patients with strategies for self-analysis and self-correction, promoting resilience and autonomy (Werner, 2012).

In summary, Cognitive Emotive Behavioral Therapy marks progress in addressing mood disorders. By combining Emotional Intelligence skills with the fundamental principles of CBT and REBT, CEBT establishes itself as an effective therapeutic methodology for inducing lasting emotional, cognitive, and behavioral changes. This integration not only facilitates short-term symptom relief but also promotes long-term emotional well-being and a fuller life (David, 2016).

Research Evidence

Cognitive Emotive Behavioral Therapy is supported by a solid scientific basis that demonstrates the interrelation between cognitive, emotional, and behavioral processes in psychopathology and mental health. The fundamental theories of Beck (1976) and Ellis (1962) have established that thoughts, emotions, and behaviors are intrinsically linked, serving as pillars for Cognitive Therapy and Rational Emotive Therapy, respectively. These theories assert that emotional responses and behavior patterns are significantly influenced by automatic thoughts and beliefs, whether rational or irrational.

Beck proposed that it is personal interpretations of events, rather than the events themselves, that determine emotional and behavioral responses. Ellis, on the other hand, highlighted that disturbing emotions originate not from adverse situations directly but from irrational beliefs about those situations.

Furthermore, Gross and John (2003) investigated the connection between cognition and emotion in their Emotional Regulation Processes Model, demonstrating how emotional regulation strategies, such as cognitive reappraisal and expressive suppression, affect emotional experience and response. Studies following this model have confirmed that cognitive distortions can exacerbate the intensity and duration of negative emotions, leading to maladaptive behaviors.

In another vein, cognitive neuroscience has provided evidence on the neural basis of the interaction between thoughts and emotions.

Research with brain imaging techniques has revealed that cognitive reappraisal activates prefrontal areas that modulate the activity of limbic regions responsible for generating emotions (Ochsner et al., 2012).

There is scientific consensus on the efficacy of CBT and REBT in treating mood disorders, such as depression and anxiety, corroborated in meta-analyses and systematic reviews (Hofmann et al., 2012). This consensus reinforces the foundation of this new proposal. Cognitive distortions have been recognized as playing a crucial role in emotional regulation and contributing to various mental disorders. Research emphasizes that intervening in dysfunctional cognitive patterns, which can trigger or maintain negative emotional states, is beneficial for symptomatic relief and functional improvement in affected individuals (Clark & Beck, 2010).

Controlled and randomized studies have shown that modifying irrational beliefs and restructuring negative thoughts facilitate positive changes in both emotions and behaviors. These changes result in a reduction of depression and anxiety symptoms and an increase in quality of life and emotional well-being. Therefore, CBT and REBT are considered fundamental interventions for treating these disorders. By combining these therapies with Emotional Intelligence strategies, interventions aimed at improving psychosocial adaptation and preventing mood disorders could be further enhanced, and this is what CEBT seeks to achieve.

Instructions

Integration of CEBT
in the Management of Mood Disorders

Objective

The following exercise introduces an innovative approach in the field of mental health: Cognitive Emotive Behavioral Therapy. This therapeutic methodology is based on the principle that our cognitive processes, namely the thoughts and beliefs that flood our minds, play a crucial role in how we experience and manage our emotions and behaviors.

The core of this exercise is cognitive restructuring, aimed at increasing awareness of the automatic thoughts that arise in various situations and confronting the cognitive distortions that warp our perception of reality, leading to unwanted negative emotions. Through this process, you will learn to identify and modify harmful or unproductive thoughts with more balanced and rational ones, which is essential for reducing emotional tension and improving overall well-being. However, the key aspect of this new proposal is the integration of Emotional Intelligence skills. By merging the identification, understanding, and management of emotions (EI) with the detection of automatic thoughts and cognitive distortions (CBT), following the structure of Albert Ellis's ABC model (REBT), the therapeutic process is expected to be more efficacious and effective.

By actively engaging with this exercise, you will develop key skills in emotional self-management and behavior modification. Each phase of Cognitive Emotive Behavioral Therapy, from identifying emotions to reflection and constant adjustment, will guide you towards a deeper understanding of your emotions, thoughts, and actions. This process will help you build a solid foundation for a healthy emotional life and promote more satisfying and enriching interpersonal relationships.

Step 1: Emotional Recognition

The first step in Cognitive Emotional Behavioral Therapy is Emotional Recognition, a key phase for identifying and accepting current emotions. Take, for example, a situation that generates social anxiety.

In this step, the focus is on identifying not only the main emotion, such as anxiety but also its nuances and specific manifestations in you. This analysis requires introspection, observing both the physical and cognitive responses associated with these emotions in specific social contexts, such as a meeting or a public presentation.

At this moment, it is important to pause and deeply reflect on your internal experience. With your personal journal by your side, use tools like the emotional meter (detailed in Appendix 9) to rate and better understand the intensity and character of your anxiety. Ask yourself questions like: "How does this anxiety physically manifest in my body? What automatic thoughts emerge at the idea of interacting in a social environment or speaking in public?".

Record these observations in detail in your journal, including any physical sensation (such as muscle tension, sweating, or palpitations) and specific thoughts that arise. This process of self-exploration is essential for developing greater emotional and cognitive awareness, which facilitates the process of change and adaptation in the later stages of therapy. This initial step is fundamental to establishing a solid foundation on which subsequent interventions will be built, allowing you to face emotional and cognitive challenges more effectively and consciously.

Example:

In the context of Cognitive Emotional Behavioral Therapy, the example of Emotional Recognition can be clearly illustrated in a situation like entering a social meeting, a common scenario that often triggers anxiety. Imagine you are in this situation and notice the physical signs of anxiety: your breathing accelerates, your heart beats more forcefully, and your hands start to tremble slightly. These signals are clear physical indicators of anxiety. Simultaneously, it is important to pay attention to your thoughts. You may be anticipating criticism or negative judgments from others, manifesting defeatist, or negative thoughts.

At this point, the essential step is to recognize and label these reactions for what they are: manifestations of anxiety in a social interaction situation. In your personal journal, it is important to describe these sensations and thoughts in detail. For example, you could write: "As I approach the meeting, I notice my heart beating faster and my breathing becomes shallow. My hands tremble slightly. Mentally, I worry about the possibility of being judged or perceived as uninteresting by others".

This act of recognition and detailed description is a crucial step towards understanding and managing your emotions. By doing so, you not only identify the emotions and physical sensations but also begin to understand the relationship between the specific situation, your automatic thoughts, and emotional responses. This awareness is a pillar in Cognitive Emotional Behavioral Therapy, as it establishes the foundation for later stages of treatment focused on emotional regulation and cognitive restructuring.

This level of self-awareness is key to more effectively addressing the emotional and cognitive challenges that arise in social contexts, preparing you for the next steps towards emotional well-being and behavioral adaptation. With this approach, you begin to develop a deeper understanding of how emotions interact with thoughts and behaviors, and a clear path is established for intervention and positive change.

Step 2: Identification of Automatic Thoughts and Cognitive Distortions

Following the first step of emotional recognition in Cognitive Emotional Behavioral Therapy, the focus shifts to automatic thoughts, which are instant and often unexamined reactions that tend to distort reality. These thoughts are usually critical and negative and can be filled with cognitive distortions. These distortions are errors in information processing that can lead to incorrect interpretations and exacerbation of negative emotions like anxiety.

It's crucial in therapy to identify and analyze these cognitive distortions. Among the most common are "all-or-nothing thinking", which involves viewing situations in absolute terms without nuances; "catastrophizing", which leads to anticipating the worst possible scenario; and "overgeneralization", which involves extrapolating a negative experience to all similar situations. These distortions are detailed in Annex 10 for your reference.

When recording your thoughts in your personal journal, it's essential to assess their accuracy and usefulness. Consider whether these thoughts are based on real facts or are influenced by unfounded fears Do these bring you any benefits or just problems? Additionally, identify any specific cognitive distortion. For example, if after an uncomfortable social interaction, you think "I'm always clumsy in meetings", you might be overgeneralizing based on a single event.

Recognizing and analyzing these automatic thoughts and cognitive distortions are crucial steps in the therapeutic process. By identifying them, you begin to unveil how thoughts influence emotions and behaviors, and in turn, how these affect the perception of situations. This step is fundamental for cognitive restructuring and emotional regulation, key elements of CEBT. This process will help you transform your view of the world and your interaction with it into a more balanced and healthy manner, thus improving your emotional well-being and your ability to handle challenging situations more effectively.

Example:

In the context of Cognitive Emotional Behavioral Therapy, consider the example of the social event and the moment when you need to start a conversation. An automatic thought emerges: "If I make a mistake while talking, everyone will think I'm incompetent". This thought is a typical example of "catastrophizing", a cognitive distortion in which an extreme negative judgment by others is anticipated due to a mistake, even though there is no concrete evidence to support this assumption.

The next essential step is to question this automatic thought. Reflect on the reality of this statement. Does a mistake in conversation truly define you as incompetent to everyone present? Consider that it's likely others have also made mistakes in speaking and were not considered incompetent. Recall situations where you've witnessed others' mistakes in similar contexts. Did you really consider them incompetent, or were you more understanding, realizing that making mistakes is human?

This introspection is crucial for identifying the unreal nature of the cognitive distortion and beginning to question the truthfulness and usefulness of these automatic thoughts. By recognizing that your perception of others' reactions to a mistake is probably exaggerated and not based on reality, you take an essential step in changing how you perceive yourself and how you interact in your social environment.

The process of identifying automatic thoughts and cognitive distortions is a fundamental act of self-awareness in Cognitive Emotional Behavioral Therapy. With constant practice, not only is more accurate and reality-adjusted thinking achieved, but also a significant reduction in social anxiety. This internal reflection exercise paves the way for deeper cognitive restructuring, allowing for a healthier management of emotions and stressful situations, and contributing to a more relaxed and confident social interaction. This ability to challenge and modify negative automatic thoughts is key to developing a more balanced and constructive perspective on social interactions and oneself.

Step 3: Unraveling Core Beliefs

The third step is the detailed analysis of core beliefs. These are deep-seated fundamental convictions that form the basis of how you perceive yourself, others, and the world. Generally established in early stages of life, these beliefs can significantly influence the interpretation of everyday experiences and situations, often without being questioned.

These core beliefs are usually absolute, rigid, and global. They can manifest in the form of critical and punitive imperatives, like "must", "have to", or in inflexible labels about oneself, such as "I'm a failure", "I'm inadequate", or "nobody loves me". To progress in your personal and emotional development, it's crucial to interrogate and assess these deeply ingrained beliefs.

It's important to reflect on the origin of these beliefs. Consider if they originated from past experiences or were instilled by authority figures or society. It's essential to identify their origin and question the validity of these beliefs considering current evidence. Evaluate if these absolutist and rigid views are overlooking the nuances and complexity of your current reality, as well as your capacity to change and adapt.

This step is crucial, as questioning and understanding the origin and influence of core beliefs pave the way for their transformation. Through this process, you can begin to perceive and experience the world, others, and yourself in a more nuanced and realistic way. This analysis is essential for achieving a healthier and more balanced emotional life.

Reviewing these core beliefs is a key moment in your journey of holistic transformation, allowing you to redefine your identity and your relationship with the world in a more adaptive and positive way. With this step, you establish a path towards greater understanding and acceptance of yourself, which is fundamental for lasting and profound emotional and psychological well-being.

Example:

This example involves deep introspection to question and understand the fundamental beliefs underlying automatic thoughts and influencing how we perceive the world and ourselves. This step requires a detailed examination of the convictions that have shaped our self-perception and our interactions with the environment.

Take, for example, a core belief like: "If I'm not absolutely eloquent and charismatic in social events, then I'm not valuable or deserving of respect". It's important to reflect on the origin of this belief. Perhaps during your childhood or adolescence, authority figures overly emphasized the importance of making a good impression and the weight of social judgment. Or maybe a humiliating experience at school, like a failed presentation, left a negative mark on your self-esteem.

The next step is to question the current validity of this belief. Ask yourself if it's truly necessary to always be the most eloquent to be valued and respected. Recall moments in your life where you've been appreciated and accepted for simply being yourself, without needing to meet expectations of eloquence and charisma.

This questioning process helps to understand that your value as a person does not depend on meeting unrealistic expectations of social behavior. You are more than your past mistakes or the judgments of others. Recognizing this can relieve the anxiety associated with social interactions and allow you to approach these situations with a more realistic and less critical perspective. By understanding that your value is not conditioned on perfection in social interactions, you can begin to free yourself from these oppressive expectations and live in a more authentic and free manner.

This step is crucial in Cognitive Emotional Behavioral Therapy, as it promotes a significant transformation in self-perception and the way of interacting with the world. By unraveling and reshaping these core beliefs, the door is opened to greater emotional well-being, increased self-confidence, and healthier and more authentic relationships. This process of self-exploration and cognitive change is a vital step towards deep and meaningful personal growth.

Step 4: Reviewing Emotional Experience

The fourth step in Cognitive Emotional Behavioral Therapy, dedicated to "Reviewing the Emotional Experience", involves a thorough analysis of how we experience, interpret, and express our emotions. This step is vital to understanding the interrelationship between emotions, thoughts, and behaviors.

After examining the core beliefs that influence your behavior and perceptions, it's crucial to reflect on the impact of these beliefs on your emotional experience. The internal emotional experience encompasses the sensations, emotions, and feelings that emerge in response to your thoughts and beliefs. These internal emotions are key, as they provide essential information on how these beliefs affect your emotional and psychological well-being.

To delve deeper into this step, reconsider the previously analyzed situation of social anxiety. Reflect on how your underlying beliefs have shaped your level of anxiety, your overall mood, and your willingness to participate in social situations. Evaluate whether the anxiety you experience is proportional to the reality of the situation, or if it's magnified by unfounded beliefs about your worth and abilities.

Also, contemplate how these beliefs and emotions manifest in your behavior. Do you tend to avoid certain social situations because of these beliefs? How do you express your emotions in these contexts? These reflections will allow you to better understand the interaction between your thoughts, emotions, and actions, and help you identify areas of opportunity to improve your emotional health. Remember that each experience leaves an emotional mark that we sometimes overlook.

Through this analysis, you may discover emotional patterns that you hadn't recognized before but play a significant role in your everyday life. This understanding is an essential component in CEBT, as it not only facilitates addressing and transforming your thoughts and beliefs but also improving your relationship with your emotions and how they influence your actions. This step represents a key advance in your emotional and cognitive development, providing you with the necessary tools for more effective emotional management and overall well-being.

Example:

Imagine facing social situations that trigger negative emotions, stemming from the core beliefs you've previously identified. Suppose one of these beliefs is the need to be extremely eloquent to gain acceptance and respect. This belief can create significant internal pressure, manifesting as anxiety. In extreme cases, this anxiety could be so intense that it leads you to avoid social interactions, thus perpetuating a cycle of anxiety and avoidance.

In this crucial step, you are encouraged to evaluate the proportionality of your anxiety to the reality of the situation. Reflect on whether it's reasonable to feel so overwhelmed by the pressure to be eloquent. By analyzing your internal emotions, you might discover that the anxious anticipation of a social event decreases when questioning the validity of your core beliefs. By challenging the notion that you must always be the center of attention or the most charismatic person, you can start to experience more genuine and rewarding social interactions.

This introspective process helps you better understand how your beliefs affect your emotions and behaviors. By recognizing that social situations do not require exceptional eloquence to be rewarding, you begin to experience a reduction in your anxiety. This step is fundamental to initiating a transformation in your emotional response, granting you the ability to regulate your emotions more effectively and reduce unnecessary anxiety. This change benefits not only your emotional well-being but also enriches your ability to interact socially in a more relaxed and authentic manner, which in turn contributes to a more satisfying and enriching social experience.

Step 5: Implementation of the ABC Model

Begin by identifying a specific event (A), such as a social gathering or a public presentation, that has triggered anxiety. Then, reflect on the beliefs (B) associated with this event. These may include irrational or limiting perceptions, such as the notion that you need to be constantly eloquent to gain recognition.

Next, assess how these beliefs impact your emotions and behaviors (C). For example, the belief that making a mistake while speaking equates to total failure could trigger intense anxiety and lead you to avoid social situations.

The purpose of this step is to challenge and restructure these irrational beliefs. Question their basis: Are there real proofs supporting them? Are there more rational and benevolent ways to interpret the situation? Question, for example, whether making a speaking error truly signifies failure. How would you react if someone else made a similar mistake?

By challenging and modifying these irrational beliefs towards more rational and empathetic interpretations, you initiate a change in your emotional and behavioral response to the event. This process is key to developing a more balanced and healthy reaction to previously anxiety-inducing situations, combining emotional intelligence with cognitive restructuring. This approach promotes a greater understanding of oneself and a more solid well-being, helping you to effectively face and manage situations that previously caused you anxiety.

Example:

Within the framework of Cognitive Emotional Behavioral Therapy, applying the ABC Model from Rational Emotive Behavioral Therapy, we address a case of social anxiety. The trigger is an invitation to a social event (Activated Event - A), which immediately awakens automatic thoughts related to the pressure of being the center of attention. This reaction stems from a belief (B) possibly formed by previous experiences or internalized social expectations.

Reflecting on this situation, you identify anxiety as the initial response, driven by the belief that you need to be exceptionally eloquent and charismatic to be appreciated (B). By questioning this belief, its lack of realistic basis is revealed: Is it truly necessary to be the focus of attention to enjoy social interaction? Could it be that the anxiety is simply an overreaction to a self-imposed demand?

Evaluating the consequences (C) of holding this belief, it becomes evident that it has provoked paralyzing fear and prevented you from fully enjoying social events, even leading you to avoid them. Now, instead of declining the invitation out of fear, you decide to face the situation with emotional regulation techniques, accepting that a certain level of nervousness is normal and manageable.

With this new perspective, you decide to attend the event with the goal of being authentic and enjoying the company, rather than fretting about being the center of all eyes. This shift in focus represents a significant step toward greater self-confidence and reduced anxiety in social contexts. The implementation of the ABC Model has allowed you to effectively restructure your thoughts and behaviors, preparing you to participate in the event with a more serene and open attitude.

Step 6: Cognitive Restructuring and Emotional Education

Cognitive restructuring, a key component of Cognitive Emotional Behavioral Therapy, encourages you to review and modify erroneous or maladaptive thoughts that affect your emotional well-being and behavior. For instance, when faced with a thought like "I always fail in social situations", you are encouraged to replace it with a more balanced perspective, such as "Sometimes I succeed in social situations, and in times when I don't, I can learn from the experience". This shift in thinking opens a path toward a more realistic and less critical interpretation of your social experiences.

Simultaneously, emotional education deepens your knowledge and understanding of your emotions. This process involves learning to clearly identify the emotions you experience, understand their origins, and recognize how they influence your behavior. For example, when feeling anxiety before a social event, you'll be able to explore the causes of this anxiety and develop strategies to respond in a more adaptive and healthy manner.

The integration of Emotional Intelligence in this process enriches cognitive restructuring. Using your emotional awareness to analyze how thoughts affect your emotions and vice versa allows for a more comprehensive approach. For example, realizing that your anxiety stems from an irrational belief enables you to actively challenge and change the underlying thought, thereby mitigating the anxiety.

Together, cognitive restructuring and emotional education equip you with valuable tools to modify your internal dialogue and improve your emotional management. This results in enhanced adaptability and emotional well-being. With practice and dedication, these skills become an essential resource for facing daily challenges, bolstering your ability to live a more fulfilling and emotionally balanced life.

Example:

The practical application of cognitive restructuring and emotional education, especially in preparation for a social event that initially generates anxiety, unfolds through several fundamental steps:

Questioning Irrational Beliefs: You address the belief that it's necessary to be the center of attention at the social event. Upon critical reflection, you conclude that this expectation is unrealistic and not essential for social acceptance or personal well-being. This questioning allows for a reevaluation of the importance and necessity of adhering to such a belief.

Emotional Analysis: You examine and acknowledge the anxiety prior to the event, understanding it as a normal response to unknown or potentially uncomfortable situations. This stage is enriched with Emotional Intelligence, allowing you to view emotions as valuable indicators rather than insurmountable barriers.

Perspective Transformation: You decide to adopt a more relaxed and flexible approach to the social event. Accepting anxiety as a natural reaction and understanding that perfection in social performance is not necessary. This mindset shift helps you prepare for the event with a more open and less critical attitude.

Emotional Regulation: You apply emotional regulation techniques to transform anxious anticipation into a moderate and positive expectation. Techniques range from mindful breathing to visualization, tailored to individual needs and preferences for more effective emotion management.

Preparation for Action: Armed with this new attitude, you are ready to face the social event. This preparation not only improves your ability to handle the current situation more effectively but also strengthens resilience and emotional understanding for similar future situations.

In summary, this example illustrates the synergy between cognitive restructuring and emotional education. It addresses not only the cognitive dimension of thoughts and beliefs but also leverages emotional understanding for more effective management of emotional and behavioral responses. This integrated approach is crucial for the development of greater adaptability and emotional well-being.

Step 7: Cultivating Self-Compassion and Empathy

The seventh step in Cognitive Emotional Behavioral Therapy is a critical point in personal and emotional development, focusing on fostering self-compassion and empathy. This approach is essential for learning to treat oneself with kindness and understanding, as well as for developing the ability to empathize with others.

During this step, the importance of adopting a compassionate attitude towards oneself, especially in difficult situations or errors, is emphasized. Self-compassion involves understanding that challenges and mistakes are part of the common human experience and do not define personal worth. It promotes the idea of responding to one's own difficulties with the same empathy and consideration that would be given to a close friend, instead of succumbing to destructive self-criticism or negative self-assessment.

To incorporate self-compassion into daily life, practicing internal dialogue in a kind and comforting tone, particularly during challenging moments, proves effective. The use of positive affirmations and reminders of shared humanity helps foster this attitude. Self-compassion not only improves the relationship with oneself but also strengthens the ability to face difficulties more effectively.

Parallelly, this step also focuses on cultivating empathy, both towards oneself and others. Empathy involves a conscious effort to understand and share the feelings of other people, leading to deeper relationships and more effective interpersonal communication. By striving to see situations from others' perspectives and understanding their emotions and reactions, the capacity for meaningful connection is strengthened.

Empathy towards oneself is equally important, consisting of recognizing and validating one's own emotions, allowing oneself to experience them without judging them as good or bad. This practice leads to a deeper emotional understanding and acceptance of internal experiences.

To cultivate self-compassion and empathy, practicing reflective writing in a journal is recommended, dedicating time daily to contemplate experiences from a compassionate perspective. Self-compassion meditation, with guided meditations that promote a compassionate focus towards oneself, is another valuable tool. Additionally, perspective-taking exercises, which involve understanding situations from different viewpoints, can be very useful in enhancing empathy.

This step is vital in Cognitive Emotional Behavioral Therapy, as it links emotional understanding with cognitive and behavioral skills. By integrating self-compassion and empathy into your life, you not only improve your relationship with yourself and others but also lay the groundwork for lasting emotional well-being. Cultivating these elements reflects a commitment to holistic and sustainable personal growth.

Example:

The example provided for the seventh step in Cognitive Emotional Behavioral Therapy, dedicated to "Cultivating Self-Compassion and Empathy", illustrates how these essential skills can be effectively applied in situations of social anxiety.

Imagine preparing to attend a social event, a circumstance that commonly awakens anxiety and nervousness. In this context, the first step is to apply self-compassion. This means recognizing and accepting that feeling anxious before a social event is a normal human response. Instead of punishing yourself or feeling ashamed for these feelings, accept them as part of the shared human experience.

Then, employ empathy towards yourself to foster a kind and understanding internal dialogue, like what you would have with a friend in a similar situation. Instead of reproaching yourself for the nerves or the pressure to behave in a specific way, remind yourself that your authenticity is the most valuable and that your personal worth is not tied to how you present yourself in social situations.

An example of this internal dialogue could be: "It's understandable to feel nervous; I don't need to be perfect or the center of attention to be valued or enjoy interacting with others. Being myself and showing my true personality is more than enough. We are all in a continuous process of learning and developing our social skills, and that includes learning to manage anxiety."

This approach to self-dialogue not only mitigates the anxiety and pressure before the event but also provides a valuable tool for handling similar situations in the future. The practice of self-compassion and empathy becomes emotional pillars, endowing you with the ability to face challenges with greater kindness towards yourself and, therefore, with reinforced emotional strength. This practice allows you to attend the event with a more relaxed and open mindset, which reduces anxiety and enables a better experience.

Step 8: Formulation of New Beliefs and Behaviors

This step in Cognitive Emotional Behavioral Therapy marks a significant advance in your self-development process. Having confronted and reformulated irrational beliefs, and having developed self-compassion and empathy, you are now in an optimal position to establish and adopt more realistic and rational beliefs. These new beliefs will be the foundation for fostering healthier and more constructive behaviors, which will be in harmony with your deeper emotional and cognitive understanding.

Creating these new beliefs requires careful introspection and a review of previous thoughts that negatively affected your emotions and behaviors. This process represents a significant step toward redefining your internal dialogue, now based on a more empathetic and profound understanding of your own needs and limitations. You are learning to view your experiences with a more nuanced and compassionate perspective, moving away from restrictive and outdated patterns of thought.

This change involves not just a transformation in how you think but also in how you behave. With strengthened new beliefs, you'll be better equipped to handle challenging situations in a more positive and effective manner. For example, by replacing the limiting belief that "I need to be perfect in social events to be valued" with a healthier one like "it's natural to make mistakes, and I can be appreciated for my authenticity," you'll foster a healthier and more relaxed approach in your social interactions. This change in your beliefs will beneficially influence your actions, allowing you to face social situations with more confidence and less anxiety.

In summary, this step is crucial for securing a positive and lasting change in your life. By integrating new beliefs and behaviors, you not only improve your emotional and mental well-being but also strengthen yourself to face future situations with greater resilience and effectiveness. This progress in therapy marks a milestone on your journey toward a more fulfilling and satisfying life.

Example:

The reformulation of beliefs and behaviors in Cognitive Emotional Behavioral Therapy is a key process, especially when addressing social anxiety. By adopting new perspectives, based on a deeper cognitive and emotional understanding, you prepare to engage in social situations in a healthier and more constructive manner.

Instead of holding onto the belief that you need to be the center of attention to be valued, you decide to adopt a more realistic and beneficial view. Now, you believe that each social interaction is an opportunity to genuinely connect with others, letting go of disproportionate personal demands. This renewed belief facilitates attending social events with a more open mindset and free from pressures.

You remind yourself: "I don't need to meet others' expectations to justify my presence. I prefer to focus on enjoying the moment, interacting naturally, and opening myself to the experience, without the need to behave in a specific way".

In terms of behavior, this new attitude manifests in concrete actions. You initiate conversations without the burden of having to be witty or exceptionally attractive, allowing yourself to be authentic, listening actively, and responding honestly. You even give yourself the freedom to step away when deemed necessary, prioritizing your well-being over social conventions.

This change in your mindset not only enables you to face social interactions calmer and confidence but also to enjoy these moments more. By aligning your beliefs with behaviors that reflect your true self and personal values, you achieve greater coherence and authenticity in your interactions. This approach not only improves your experience in social situations but also enriches your overall well-being. With each step in this direction, you strengthen your capacity to live more fully and satisfactorily.

Step 9: Integration and Daily Practice of EI and CBT Skills

This step focuses on the integration and daily practice of Emotional Intelligence and CBT skills. This is a crucial moment in your personal development, where you actively apply what you've learned to reinforce positive changes in your daily life.

Begin by reflecting on how your new skills can influence everyday situations. For example, in social contexts that previously generated anxiety, apply cognitive restructuring and emotional regulation techniques. View each social interaction as an opportunity to practice skills like active listening and assertive expression, thus improving your emotional management.

In moments of stress or challenge, focus on replacing negative thoughts with more balanced and constructive ones. For example, faced with a work challenge, instead of thinking, "this is impossible", adopt the attitude of, "this is a challenge, but I have the skills to face it".

Integrate self-compassion into your daily life. In difficult situations or after making mistakes, speak to yourself with kindness and understanding, rather than falling into self-criticism. Accept mistakes as part of human learning and growth.

Practice empathy towards yourself and others. In your interactions, strive to understand the feelings and perspectives of other people, thus improving your interpersonal relationships.

Maintain a record in your personal journal of your experiences and reflections. This log will help you track your progress, identify areas for improvement, and celebrate your successes.

The constant practice of these skills in your daily life is key to lasting emotional and behavioral transformation. With each step you take, you move closer to a life where your emotions and thoughts support you in the pursuit of personal balance and well-being.

Example:

When facing a usual situation at work, like an important meeting with colleagues, you can apply the tools acquired in Cognitive Emotional Behavioral Therapy to transform your experience. Previously, these meetings might have generated a high degree of anxiety, worry about how you would be perceived, and fear of expressing your ideas. Now, with a renewed focus, your approach will be different.

Start by accepting and acknowledging your emotions. When you feel anxiety emerging, take a moment to perform deep breaths, embracing that emotion as a normal human reaction to the anticipation of a significant event.

Next, challenge your negative automatic thoughts through cognitive restructuring. Transform thoughts like "I'm going to make a mistake, and everyone will judge me" into "Everyone at the meeting is focused on the issues at hand, not on judging me. My ideas are valuable and deserve to be shared".

Focusing on your emotional education, recognize that anxiety is a signal of the importance of the event to you, and that it's natural to feel some nervousness. Use this energy as motivation for more thorough preparation, instead of letting it paralyze you.

During the meeting, apply Emotional Intelligence skills like active listening and empathy. This will not only improve your communication with colleagues but also help decrease your anxiety by focusing more on the conversation and less on yourself.

After the meeting, take time to reflect on the experience. Assess how you felt implementing these new skills and if you noticed improvements in your anxiety management and in your ability to effectively participate.

This process illustrates the practical integration of EI and CBT skills into your daily life. As you continue practicing them, these techniques will become more natural and effective, allowing you to handle challenging emotions and thoughts in various situations with greater ease, thus promoting your continuous personal and professional growth.

Step 10: Post-Action Reflection and Continuous Adjustment

Post-action reflection is a vital component in your development process through Cognitive Emotional Behavioral Therapy. This step focuses on an introspective and detailed evaluation of your recent experiences, adopting both a critical and compassionate perspective. This analysis will provide you with a deep understanding of the interaction between your emotions, thoughts, and actions, and offer valuable lessons for the future.

At this reflection moment, it's important to consider not only the successes and positive aspects of your experience but also to identify and acknowledge areas that need improvement. For example, you might reflect on how you managed anxiety at a recent social event. Evaluate the effectiveness of your new thinking and behavior strategies.

Ask yourself how they influenced your level of comfort and participation in the event, and whether they contributed to achieving your personal and emotional goals.

This self-evaluation process is a dynamic exercise in adjustment and recalibration. It allows you to modify and enhance your personal strategies and coping techniques for similar situations in the future. Carefully analyze the emotional responses that arose and determine if the emotional regulation and cognitive restructuring techniques you applied were appropriate and effective. Reflect on moments when your reaction was different than expected and consider what you could do differently in the future to achieve results more aligned with your personal goals.

Additionally, contemplate how these new ways of thinking and acting align with your values and long-term goals. Evaluate whether you are moving toward the version of yourself you wish to be and what adjustments you could implement to ensure that your actions more accurately reflect your renewed beliefs and values.

Finally, this step of post-action reflection and continuous adjustment is crucial to solidifying the changes you've made and ensuring that the transformation experienced through CEBT is lasting and meaningful. By dedicating time regularly to this introspective reflection, you will strengthen your ability to tackle emotional and cognitive challenges proactively and consciously, thereby advancing on your path toward personal growth and emotional well-being.

Example:

The post-action reflection you conducted after participating in a social event is a crucial step in your personal development process through Cognitive Emotional Behavioral Therapy. Despite initially facing a sense of anxiety, you applied the new belief that you've integrated into your life: your goal was simply to be present and enjoy the experience. This mindset facilitated a more relaxed and open approach to the situation, increasing your ability to genuinely enjoy the interactions and environment.

During your reflection, you identified that, although the anxiety did not disappear completely, you were able to manage it effectively. This management allowed you to feel less pressured and more in control of the situation. However, you also recognized moments when doubt and insecurity tried to surface, leading you to withdraw or not participate in potentially enriching conversations. This awareness becomes a valuable opportunity to adjust your approach in future situations.

Based on these reflections, you begin planning how you could further improve managing your anxiety and participating in future social events. You consider challenges like initiating at least one conversation with someone new or preparing conversation topics in advance to increase your confidence. This process of post-action reflection and continuous adjustment is essential in CEBT, as it provides an opportunity to learn from your experiences, adjust your coping strategies and tactics, and continue advancing in your personal and emotional development. The conscious application of these lessons will allow you to approach similar situations in the future with greater confidence and less anxiety, contributing to your personal growth and achieving deeper and more sustainable emotional well-being.

Conclusion

Summary and Reflection

Concluding the Cognitive Emotional Behavioral Therapy program, a significant transformation has been achieved by merging techniques from Cognitive Behavioral Therapy, Rational Emotive Behavioral Therapy, and elements of Emotional Intelligence, advancing in the treatment of emotional disorders.

This therapeutic method has allowed for the identification and modification of limiting thoughts and beliefs, improving emotional regulation. Throughout the program, skills for constructive emotional management and a positive internal narrative have been developed, increasing well-being and resilience.

Elements such as unconditional self-acceptance and empathy have strengthened mental well-being and relationships, expanding the social support network. CEBT has equipped for self-diagnosis and self-correction, favoring autonomy in handling future emotional challenges, and promoting sustainable cognitive and behavioral changes.

In summary, CEBT has enriched life with greater self-awareness and emotional adaptability. The principles and skills acquired are essential for facing current and future challenges, marking a commitment to personal growth and the ability to manage emotional complexity.

Step Nine

Learning Consolidation and Healthy Habits

Introduction to the Topic

This chapter focuses on consolidating the learning and knowledge previously acquired, emphasizing the creation and maintenance of healthy habits that promote mental health and resilience. It seeks to effectively integrate these skills and knowledge into everyday life to foster sustainable and long-lasting emotional and psychological well-being.

Learning consolidation, a key process in educational and developmental psychology, involves integrating new knowledge and experiences into long-term memory (Schacter, Gilbert, Wegner, & Nock, 2018). This process is essential for skills and knowledge to become part of the individual's behavioral and cognitive repertoire, allowing for their effective application in various life situations.

From a neuroscientific perspective, learning consolidation involves the reorganization and strengthening of neural connections in the brain, facilitated by constant repetition and practice (Dudai, Karni, & Born, 2015). Thus, repeating and practicing learned skills, such as emotional regulation and mindfulness, promotes their internalization and automation.

Forming healthy habits is crucial in managing mood disorders. Defined as automatic behaviors triggered by contextual cues, these habits have a significant impact on mental and physical health (Wood & Rünger, 2016). Regular physical exercise, for example, has been shown to be effective in reducing symptoms of depression and anxiety, possibly due to its influence on neurotransmitter regulation and self-esteem improvement (Schuch et al., 2016).

Implementing mindfulness and meditation routines can also improve emotional regulation, reduce stress reactivity, and increase awareness and acceptance of emotional experiences (Guendelman, Medeiros, & Rampes, 2017). These practices foster an attitude of observation and non-judgment towards thoughts and emotions, essential for managing mood disorders.

In summary, the consolidation of learning and the formation of healthy habits are fundamental to promoting mental health and resilience. Integrating these practices into everyday life facilitates effective management of mood disorders and promotes lasting well-being. The constant application of these skills and knowledge can result in significant changes in brain structure and function, improving life quality and personal satisfaction.

Research Evidence

The formation and consolidation of healthy habits play a crucial role in the treatment and management of mood disorders such as depression and anxiety. Recent research has shown that adopting habits like regular physical activity, a balanced diet, and mindfulness practice can positively impact mental health (Kvam, Kleppe, Nordhus, & Hovland, 2016).

A study in the "American Journal of Psychiatry" indicates that even one hour of exercise per week can prevent between 12% and 17% of depression cases (Harvey et al., 2018). Exercise stimulates the release of endorphins, known as well-being hormones, and regulates neurotransmitters linked to depression and anxiety, such as serotonin and norepinephrine.

Similarly, a diet rich in fruits, vegetables, whole grains, and omega-3 fatty acids has been associated with a lower risk of depressive symptoms. A study in "BMC Medicine" revealed that dietary interventions could be effective in treating major depression (Jacka et al., 2017).

Mindfulness meditation has been shown to be effective in reducing anxiety and depression. Research in "JAMA Internal Medicine" showed that this practice could significantly decrease symptoms of anxiety and depression (Goyal et al., 2014).

Learning consolidation, from a neuronal perspective, involves the strengthening of neural connections through repetition and practice. During learning, certain neural pathways are activated in the brain. Repetition and practice strengthen these pathways, consolidating learning from short-term to long-term memory (Dudai, Karni, & Born, 2015).

This process benefits from the brain's reward system, which releases dopamine, crucial in motivation and pleasure. Dopamine not only improves mood but also reinforces neural connections related to learning (Schultz, 2016).

Therefore, the consolidation of healthy habits and the creation of new neural pathways through active learning present promising methods for the treatment and management of mood disorders. These strategies offer not only symptomatic relief but also promote lasting changes in the brain, enhancing sustained improvement in mental health and overall well-being.

Instructions

Learning Reflection and Creation
of Healthy Habits

Objective

The main goal of this exercise is to guide you through a detailed reflection on the emotional intelligence skills, identification of beliefs, and cognitive restructuring acquired in previous chapters. It focuses on how to apply this knowledge to form daily habits that promote your mental health and increase your emotional resilience, crucial elements for the effective management of mood disorders and the promotion of lasting well-being.

Learning consolidation, a neural process essential for the formation of long-term memory, strengthens synaptic connections in the brain, facilitating the incorporation of knowledge and skills into daily life. Dudai, Karni, and Born (2015) highlight the importance of repetition and reflection in this process, allowing the learned skills to be integrated into your behavioral repertoire.

By completing this exercise, you will have not only acquired useful knowledge for managing mental health but also developed a series of daily habits that support your emotional and mental well-being. The constant practice of these techniques provides tools to proactively address mood disorders and cultivate a more stable and enduring state of well-being.

This ongoing process of learning and growth is essential for reinforcing your capacity for adaptation and emotional management, which significantly contributes to a richer and more satisfying life. Integrating these skills into your daily routine not only improves your mental health but also your overall well-being, preparing you to face life's challenges with greater confidence and stability.

Step 1: Learning Review and Reflection

This initial step in your journey towards enhanced emotional well-being invites you to deep introspection about the knowledge gained in emotional intelligence and behavioral therapies. This process includes reflecting on the development of social skills, practicing self-compassion, exercising assertiveness, and incorporating healthy habits into daily life. It represents a crucial moment to meditate on the integration of these essential insights into your daily life and evaluate the significant impact they have had on your emotional and mental state.

Begin by reviewing the fundamental concepts and notes accumulated in your personal journal. This exercise not only deepens your understanding of the topics covered but also provides you with an overview of how these skills have been implemented in your life, highlighting both the positive changes made and the challenges faced. This is a moment to acknowledge your progress, reflect on the difficulties, and consider adjustments to optimize the application of these learnings in the future.

You are encouraged to critically evaluate both your successes and the obstacles encountered. Reflect on the instances when you successfully applied the learned skills, as well as those situations where you faced difficulties. This analysis will help you identify specific areas for improvement and adjust your approach for future applications.

This step is fundamental not only for assessing the progress made but also for proactively planning your continued development. By dedicating time to this reflection, you commit to a constant process of personal improvement, essential for reinforcing your emotional and mental health. This commitment to your personal and emotional growth establishes a solid foundation for future successes on your path to a more balanced and fulfilling life.

Example:

Imagine that during the week, you used your personal journal to detail your thoughts and emotions, especially in moments of stress or challenge. This introspection allowed you to identify the automatic thoughts and irrational beliefs that influence your behavior and emotional well-being. You discovered, for example, that certain recurring ideas about your work performance stem from unfounded beliefs about your capabilities, rather than concrete facts.

This reflective exercise also revealed difficulties in directly connecting your intense emotions to those underlying beliefs. While you recorded situations that triggered strong emotional responses in your journal, drawing a clear link to a specific belief proved complex. This finding is crucial because it points to areas for deeper exploration, improving your understanding and management of these dynamics.

In response, consider investing more time in self-exploration and, if deemed necessary, seeking additional support through therapy or counseling. This will help you achieve a more detailed understanding of your fundamental beliefs and their impact on your emotions and behaviors.

This evaluation and reflection process is essential for your continuous development in emotional intelligence and coping strategies. It not only offers you the chance to recognize and appreciate your progress but also motivates you to proactively plan your personal and emotional evolution. By committing to this practice, you are laying the groundwork for greater self-awareness and a more balanced and enriched emotional life, marking a turning point in your journey towards emotional and mental well-being.

Step 2: Implementation of SMART Goals

Setting goals is a fundamental pillar on the path to enriching emotional well-being and the effective integration of key learnings, especially in areas such as emotional intelligence and behavioral therapies. Adopting the SMART method (Specific, Measurable, Achievable, Relevant, and Time-bound) for defining your goals not only provides an organized framework for your ambitions but also facilitates an accurate evaluation of your progress.

This moment is appropriate to discern in which aspects of your life the application of this knowledge would be most beneficial. For instance, you might set the goal to improve your emotional management under pressure, enhance your conflict resolution skills, or establish a constant practice of mindfulness to mitigate daily stress.

For each goal you set, it's crucial to detail precisely your intentions, ensuring they are quantifiable for effective tracking of your evolution. Ensure that your goals are realistic, tailored to your current resources and abilities, and verify their relevance for your overall well-being. Additionally, define specific timelines for their achievement, thus maintaining a clear direction and motivation.

With your SMART goals already outlined, sketch concrete steps and incremental strategies that will guide you toward their accomplishment. This method will keep you motivated and allow you to adjust your tactics as you progress in your personal development.

Initiating this goal-setting process means committing to incessant growth. The specificity and methodology behind your SMART goals will be catalysts for significant improvements in your emotional well-being and your ability to face challenges, enhancing your resilience and strengthening your mental health in a lasting manner. Now is the time to turn your learnings into meaningful actions that reflect your dedication to a more fulfilling and harmonious existence.

Example:

Reflecting on your daily logs, you've realized the importance of documenting your thoughts and emotions to detect negative trends. However, you identify an opportunity for improvement in organizing these reflections. Therefore, you set a specific goal: "I will commit to spending an additional 10 minutes each night, for the next two weeks, to organize my journal entries, categorizing my thoughts and emotions into well-defined categories".

Additionally, you recognize that delving into the identification of your core beliefs still presents challenges. To address this, you establish another SMART goal: "I will dedicate 15 minutes daily to identify, at least once a week, a core belief, relating it to the day's events and its connection with my deepest convictions". To ensure progress in this area, you consider scheduling a monthly session with a psychology specialist or counselor.

These objectives, defined by their specificity, measurability, achievability, relevance, and timeliness, are designed to be effectively incorporated into your daily routine. Their implementation will mark a significant advance in your capacity for conscious mental health management. With defined deadlines and practical measures, you're heading towards a constant practice that will not only foster your personal and emotional development but also consolidate your well-being in a comprehensive and enduring way. This proactive strategy will facilitate maintaining your path of self-exploration and emotional self-management, establishing beneficial routines that will support your long-term well-being.

Step 3: Planning Healthy Habits

The "Planning Healthy Habits" stage is crucial on your journey toward enhanced emotional well-being. This step involves defining daily practices that benefit the body, mind, and spirit. Begin by reflecting on the knowledge acquired, especially in emotional intelligence and stress management techniques you've learned.

Effective planning of healthy habits requires selecting specific activities you wish to adopt regularly. This could range from adopting a balanced diet, practicing consistent physical exercise, to ensuring restorative sleep. Each of these aspects is crucial for balancing your mood and cultivating emotional resilience, strengthening your ability to overcome daily challenges, and improving your long-term mental well-being.

For these changes to be enduring, set clear and realistic goals. Apply the SMART method to define specific goals, such as "I will dedicate 30 minutes daily to walking, five days a week" or "I will practice meditation for 10 minutes every morning". Choose activities that you find rewarding and that hold personal meaning, which will increase the likelihood of them becoming an integral part of your life. Also include mindfulness practices and relaxation techniques in your plan. These strategies will connect you with yourself on a deep level, promoting a state of awareness that will facilitate the identification and management of your emotions more effectively. Mindfulness and meditation not only reduce stress but also generate a sense of calm and well-being in your daily life.

Adopting these healthy habits should be a gradual process. Progress at your own pace, valuing each advancement, no matter how small. This patient and self-compassionate approach to change will establish a solid foundation for your emotional and physical health, allowing you to live in a more harmonious and satisfying manner.

Example:

After reflecting on your learnings in emotional intelligence and behavioral therapies, you decide to take concrete actions to foster your emotional well-being, committing to the development of healthy habits. This step towards self-care involves making significant adjustments to your daily routine, seeking harmony that benefits both your mind and body.

Initially, you choose to adopt a healthier diet, recognizing the direct impact of nutrition on your mood and energy level. You plan to enrich your meals with a variety of fruits and vegetables and decide to reduce the consumption of processed foods and sugars, organizing your weekly menus every Sunday.

Recognizing the value of physical exercise for your mental health, you commit to engaging in activities that bring you joy, such as walking, yoga, or swimming, at least three times a week. This commitment not only benefits your physical state but also becomes an effective strategy for stress management and overall well-being enhancement.

Adequate rest emerges as another essential pillar of your plan. To promote restorative sleep, you implement a nighttime routine that includes limiting screen exposure before bedtime, preparing a calm environment in your bedroom, and establishing regular sleep schedules.

Additionally, you decide to integrate the practice of mindfulness and meditation into your daily life, setting specific times to practice mindfulness, such as upon waking or before meals, thus fostering a constant connection with the present and reducing anxiety.

Throughout this process, you use your personal journal to document both your progress and the challenges faced, reflecting on the impact of these habits on your mood and emotional health. This tracking proves to be a key tool for assessing the effectiveness of the changes made and making necessary adjustments.

After a few weeks, you'll notice the beneficial effect of integrating these healthy habits into your life. You experience an increase in your energy and balance, as well as a greater capacity to face daily challenges with emotional strength. This change underscores the importance of an integrated approach to well-being, where simultaneous care of the body and mind is essential for achieving full emotional health.

Step 4: Integrating Mindfulness Practice

Incorporating mindfulness practice into your daily routine stands out as an essential step towards enriching your emotional well-being and developing lasting resilience in the face of adversity. This technique, which promotes full awareness of the present moment, equips you with the ability to observe your thoughts, emotions, and physical sensations from an impartial perspective, avoiding hasty judgments. Beyond reducing stress and improving concentration, mindfulness fosters a more harmonious and compassionate relationship with oneself.

Adopting mindfulness initiates a profound change in how you perceive your mental and emotional processes. This advancement is based on the ability to recognize and accept your internal experiences without fully identifying with them, thus facilitating a more balanced and mindful reaction to daily challenges. Through mindful attention, you learn to unravel the web of automatic thoughts and to approach challenging emotions with serenity and understanding, preventing excessive reactivity or the repression of feelings.

To integrate mindfulness into your life, you can start with simple and direct practices. Dedicate a few minutes each morning to focus on your breathing, appreciating each inhalation and exhalation as an opportunity to anchor your attention in the now. Apply mindfulness to daily activities, such as eating or walking, paying complete attention to the sensations and experiences of the moment. These exercises, however brief, act as potent reminders of your ability to remain centered and conscious throughout the day.

Mindfulness also promotes self-compassion and acceptance, crucial virtues for managing emotional fluctuations with care and benevolence towards oneself. By cultivating a space of non-judgmental observation, it becomes easier to identify and modify limiting beliefs, strengthening your ability to adapt and thrive in the face of life's challenges.

With continuous mindfulness practice, you will notice its transformative effects: a reduction in stress, increased mental clarity, and strengthened emotional well-being. This method allows you to approach life with greater calm, clarity, and confidence, establishing mindfulness as a vital support on your path to a fulfilled and balanced existence.

Example:

Recognizing the transformative impact of mindfulness, you decide to make this practice an integral part of your daily life, with the goal of reinforcing your mental and emotional well-being. This commitment begins each morning, dedicating 10 to 15 minutes to focused breathing meditation, in a quiet place where you can be without distractions. This moment of morning serenity becomes a fundamental pillar to start the day, providing you with a foundation of peace and concentration that prepares you to face any challenge serenely.

Motivated by the positive effects of these morning sessions, you decide to extend the practice of mindfulness to other critical moments of the day. You introduce brief mindful pauses during lunch and establish a meditation ritual before bedtime. These intervals of mindfulness offer opportunities to reconnect with the present moment, significantly decreasing the inclination towards rumination and anxiety. As you continue with this practice, your appreciation of the now deepens, enriching your daily experience with a more intense feeling of peace and satisfaction.

The habitual incorporation of mindfulness into your routine not only elevates your ability to manage stress and complex emotions but also fosters an environment conducive to personal and emotional growth. By adopting mindfulness as a daily habit, you not only face life with greater calm and clarity but also stimulate a significant transformation in your overall well-being. This commitment to mindful practice becomes a resource of strength and well-being, marking a substantial change in your ability to enjoy a full and resilient existence.

Step 5: Exercise and Nutrition Implementation

The integration of an exercise routine and healthy eating habits is crucial for overall well-being, positively affecting both physical and mental health. Regular physical activity and a balanced diet are essential pillars for maintaining an emotional equilibrium and promoting good psychological health.

Physical activity plays a key role in mood enhancement, thanks to the release of endorphins, known as the "happiness hormones". These natural brain chemicals can reduce pain perception and generating feelings of well-being and joy. The importance of exercise extends to the prevention and mitigation of symptoms associated with depression and anxiety, offering an effective method to improve life quality.

Simultaneously, maintaining a rich and balanced diet is vital for proper brain functioning and emotional management. Nutrient-rich foods, such as fruits, vegetables, lean proteins, whole grains, and omega-3 fatty acids, significantly contribute to improving concentration, increasing mental clarity, and stabilizing moods. Adequate nutrition is, therefore, a key component to strengthen mental health and foster emotional balance.

Consciously implementing these elements in daily life not only represents an effective strategy for stress management and energy increase but also promotes a healthier and more rewarding lifestyle. By adopting healthy exercise and nutrition practices, you invest in your physical and emotional health, laying the foundation for comprehensive and lasting well-being.

This holistic approach to self-care underscores the interrelation between physical and mental health, encouraging you to commit to a lifestyle that benefits both body and mind. By integrating exercise routines and healthy eating patterns into your daily life, you embark on a journey towards a more balanced, enriched, and full life, establishing a deep commitment to your personal well-being.

Example:

Actively deciding to improve your overall well-being, you recognize the fundamental importance of nutrition and exercise in mental health. Following a nutritionist's advice, you introduce probiotics into your breakfast, based on evidence linking optimal gut health with more positive moods and reduced anxiety.

Additionally, you reformulate your dinner to include lighter and nutrient-rich options, excluding complex carbohydrates to favor a healthy sleep cycle. This dietary adjustment is strategic for improving the quality of your nighttime rest, a pillar for emotional stability and effective stress management.

Parallelly, you commit to an exercise routine designed according to your tastes and personal goals. You prefer activities you enjoy, such as running outdoors or swimming, and plan training sessions three times a week. This commitment not only strengthens your physical condition but also improves your self-esteem and contributes to your personal satisfaction.

The effects of this dual strategy soon become evident. You experience a notable increase in your daily energy, greater emotional stability, and more restorative sleep. The adjustments made in your diet and exercise regimen reveal themselves as fundamental pillars for your emotional health, demonstrating the positive influence lifestyle changes can have on overall well-being.

By integrating these healthy habits into your life, you are laying the groundwork for lasting mental and physical well-being, highlighting the relevance of a holistic approach to self-care. The conscious adoption of proper nutrition and regular physical activity confirms as effective tactics to increase your emotional resilience and cultivate a more balanced and fulfilling lifestyle.

Step 6: Gratitude Journal

Cultivating a gratitude journal is identified as a powerfully transformative practice, aimed at fostering a spirit of thankfulness for the positive aspects of existence. Dedicating time daily to reflect and jot down in a journal the progress made in adopting healthy habits and advancing emotional intelligence skills, as well as expressing gratitude for both the small and significant blessings of each day, becomes a valuable tool for emotional enrichment.

Research in positive psychology has confirmed that gratitude brings numerous benefits to emotional well-being, such as an increase in happiness, a reduction of stress, and an enhancement of self-esteem. Focusing on the valuable and positive aspects of life facilitates a shift in focus from what is lacking to what is plentiful, transforming the perception of the world and improving interactions with it.

The act of writing in a gratitude journal promotes deep reflection on personal achievements and daily joys, encouraging appreciation for both significant successes and moments of bliss. This daily practice of acknowledgment and thankfulness cultivates an optimistic and content mindset, significantly contributing to present emotional well-being and laying the foundation for a more fulfilling future.

Integrating gratitude into your daily routine emerges as an effective method to adopt a more positive life perspective and value your experiences and advancements. By committing to gratitude regularly, not only do you enhance your day-to-day life but also strengthen your mental health, establishing thankfulness as an essential pillar for enriching and lasting emotional balance.

Example:

Imagine routinely, after reviewing your personal diary, taking 10 to 15 minutes each day to write in your gratitude and progress journal. This time is dedicated to illuminating the positive aspects of the day, such as maintaining calmness in the face of a work challenge or dedicating time to your mindfulness practice. Then, focus on expressing gratitude for life's blessings, whether for your health, family, friends, or even the small daily moments of joy.

Additionally, this time allows you to value your qualities and celebrate your achievements, appreciating your efforts and victories, no matter their size. This nightly exercise becomes a key ritual, helping you end the day on a positive note, significantly contributing to your overall well-being and happiness.

With the constant incorporation of this practice into your daily life, you notice a notable transformation in your perception of the world. You adopt a more optimistic attitude, become more aware of life's gifts, and more compassionate towards yourself. Gratitude and recognition of your progress nourish your self-esteem and improve your ability to face difficulties with optimism and resilience. This habit of thankfulness stands as an essential support of your emotional stability, providing a robust foundation for lasting and enriched mental and emotional health.

Step 7: Strengthening Social Connections

In this pivotal step towards optimal mental and emotional health, you focus on strengthening your social connections, which are fundamental to your well-being. Meaningful relationships provide support, understanding, and a valuable sense of belonging. The ability to forge and sustain these ties depends on efficient communication and a developed emotional intelligence, skills you have been consciously working on.

Begin by evaluating your current network of relationships, distinguishing those that add value to your life and identifying areas that could be improved. You may wish to strengthen the connection with certain friends, family members, or even colleagues. It's crucial to recognize that each relationship requires effort and commitment for its development and maintenance.

Next, develop a plan to perfect your communication skills, encompassing active listening techniques, the clear and respectful articulation of your ideas and feelings, and the willingness to understand others' perspectives. These abilities are vital for establishing deep and genuine interactions.

Commit also to regularly dedicating time to cultivate these relationships, whether through meetings, calls, or messages. The key lies in the intentionality of these interactions, always seeking to reinforce the bond.

To expand your support network, participate in groups or activities that resonate with your interests or values, thus finding like-minded communities. These new relationships not only diversify your social environment but also provide additional support when needed.

Finally, the practice of gratitude and recognition plays a crucial role in your relationships. Valuing and thanking the people in your life deepens connections and promotes a reciprocal support environment. Celebrating others' successes and being there in difficult times are actions that solidify these ties.

This effort to strengthen your social connections is an invaluable investment in your mental health and emotional well-being. Developing and maintaining meaningful relationships enriches your social life and builds a fundamental support network to overcome adversities. Each interaction brings you closer to balanced emotional well-being, increasing your emotional resilience in the face of life's challenges.

Example:

After recognizing the importance of strengthening your social bonds, you decide to take concrete actions to improve your communication skills and expand your circle of support. You are aware that, despite personal advancements and emotional management achievements, a network of strengthened relationships constitutes an essential pillar for your emotional balance.

With this purpose, you set a specific goal: to initiate meaningful conversations with at least two people from your close circle weekly. This initiative could focus on colleagues with whom you wish to improve ties or friends or family members with whom you've lost contact. The goal is to transcend superficial exchanges, delving into topics of mutual interest that foster a deeper bond.

Simultaneously, you decide to participate in a group or association aligned with your hobbies or interests, such as a book club, a hiking collective, or an art workshop. This involvement not only allows you to meet individuals with shared affinities but also provides an ideal setting to practice your communication skills and forge bonds in a friendly and supportive context.

Committing to cultivating authentic and substantial relationships, you adopt active listening in every conversation, genuinely striving to understand others' perspectives and feelings. This involves asking open-ended questions, echoing what you've understood, and demonstrating empathy.

Additionally, you establish a routine to maintain and nurture these ties. This can mean organizing regular calls with distant loved ones or scheduling monthly meetups with new friends from the group you've joined. The purpose is to ensure the development and consolidation of these relationships.

By implementing these strategies, you notice how your support network diversifies and your interaction skills enrich. This increased connection and mutual understanding reinforce your ability to face adversities, offering you a sense of community and significantly contributing to your emotional stability.

This commitment to enriching your social bonds not only beautifies your life with valuable relationships but also builds a crucial support structure for difficult times, elevating your mental and emotional well-being. This conscious approach to social interaction proves fundamental for an emotionally rich and balanced life.

Step 8: Time Management and Stress Reduction

Effective time management and stress reduction are essential pillars for maintaining a healthy balance in your life, positively affecting both your mental and physical well-being. This step focuses on providing you with practical strategies for optimal time organization, which will help you focus on the fundamental aspects of your life while minimizing stress levels that could undermine your emotional health.

Begin this process by conducting an accurate assessment of how you currently manage your time. Identify activities that drain your energy without offering real benefits or divert you from your personal goals. This self-knowledge analysis will reveal opportunities to readjust your time distribution and optimize your energy towards more fruitful activities.

After this introspection, learn to prioritize your activities based on their relevance and urgency, applying techniques such as the Eisenhower matrix. This method will guide you to focus on tasks crucial for your personal and professional growth, ensuring that you invest your time in what is genuinely important.

Integrating conscious breaks throughout the day is fundamental for self-care and stress mitigation. These intervals can range from brief mindfulness exercises and breathing techniques to moments of tranquility to reconnect with yourself. Schedule these breaks, especially during times of high workload or stress, allowing you to rejuvenate your mind and maintain a serene perspective.

For sustainable and effective time management, create a weekly schedule that incorporates your essential obligations, as well as periods dedicated to exercise, balanced eating, adequate rest, and activities that bring you joy and satisfaction. The challenge lies in finding a balance that supports your personal and work aspirations without compromising your mental and physical health.

Periodically evaluate the impact of these time management and stress reduction techniques on your daily life. Adjust your planning as needed to perpetuate your well-being. By adhering to this method, you will not only increase your productivity and efficiency but also strengthen your emotional resilience, optimally positioning yourself to face life's challenges with a positive and proactive approach. This holistic commitment to your development will enable you to enjoy an enriching and balanced existence, with well-being and harmony as your faithful allies.

Example:

After delving into emotional intelligence and cognitive restructuring, you decide to apply this knowledge to tackle the challenge of optimizing time management and reducing stress. You are aware that much of your anxiety originates from the feeling of being perpetually against the clock, overwhelmed by multiple tasks.

You begin this process by thoroughly evaluating your weekly activities and commitments, distinguishing between those essential and those that can be delegated or discarded. This analysis provides a clear view of your time distribution, revealing areas for potential improvement or excessive responsibilities.

Based on this understanding, you define a specific SMART goal: "I will allocate two hours every Sunday afternoon for weekly planning, ensuring a balanced distribution of time between work, rest, exercise, and self-care". This goal, clearly defined, measurable, realistic, relevant, and time-bound, offers a framework for its ongoing tracking and adjustment.

To facilitate disconnection and self-care, you incorporate five-minute mindfulness breaks at the start of the workday, during lunch, and before sleep. These brief interludes promote a momentary disconnection from daily pressures, focusing on the present and reducing accumulated stress.

This strategy results in a notable improvement in your stress management and ability to concentrate and remain calm in the face of daily challenges. Active time management and the integration of relaxation techniques not only increase your efficiency and personal satisfaction but also strengthen your emotional resilience, offering you a more controlled and balanced life approach.

Consciously adopting these practices in your daily life equips you with essential tools to navigate life with greater ease and confidence. This commitment to yourself reveals the value of self-efficacy and how minor adjustments in your routines can have a substantial impact on your overall well-being.

Step 9: Continuous Assessment and Goal Adjustment

Continuous assessment and adjustment of your goals are essential on the path to optimal emotional and mental state. This practice not only facilitates tracking your progress but also highlights the need for modifications to stay on course toward your aspirations. Regular self-assessment emerges as an invaluable tool, allowing you to reflect on your advances, celebrate your achievements, and recalibrate in less developed areas or where previous approaches have been less effective.

Begin this process by setting aside weekly time to review your established goals, analyzing your progress in each honestly. Question your actions and their alignment with these objectives, identifying both achievements and obstacles that have arisen. This introspection will help you discern your areas of strength and those where deviations from the initial plan require your attention.

This assessment exercise also provides you the flexibility to readjust your goals based on the life changes you experience. Some goals may lose relevance, or new priorities may emerge, reflecting your personal evolution and the challenges overcome. Adapting your objectives reflects growth and keeps you focused on what truly contributes to your well-being.

Take time to contemplate how the emotional intelligence competencies you've cultivated influence your daily life. Examine the perceived changes in stress management and in your relationships, assessing the effectiveness of the learned skills. These reflections will allow you to appreciate the real impact of your efforts and adjust your strategies as necessary.

It's crucial to maintain an open and adaptable mindset, recognizing that change is inherent to growth. Accepting this dynamic will equips you to face the unpredictable with resilience, focusing more on consistency and adaptability than the speed of your achievements.

Committing to continuous evaluation and adjustment of your goals reinforces your dedication to self-development and improving your emotional well-being. This process ensures you remain true to your values and aspirations, leading you toward a life enriched by sustained learning and growth.

Example:

After months of dedication to your personalized 10-step program for improving emotional and mental well-being, you decide to undertake a detailed reflection to evaluate and possibly recalibrate your goals. This moment of introspection is crucial for analyzing the journey toward the objectives you set at the beginning of this journey.

In a serene environment, you open your journal, where you have meticulously recorded your aspirations and progress. You begin a deep examination of each goal, questioning your progress, the challenges faced, and the solutions found. You also consider how new situations that have arisen could influence the redefinition of your goals.

You notice significant achievements in some areas, such as the effective implementation of mindfulness and the enrichment of your personal relationships. However, you identify that time management and stress control still represent significant challenges, revealing the need for a more concrete methodology to address these goals.

Based on this introspection, you set renewed and realistic goals, such as applying the Eisenhower quadrant to prioritize tasks, distinguishing the urgent from the truly important. You commit to dedicating daily time to activities that promote your self-care and relieve stress.

This assessment leads you to a deeper understanding of the importance of adaptability in your personal growth. You opt to conduct monthly checks of your progress, allowing you to dynamically adjust your plans and ensure continuous progress toward your well-being.

The practice of reviewing and adjusting your goals becomes an essential component of your commitment to self-development. Concluding this exercise, you will feel revitalized, with a clear plan to move forward toward a state of emotional balance and mental health, underscoring the value of flexibility and adaptation as fundamental pillars in your personal development.

Step 10: Celebrating Achievements and Reflection

As you reach the conclusion of this significant journey of personal and emotional development, you find yourself at the threshold of the final step: Celebrating Achievements and Deep Reflection. This moment marks a significant pause, giving you the chance to look back and appreciate every achievement gained. Throughout this 10-step program, you have made a conscious effort to enrich your emotional well-being and hone your emotional intelligence skills, and now is the moment to recognize and honor that dedication.

Begin this phase by reminiscing about your journey. Reflect on the obstacles you've overcome and how you triumphed over them. Recall moments of uncertainty and how you found the determination to persevere. Each of these episodes is undeniable evidence of your evolution and strength.

Open your journal to document your triumphs. Focus not only on the most notable achievements but also on the smaller victories that together have shaped the essence of your progress. Perhaps you've established and maintained beneficial habits, cultivated your interpersonal relationships, or discovered more effective stress management strategies. Every success, no matter how small, is worthy of celebration.

Then, ponder the personal lessons learned. Question which beliefs you've transformed and how your understanding of emotional intelligence and its integration into your daily life has changed. These introspections will allow you to appreciate the depth of change you've experienced.

After recognizing your conquests, formulate intentions for your future growth. Reflect on ways you can continue applying the skills and knowledge acquired to new challenges and aspirations. Celebrating your successes marks not just a conclusion, but also the beginning of your ongoing emotional and personal evolution.

Lastly, share your experiences. Talk with friends, family, or support groups about your journey. Sharing not only solidifies your own achievements but can also serve as inspiration and encouragement for others on their paths to emotional well-being.

This step invites you to look back with gratitude, inward with acknowledgment, and forward with optimism. It serves as a reminder that personal growth is a continuous journey, where every advancement deserves to be celebrated.

Conclusion

Summary and Reflection

As you conclude this chapter, you find yourself at a pivotal moment for your emotional health and resilience. It's crucial to put into daily practice the lessons learned, developing habits that support and enhance your mental well-being. This effort not only safeguards your emotional health but is also crucial for your ongoing personal growth.

You have made significant progress, from reflecting and setting goals to practicing mindfulness and adopting a healthy lifestyle. You have learned to appreciate each step forward, preparing yourself for future challenges with self-compassion and gratitude.

The importance of this chapter lies in your ability to sustain and expand upon the achievements gained. By integrating these practices into your routine, you promote not just present well-being but also enduring and profound personal development. With greater clarity and optimism, celebrate everyday achievements and cultivate gratitude for the simple things.

This process represents a comprehensive transformation. The combination of emotional intelligence, mindfulness, and a healthy lifestyle enhances your well-being. It's important to create a life where mental and emotional health are priorities.

Remember, the journey towards resilience and emotional well-being is ongoing, with challenges you can now face with confidence. Celebrate your successes and approach the future with hope. Your commitment demonstrates your strength and aspiration for a richly fulfilled life.

Step Ten

Maintenance of Changes
and Relapse Prevention

Introduction to the Topic

This chapter focuses on a critical aspect of the treatment and management of mood disorders: how to preserve the positive changes achieved and prevent potential relapses. In the process of recovery and improvement of mental well-being, it's not enough to achieve progress; it is imperative to maintain these advances and prepare to face future challenges.

Preserving positive changes is a dynamic and ongoing task, requiring uninterrupted commitment and adaptability to new circumstances and experiences. This chapter proposes practical and effective strategies to incorporate into daily life, aiming to reinforce mental and emotional health sustainably and reduce the risk of relapse.

We will address techniques such as constant monitoring of emotions and thoughts, crucial to identify early any sign of alarm and act preventively. Also, the importance of developing a personalized plan to face adverse situations will be analyzed, including adaptive coping methods and problem-solving strategies.

A fundamental element will be the emphasis on the importance of support networks and their promotion. Having an effective support system, whether through personal relationships, support groups, or mental health professionals, is vital in the process of maintenance and relapse prevention. Additionally, the importance of self-care, such as regular exercise, a balanced diet, and relaxation techniques, highlighting their positive influence on the emotional and mental state, will be examined.

By the end of this chapter, the reader will have gained an expanded understanding of how to preserve the achievements obtained and will be better prepared to manage future challenges, thus facilitating the path toward a more emotionally fulfilling and balanced life.

Research Evidence

Research in the field of clinical psychology and behavioral therapy has underscored the crucial importance of maintaining positive behavioral and emotional changes in addressing mood disorders. Moore et al. (2016) highlight that relapse prevention is as important as the initial treatment.

Continuous monitoring emerges as a key strategy in this area. For many individuals, regular tracking of thought patterns and behavior through personal journals or mental health apps becomes essential. This technique facilitates constant observation of mood states and emotional responses, allowing early identification of signs of a possible relapse and enabling timely interventions.

Additionally, preparing to face challenging situations is of paramount importance. Developing action plans and coping strategies, particularly for circumstances that historically triggered adverse emotional responses, is crucial. According to Roemer and Orsillo (2019), tools such as mindfulness and cognitive-behavioral therapy represent valuable resources to anticipate and manage stressful situations.

The relevance of support networks cannot be underestimated. Participation in support groups or the consolidation of a robust social support network, as Johnson et al. (2011) indicate, is fundamental in preserving mental health. These groups provide a safe environment for sharing experiences and receiving support.

Lastly, self-care strategies, including regular exercise, a balanced diet, and relaxation techniques, are highlighted as vital elements. These practices minimize stress and promote overall well-being, playing a significant role in preventing relapses and maintaining emotional balance.

In conclusion, a comprehensive approach that integrates continuous vigilance, preparation for challenges, social support, and self-care is essential in preventing relapses and conserving mental health is clearly evidenced.

Instructions

Coping Strategies and Preparation
for Future Challenges

Objective

The aim of this exercise is to develop and reinforce your ability to sustain positive changes durably and to formulate a comprehensive action plan to prevent relapses in the context of mood disorders. This exercise transcends the mere consolidation of improvements achieved, focusing on the proactive implementation of strategies for future emotional and psychological challenges.

Throughout the previous chapters, various tools and skills have been acquired, including stress management techniques, mindfulness practices, and cognitive-behavioral coping strategies. The challenge is to integrate these skills into your daily life in such a way that they become part of your habitual behavior, thus establishing a solid foundation for long-term emotional well-being.

It is essential to learn to recognize and value the positive changes made, not only as isolated achievements but as elements of a continuous process of growth and personal development. This involves the ability to identify and celebrate your successes and to see setbacks as learning opportunities.

Developing an action plan to prevent relapses is a key aspect of this exercise. Such a plan should be personalized, considering your circumstances, challenges, and needs. It should include specific strategies to detect and manage early signs of stress, anxiety, or depression, and define proactive actions to address potentially triggering situations.

Furthermore, the importance of developing and sustaining an effective support network is emphasized, promoting meaningful relationships with family, friends, and mental health professionals who can provide support and understanding when needed.

Finally, this exercise seeks to empower you to take an active role in caring for your mental health and emotional well-being. Upon completing this exercise, you will not only have strengthened your ability to maintain positive changes but will also have a set of personalized strategies to prevent relapses and face future challenges with confidence and resilience.

Title: Step 1: Incorporation of Continuous Assessment

Integrating constant evaluation into your journey towards emotional well-being is a key element in maintaining and enhancing the progress achieved in your mental health. This method enables you to closely monitor your evolution and immediately recognize any signs of setback, allowing for the appropriate adjustments in your coping methods.

Regular consultations with a mental health professional are an essential component of this dynamic, providing you with an expert assessment that enriches your self-examinations. These interactions offer objective perspectives about your emotional condition, facilitating the identification of trends or specific challenges that may require specialized attention.

The use of self-assessment tools, such as the Beck Depression Inventory and the Beck Anxiety Inventory (both available online), contributes to obtaining a precise overview of your anxiety levels and mood state. Although these resources do not replace professional evaluation, they are beneficial for self-monitoring and introspection.

Incorporating continuous assessment from the beginning is crucial for developing a comprehensive approach aimed at relapse prevention. This approach not only enables you to preserve the improvements made but also to proactively anticipate potential emotional and psychological obstacles in the future. By adopting these measures in your daily life, you reinforce your ability to optimally manage your mental health, ensuring steady progress towards a state of lasting well-being and emotional strength.

Example:

Adopting continuous evaluation in your journey towards recovery and maintaining your mental health is an essential tactic to ensure lasting progress and avoid potential setbacks. Imagine that, after facing periods of anxiety and depression, you choose to fervently dedicate yourself to your emotional well-being, adopting a proactive stance towards self-assessment and constant monitoring of your emotional state.

This commitment is realized through regular appointments with a psychologist, which offer a reliable environment to examine your emotions, challenges, and progress. These meetings provide you with a deeper understanding of your mental and behavioral patterns, offering you personalized tactics for stress management and enhancing your resilience.

Parallelly, you choose to enrich these consultations with the periodic use of the Beck Depression Inventory. This self-assessment tool facilitates tracking your depressive states every two weeks. While aware that this resource does not replace professional guidance, it acts as a valuable complement to exercise active control over your emotional health, giving you the ability to detect and respond to any concerning signs more promptly.

This mechanism of constant evaluation stands as a key support in your improvement process, not only allowing you to preserve the achievements made but also preparing you to tackle future emotional challenges with renewed security and efficiency. The sessions with your psychologist, alongside systematic self-monitoring, equip you for an uninterrupted evolution process, in which every advance is celebrated, and every obstacle is transformed into an opportunity to learn and progress.

Step 2: Identification of Warning Signs

Early recognition of warning signs associated with stress, anxiety, and depression is a vital element in preserving your mental well-being. Often, these preliminary indicators, such as sleep disturbances, increased irritability, or a loss of interest in previously enjoyable activities, can be underestimated due to their seeming insignificance. However, the ability to identify these symptoms in their initial stages enables you to actively address them, preventing their escalation.

This aspect of the process emphasizes the need to cultivate a detailed self-awareness that allows you to perceive subtle variations in both your emotional and physical well-being. Being alert to these early signals gives you a privileged opportunity to implement preventive measures and manage them effectively before they evolve.

Building a personalized action plan, tailored to your circumstances, that incorporates various strategies–from relaxation techniques and mindfulness to regular physical activity and a balanced diet, complemented by psychological support when required–is essential to respond to these signs.

Proper detection of these signals and the execution of a personal action plan are indispensable steps towards effective management of your mental health. This preventive approach not only facilitates early symptom relief but also expands your capacity to handle future emotional challenges, thus laying a robust foundation for your lasting emotional stability.

Example:

Anticipation and recognition of warning signs are crucial to preventing the escalation of stress, anxiety, or depression. Suppose you have noticed subtle changes in your mood, such as increasing irritability or problems concentrating, negatively impacting both your interpersonal relationships and your job performance. Initially, you might minimize these symptoms, considering them merely the result of fatigue or transient stress. However, upon deeper self-assessment, you identify these indicators as early signs of anxiety.

Determined to proactively address these symptoms, you implement a series of strategies aimed at strengthening your mental and physical health. You introduce mindfulness practices into your daily routine, dedicating time each morning to meditation to promote serenity and concentration before facing the day. Aware of the positive impact of exercise on mental health, you enroll in swimming classes twice a week, seeking both physical activity and a moment to clear your mind.

Furthermore, aiming to improve your mood, you review and adjust your diet to include foods rich in omega-3 and antioxidants, recognized for their mental health benefits. You also establish a more rigorous sleep routine, ensuring you get the necessary rest for optimal recovery.

After several weeks, you notice significant improvements in your stress management and a decrease in irritability and concentration difficulties. These positive advances reinforce your dedication to self-care and motivate you to continue monitoring your emotional health, adjusting your action plan as necessary to face future challenges. This holistic approach not only improves your present well-being but also lays the groundwork for effective management of stressful situations in the future, strengthening your emotional and social resilience.

Step 3: Planning Coping Strategies

Developing and personalizing coping strategies constitute the third essential step in your process towards emotional recovery and strengthening. This step is crucial for effectively managing stress, anxiety, or depression, and vital for preventing future relapses. Setting up these strategies ranges from sleep regulation and diet to including activities that promote emotional and physical well-being, tailored to your needs and personal situation.

Personalizing your coping methods can greatly benefit from the guidance of a mental health professional. They can provide you with specific techniques from Rational Emotive Behavior Therapy and Cognitive Behavioral Therapy, focusing on cognitive restructuring, to challenge and modify irrational thoughts and beliefs that influence your emotional state.

Adapting your coping strategies not only addresses symptoms more effectively but also promotes lasting practices that improve your long-term well-being. The conscious and regular application of these techniques demonstrates a solid commitment to your mental and emotional health, equipping you with tools to face future challenges with greater resilience.

This step requires continuous reflection and the flexibility to adjust your strategies as necessary, underscoring the importance of this commitment to maintaining your emotional health and preventing relapses. By personalizing coping strategies to your specific needs, you empower yourself to effectively manage stress and emotional challenges, thus establishing a solid foundation for a healthier and more balanced future.

Example:

After recognizing worrying signs in your emotional and physical well-being, you decide to take specific measures to develop effective coping methods. Understanding the crucial role of rest, exercise, and a balanced diet in managing your emotional health, you formulate a meticulous plan to incorporate these practices into your daily routine.

Initially, you focus on overcoming sleep difficulties that have adversely affected your mood. You opt to establish a night-time routine conducive to rest, including disconnecting from electronic devices an hour before sleep and engaging in relaxing activities, such as meditation or reading. Likewise, you adjust the environment of your bedroom to optimize resting conditions, regulating aspects like lighting, sound, and temperature.

Simultaneously, you recognize the importance of regular exercise for your mental well-being and decide to include physical activities that you find enjoyable, such as walking outdoors or swimming, in your weekly schedule. This commitment not only favors your sleep but also elevates your overall sense of well-being and energy.

With the support of a nutritionist, you develop a dietary regimen focused on consuming foods that promote a good mood and optimal energy levels while limiting the intake of caffeine and sugars, especially in the afternoon. This comprehensive approach to your diet provides greater balance and reduces your vulnerability to emotional ups and downs.

The application of these coping strategies leads to palpable improvements in your quality of life. Headaches decrease, your energy and concentration levels increase, and you experience a notable uplift in your mood. This proactive and personalized approach to managing stress and anxiety not only equips you to handle daily vicissitudes with greater solvency but also establishes a solid foundation for maintaining your emotional well-being in the long term.

Step 4: Creating a Support Network

The fourth step of this program focuses on creating and strengthening a social support network, a fundamental pillar for mental and emotional health. This step emphasizes the importance of cultivating meaningful relationships with family, friends, and professionals who can provide you with support, understanding, and comfort during difficult times.

Building a support network is not just about being surrounded by people; it involves establishing deep connections with those who understand and respect your journey towards recovery, providing a safe environment where you can express your feelings and experiences without fear of judgment. These bonds, founded on trust and empathy, become an invaluable source of comfort and encouragement, enhancing your ability to overcome adversities with greater strength.

To construct an effective support network, your active participation in communities or groups with similar interests or circumstances is crucial. This integration allows you not only to receive support but also to offer it, generating a sense of purpose and belonging. Involvement in group therapies or support meetings facilitates access to additional resources and new perspectives on stress, anxiety, and depression management.

This step highlights the importance of maintaining an open and receptive attitude towards establishing new relationships and strengthening existing ones. By nurturing these connections, you create a robust and reliable emotional support network, crucial for your overall well-being and an essential tool in preventing relapses. Ultimately, these interactions not only contribute to your recovery process but also enrich your existence, providing a solid foundation of support and unconditional understanding.

Example:

After recognizing the fundamental value of having a solid support system, you take the initiative to consolidate your social support network, starting by evaluating the current relationships in your life. You identify those individuals who offer true understanding and emotional backing and decide to strengthen ties with them, communicating your commitment to improving your mental health and highlighting the importance of their support in this process.

To strengthen these bonds, you organize regular meetings, both virtual and in-person, creating spaces for exchange where experiences, feelings, and mutual support can be shared. These gatherings transform into safe havens, where you feel heard and valued, increasing trust in your emotional connections.

Additionally, you join a local support group, finding a forum where individuals with similar experiences exchange management tactics and mutual compassion. Participation in this collective brings new perspectives and facilitates establishing meaningful connections with people who understand your situation.

Simultaneously, you opt for the accompaniment of a therapist, who provides professional counseling and becomes an essential part of your support circle. This specialist assists you in developing tailor-made strategies for managing stress and anxiety and provides an additional space for support and understanding.

As you cultivate and expand your support network, you become aware that you are not alone in your battle. This sense of community and mutual support not only makes it easier to face daily challenges but also proves to be a key element in your long-term recovery. The support network stands as a bastion of strength and resilience, equipping you with the emotional resources required to overcome adversities and celebrate victories on your path to well-being.

Step 5: Reviewing Goals and Values

The periodic review of your goals and values is essential on your journey towards optimal emotional health. This fifth step encourages you to examine and reassess your personal goals and fundamental principles, ensuring that your actions and decisions are fully in harmony with your authentic aspirations and values. This congruence is crucial for your mental well-being, as it fosters an existence aligned with your true desires and ethical principles.

During this introspective and growth process, it's imperative that your goals and values not only encapsulate your dreams but also reflect a deep understanding and effective management of those elements in your life that affect your emotional state. This includes the handling of automatic thoughts and the reassessment of irrational beliefs. Adjusting your goals and values contributes to forging a more balanced and harmonious lifestyle, favoring a stronger emotional stability.

This step guides you to ensure that your decisions and actions resonate with your essential values, thus enhancing your mental health. Constant evaluation of your goals and values is indispensable for maintaining lasting emotional balance, giving you the flexibility to adapt your aspirations to your current emotional and psychological needs. By ensuring that your goals and values are aligned with your emotional well-being, you are headed towards more fulfilling personal development and realization.

Example:

On your journey towards personal development, after strengthening your support network and learning to effectively manage stress signals, you take a moment for deep reflection on your personal goals and values. This introspection leads you to realize that many of your previous goals were heavily focused on external achievements, which often increased your stress and anxiety due to the pressure you placed on yourself.

From this understanding, you decide to set new goals that balance professional success with your personal well-being. For example, instead of focusing solely on achieving a promotion, you establish objectives centered on improving your stress management skills at work and dedicating time to enjoy rewarding activities, such as your hobbies or meaningful moments with your loved ones.

Similarly, you reconsider your values, giving greater importance to mental health and self-acceptance. You understand that prioritizing your emotional well-being is essential, on the same level as achieving successes in other areas of your life. This shift in focus leads you towards more conscious and healthy decisions, resulting in a notable decrease in your stress and an increase in your life satisfaction and fulfillment. This process of reassessment not only reinforces your commitment to holistic personal growth but also establishes a solid foundation for making decisions aligned with comprehensive and lasting well-being.

Step 6: Preparing for Future Challenges

"Preparing for Future Challenges" represents the sixth crucial step on your personal growth journey. This phase focuses on consolidating and proactively applying the strategies and skills acquired in anticipation of potential challenging situations. Imagine these coping techniques as an emergency toolkit, designed to be effective, practical, and readily accessible when you need them most.

The goal of this stage is to identify in advance situations that could generate stress and design a specific action plan. This includes not only general strategies for stress management but also concrete responses for scenarios you consider potential anxiety triggers. The constant and mindful practice of these techniques ensures their efficiency in critical moments.

By anticipating future challenges, you arm yourself with a repertoire of effective responses to successfully overcome adversities. This prior preparation provides you with a sense of mastery and competence, allowing you to face any situation with greater confidence and calm. This step concludes your training process, equipping you with everything necessary to maintain your emotional balance and effectively confront the challenges that arise in your life, thus strengthening your resilience and adaptability to future vicissitudes.

Example:

After strengthening your support network and aligning your goals and values, you focus on the proactive anticipation of future challenges, an essential step towards your personal growth and emotional well-being. Reflecting on past experiences that have generated stress, you develop a detailed action plan for specific situations identified as potentially challenging. For instance, facing the anxiety provoked by work presentations, you decide to implement a strategy that includes advanced preparation, pre-event relaxation techniques, and positive visualization practices.

Additionally, you integrate mental simulation exercises, visualizing yourself successfully managing these situations through the effective use of acquired strategies. This approach not only prepares you to face these challenges with serenity but also strengthens your self-confidence and your perception of the ability to control stress effectively.

To complement, you adopt general stress management strategies, such as daily meditation and regular physical activity, which become pillars of your daily routine to strengthen your resilience. Furthermore, you establish periodic reviews with your therapist to assess the progress of your plan and adjust when necessary, ensuring optimal and continuous preparation for any future challenge. This commitment to preparation and adaptation reflects your dedication to maintaining and improving your mental health, ensuring you are equipped to navigate life with confidence and balance.

Step 7: Promoting Self-Efficacy

Strengthening self-efficacy, an essential component in your journey towards recovery and maintaining a healthy emotional state, becomes the focus of this crucial step. This process involves cultivating unwavering confidence in your abilities to face adversities and fulfill your aspirations, thus establishing a solid foundation for your mental health and future relapse prevention. Here, you'll dedicate yourself to developing a deep conviction in your personal capabilities, which is vital for overcoming complex challenges and achieving significant accomplishments.

Begin this journey by valuing your previous successes, regardless of their size. Spend time reflecting on the occasions when you've overcome obstacles or achieved goals that seemed unattainable. This exercise not only provides concrete evidence of your ability to navigate difficulties but also empowers you to tackle new challenges.

Setting small and realistic goals plays a crucial role, as experiencing frequent successes will strengthen your self-confidence and affirm your sense of self-efficacy. For example, if social anxiety is a barrier, initially propose engaging in brief conversations with people in your immediate environment, gradually increasing the complexity of these interactions.

Acquiring new skills or hobbies is another pillar in this process. Discovering and mastering new abilities is a source of empowerment that validates your capacity to learn and evolve.

It's equally important to celebrate each of your achievements, regardless of their scale. Acknowledging your successes fosters motivation and reinforces confidence in your ability to overcome future challenges.

Finally, seeking constructive feedback from your support circle enriches your perception of your strengths and fosters an expanded sense of self-efficacy.

By cultivating self-efficacy, you not only reinforce your emotional well-being in the short term but also lay the groundwork for enduring resilience. This focus on self-confidence, continuous learning, and social support equips you with the necessary tools to face upcoming challenges with determination, guiding you towards a future of personal fulfillment and emotional stability.

Example:

In this crucial phase of your development, after having solidified your support network and reevaluated your goals and values, you focus on the vital task of increasing your self-efficacy. You face the challenge of public speaking, a situation that previously exacerbated your anxiety, but now you see it as an opportunity to strengthen your confidence in your own abilities, adopting an active approach to improve both your performance and your management of anxiety in these contexts.

You determine a concrete and realistic goal: to enroll in a public speaking course, for example. This step aligns with your objective to refine your communicative skills and simultaneously foster your self-efficacy. Throughout the course, you set incremental goals, such as extending the duration of your interventions or applying new strategies to captivate and retain the interest of the audience.

Simultaneously, you keep a detailed record of your progress and reflections in a journal. This tracking not only evidences your evolution over time but also allows you to identify and celebrate each victory, regardless of its size. The positive feedback from instructors and peers becomes an invaluable resource for motivation and learning, strengthening your conviction in your ability to overcome obstacles.

You also incorporate visualization practices, in which you imagine facing and successfully overcoming public speaking-related challenges. This mental preparation equips you to handle anxiety more efficiently and strengthens your confidence in your abilities to manage these situations.

On the day of your presentation, you apply everything you've learned with determination: from preparation techniques to relaxation methods and positive visualization. The experience translates into a notable success; despite initial nervousness, you manage to conduct your presentation with remarkable fluency and confidence. This milestone becomes an essential reference in your process of strengthening self-efficacy, proving to yourself that you possess the capacity to face and conquer challenges previously considered unreachable.

This journey towards fostering self-efficacy, ranging from setting realistic goals to acknowledging and celebrating your successes, not only solidifies your confidence in your ability to overcome adversities but also optimally prepares you for future challenges, positively impacting your emotional well-being and significantly contributing to the prevention of relapses.

Step 8: Cultivating Resilience

Strengthening resilience is a crucial stage in your journey toward optimized emotional well-being and effective management of mood fluctuations. This process focuses on building an internal toughness that enables you to face and overcome challenges, extracting valuable lessons from each experience to forge a more resilient and versatile version of yourself.

Initially, it's imperative to understand that resilience does not translate to the absence of adversity or suffering but to the ability to navigate through these situations and emerge with a deeper understanding of oneself and renewed strength. Accepting complex emotions as integral elements of personal growth is fundamental, preventing these from dictating your capacity to progress.

The implementation of realistic and meaningful goals is a pillar for promoting resilience, providing you with motivation and a clear purpose. It is vital that these objectives are in harmony with your core values, ensuring that every step taken reflects your deepest priorities and convictions.

The support of a solid network of relationships is equally crucial. Establishing connections with individuals who offer understanding, empathy, and encouragement is fundamental for your ability to overcome obstacles. These connections bring you new perspectives, emotional support, and practical solutions to challenges.

Introspection and constant learning are also key elements in this process. After facing an obstacle, take a moment to reflect on the events, your reaction to them, and the lessons learned. This analysis allows you to recognize and adjust thought patterns and behaviors.

Incorporating daily self-care practices is another essential strategy for fostering resilience. Activities such as meditation, exercise, reflective writing, and engaging in enjoyable hobbies provide moments of relaxation and mental clarity, boosting your mood and energy to face challenges.

Lastly, adopting a growth mindset encourages you to view challenges as opportunities for evolution and learning, rather than as insurmountable barriers. This attitude motivates you to experiment, take conscious risks, and perceive failure as an inherent component of the evolutionary process.

The development of resilience is a perpetual commitment to your personal growth, providing you with the essential tools to handle life with greater security and positivity. By adopting these strategies, you prepare not only to overcome the challenges that arise but also to thrive despite them.

Example:

After strengthening your self-efficacy and successfully overcoming various emotional challenges, you face an unexpected and considerable challenge. This scenario tests your resilience, inviting you to employ all the skills and knowledge acquired so far.

Faced with this challenge, you decide to reflect on the coping strategies you have been cultivating. You remember the fundamental role that meditation and regular exercise previously played in preserving your balance and mental clarity. With this foundation, you reinstate a daily meditation practice and reactivate your exercise routine, not only as a method to address the immediate stress but also as a measure to reinforce your future resilience.

You seek the support of your support network, opening and asking for guidance. The empathy and understanding you receive reinforce your conviction that you are not alone in this challenge, providing you with renewed strength and the impetus to persevere, underscoring the value of meaningful connections in your recovery journey.

You reevaluate your goals and values, remembering that the essence of resilience lies in the ability to navigate through pain and difficulties, extracting learnings and growth from these experiences. This introspection leads you to formulate new objectives that reflect your personal evolution and your expanded capacity to manage stress and adversities.

Armed with these resources, you approach the current challenge from a renewed perspective. Instead of perceiving it as an insurmountable obstacle, you see it as an opportunity to demonstrate your resilience and gain valuable lessons. This process increases your confidence in your ability to face and overcome challenges, further strengthening your resilience and your commitment to caring for your emotional well-being.

This proactive approach to cultivating resilience not only enables you to overcome the immediate challenge but also optimally prepares you for future adversities. With each experience, your ability to recover from difficulties is fortified, enriching your sense of well-being and life fulfillment.

Step 9: Implementing Self-Care Habits

Strengthening resilience is a crucial stage in your journey toward optimized emotional well-being and effective management of mood fluctuations. This process focuses on building an internal toughness that enables you to face and overcome challenges, extracting valuable lessons from each experience to forge a more resilient and versatile version of yourself.

Initially, it's imperative to understand that resilience does not translate to the absence of adversity or suffering but to the ability to navigate through these situations and emerge with a deeper understanding of oneself and renewed strength. Accepting complex emotions as integral elements of personal growth is fundamental, preventing these from dictating your capacity to progress.

The implementation of realistic and meaningful goals is a pillar for promoting resilience, providing you with motivation and a clear purpose. It is vital that these objectives are in harmony with your core values, ensuring that every step taken reflects your deepest priorities and convictions.

The support of a solid network of relationships is equally crucial. Establishing connections with individuals who offer understanding, empathy, and encouragement is fundamental for your ability to overcome obstacles. These connections bring you new perspectives, emotional support, and practical solutions to challenges.

Introspection and constant learning are also key elements in this process. After facing an obstacle, take a moment to reflect on the events, your reaction to them, and the lessons learned. This analysis allows you to recognize and adjust thought patterns and behaviors.

Incorporating daily self-care practices is another essential strategy for fostering resilience. Activities such as meditation, exercise, reflective writing, and engaging in enjoyable hobbies provide moments of relaxation and mental clarity, boosting your mood and energy to face challenges.

Lastly, adopting a growth mindset encourages you to view challenges as opportunities for evolution and learning, rather than as insurmountable barriers. This attitude motivates you to experiment, take conscious risks, and perceive failure as an inherent component of the evolutionary process.

The development of resilience is a perpetual commitment to your personal growth, providing you with the essential tools to handle life with greater security and positivity. By adopting these strategies, you prepare not only to overcome the challenges that arise but also to thrive despite them.

Example:

After strengthening your self-efficacy and successfully overcoming various emotional challenges, you face an unexpected and considerable challenge. This scenario tests your resilience, inviting you to employ all the skills and knowledge acquired so far.

Faced with this challenge, you decide to reflect on the coping strategies you have been cultivating. You remember the fundamental role that meditation and regular exercise previously played in preserving your balance and mental clarity. With this foundation, you reinstate a daily meditation practice and reactivate your exercise routine, not only as a method to address the immediate stress but also as a measure to reinforce your future resilience.

You seek the support of your support network, opening and asking for guidance. The empathy and understanding you receive reinforce your conviction that you are not alone in this challenge, providing you with renewed strength and the impetus to persevere, underscoring the value of meaningful connections in your recovery journey.

You reevaluate your goals and values, remembering that the essence of resilience lies in the ability to navigate through pain and difficulties, extracting learnings and growth from these experiences.

This introspection leads you to formulate new objectives that reflect your personal evolution and your expanded capacity to manage stress and adversities.

Armed with these resources, you approach the current challenge from a renewed perspective. Instead of perceiving it as an insurmountable obstacle, you see it as an opportunity to demonstrate your resilience and gain valuable lessons. This process increases your confidence in your ability to face and overcome challenges, further strengthening your resilience and your commitment to caring for your emotional well-being.

This proactive approach to cultivating resilience not only enables you to overcome the immediate challenge but also optimally prepares you for future adversities. With each experience, your ability to recover from difficulties is fortified, enriching your sense of well-being and life fulfillment.

Step 10: Strategy Evaluation and Adjustment

In this pivotal step toward your emotional well-being, you dedicate time to reviewing and refining your coping strategies. You are aware that the path to recovery and personal growth is dynamic, and changes in your life may require adaptations in how you handle stress and emotional challenges. Therefore, this moment is key to ensuring that your tactics continue to be relevant and effective for your current and future circumstances.

You begin by scheduling regular evaluations of your coping methods, marking dates on your calendar for reflection on their impact. You pose essential questions: "Do these strategies still align with your goals and values?", "Have they facilitated tangible improvements in your emotional and mental state?", "Is it necessary to modify or replace any of them to address new challenges or changes in your environment?".

During this introspection, you value the feedback from your support circle and, when feasible, from mental health specialists. Their external perspectives can enlighten you on aspects to improve or variations in your emotional needs that you may have overlooked.

Based on this reflection, you adjust your coping methods as you deem appropriate. These adjustments can range from increasing the frequency of your relaxation exercises to seeking new therapy modalities or support for more intricate challenges.

This process highlights the need for flexibility and willingness to adapt. The constant evolution of life demands that what was once effective may need to be reviewed. By committing to continuous evaluation and adjustment of your strategies, you ensure you are following the best path toward resilience and lasting well-being. This proactive approach not only empowers you to face life's vicissitudes more skillfully but also reinforces your confidence in your ability to overcome future emotional and psychological challenges, reaffirming your commitment to sustained and conscious personal development.

Example:

After integrating new self-care practices and strengthening your support circle, you face a period of significant change, whether professional or personal. This scenario marks the ideal time to apply "Strategy Evaluation and Adjustment" to ensure the effectiveness of your coping methods against these emerging challenges.

You initiate this process by analyzing the coping strategies you have used so far, reflecting on their impact considering recent changes in your life. You question the adequacy of these tactics against the new stress levels and recognize the need for adjustments to align them with your current situation.

In response, you decide to increase therapy sessions, seeking more intensive professional support during this adjustment period. You modify your exercise routine, incorporating practices like yoga or meditation that better fit your updated schedule and contribute to stress reduction. Additionally, conscious of the invaluable worth of your support network, you schedule regular meetings with friends and family to preserve and strengthen those essential social bonds for your emotional balance during times of change.

This process of review and adaptation reflects your dedication to preserving your mental health. Remaining vigilant to the effects of life changes on your emotional well-being and being willing to modify your coping strategies underscores your resilience against challenges. This adaptable approach enables you to effectively manage stress and adversities, ensuring your progress toward sustainable emotional well-being and solid recovery.

Conclusion

Summary y Reflection

At the conclusion of this program for maintaining positive changes and preventing relapse, it's time to reflect on the journey we've undertaken. We've embarked on a path of self-discovery and mental strengthening, tackling key stages for our emotional well-being.

We began by assessing our emotional state, which allowed us to understand our reactions and prepare ourselves to recognize early warning signs of stress or depression. This identification enabled us to develop effective action plans, reinforcing our coping strategies.

Building a support network highlighted the importance of having meaningful relationships and support. Reviewing our goals and values motivated us to live in a way that's coherent with our ideals. Additionally, we prepared for future challenges, gaining confidence in our emotional management skills.

Reflecting, each phase has been fundamental in establishing a strong foundation for our mental health, teaching us to effectively manage stress and face the future with optimism.

This process concludes with a renewed sense of pride and hope. Each step has reinforced our commitment to well-being and demonstrated our capacity for resilience. It encourages us to continue applying what we've learned, remembering that we are in a constant state of growth and learning.

Appendix 2: H-BCDS
Hernandez-Barrera
Cognitive Distortions Scale

Cognitive distortions are biased ways of thinking that often manifest in patterns of misinterpreting reality. They are central elements in many psychological and emotional disorders, and their identification and management are key in the process of Cognitive Behavioral Therapy and everyday life.

These cognitive biases can affect a person in various ways, including how they perceive themselves, how they interpret interactions with others, and how they anticipate future events. These thinking patterns can fuel negative emotions, such as anxiety and depression, and can lead to self-destructive behaviors.

The Hernandez-Barrera Cognitive Distortions Scale (H-BCDS) is an experimental tool that allows for the identification and measurement of these cognitive distortions. This inventory consists of 60 items that address 15 of the most common and harmful cognitive distortions, such as "mental filtering", "mind reading", and "control fallacy", among others.

By responding to this inventory, you will provide valuable information about your own thought patterns. This self-recognition is a crucial first step in the process of modifying these distortions, thus allowing for significant improvement in your mental health.

It is important to note that the H-BCDS is a self-report tool. This means that the results are based on your personal perception and self-assessment of your thinking. While this tool provides an initial valuable insight, it is recommended to use it in conjunction with professional counseling for a more comprehensive interpretation and appropriate treatment. The H-BCDS is completely experimental and only serves as an annex to this book. Its effectiveness has not been proven, so readers are advised to take the results with great discretion.

Lastly, remember that the purpose of this inventory is not to diagnose any mental illness but to provide insight into thought patterns that may be affecting your emotional well-being. Be sure to seek the help of a mental health professional if you are experiencing psychological difficulties.

Instructions

Proceed to carefully examine each statement present in this inventory. Your task will be to evaluate the frequency with which you find yourself experiencing each of these behaviors in your everyday life. Rate each item on a scale from 0 to 5. The number "0" represents a frequency of "never", and the number "5" indicates a frequency of "always". 1 point indicates that the behavior occurs "almost never", 2 points suggest that the behavior "sometimes" manifests, 3 points denote that it is "habitual", 4 points imply that the behavior occurs "almost always".

It is important to highlight that for the items marked with an asterisk (*), the scoring system is reversed. In these cases, a rating of "0" is transformed into "5", a rating of "1" turns into "4", and so on. It is also essential to understand that in this process, there are no right or wrong answers, and complete honesty in your evaluation is required. The scale is found on the following pages.

Behaviors	0	1	2	3	4	5
Despite frequently receiving positive feedback at work, you find yourself dwelling on the one criticism you received.						
You had a poor performance in an interview and assume you will do just as poorly in the next one.						
A coworker does not greet you, and you assume they are angry with you.						
When your friends are in a bad mood, you tend to think you did something wrong.						
Despite the job interview not going perfectly, you believe you can still land the job.						
When you feel anxious, you assume something bad will happen.						
Despite things going wrong, you know you can learn and improve.						
You feel guilty when things don't go as expected, even when it's out of your control.						
You get angry when you believe you have not been rewarded adequately for your work.						
You feel frustrated because your partner does not change their behavior, despite your repeated mentions.						
You focus primarily on your mistakes and not your achievements.						
You give your minor errors their proper importance as learning opportunities and highly value your achievements.						
You think that if you are not perfect, then you are a failure.						
You feel guilty for not meeting the goals you set for yourself.						
You assume your friends think you are boring because they did not laugh at your joke.						
You make a mistake on a task and consider it a total failure, ignoring the good parts.						
A friend cancels plans with you, and you conclude they will always cancel.						
You see two friends whispering and assume they are talking badly about you.						

Statement						
You think your partner is angry with you when they are distracted or tired.						
You worry that a small mistake could ruin your entire career.						
You feel incompetent, so you assume you are bad at your job, despite positive performance evaluations.						
You consider yourself "stupid" for making a mistake at work.						
You recognize that each person is responsible for their own emotional well-being.						
You feel bitter because things do not go as you believe they should.						
You feel resentful because your friends do not change their plans to accommodate your preferences.						
You prioritize the positive parts of your day and manage problems without letting them overshadow your moments of joy.						
You amplify others' achievements but minimize your own.						
You understand that making mistakes does not make us bad people.						
You criticize others for not following the rules you consider important.						
You think your boss is dissatisfied with your work because they did not praise you.						
You mainly focus on your mistakes, ignoring the positive aspects.						
You say something inappropriate in a meeting and believe you are always an idiot.						
You do not receive an immediate response to a text message and conclude the other person is ignoring you.						
You often feel you are the cause of family problems.						
You believe a small disagreement can end a long-term relationship.						
You feel your friends do not love you, so you believe it is true, even though they act in a friendly and loving manner.						
If a friend is late to a meeting with you, you think they are "irresponsible."						

You feel stressed trying to have complete control over all situations and not achieving it.						
You feel frustrated because people do not follow the same rules or standards as you.						
You feel irritated because your coworkers do not follow your methods.						
You value and focus on positive feedback while taking the negative as opportunities to improve.						
You exaggerate a problem and minimize the impact of solutions.						
If you do not win consistently, you consider yourself a loser.						
You feel frustrated because things are not as they "should" be.						
You believe your partner is upset with you because they did not respond immediately.						
You usually only remember the times your partner forgot to do something instead of the times they did.						
The person you like rejects you, and you think you will never be successful in love.						
Your boss does not comment on your report, and you assume they did not like it.						
You understand that the outcome of a team project depends on collective effort and not just on your individual performance.						
You suppose that feeling sick for a few days is a sign of a serious illness.						
Your partner shows you love every day, but you still think they do not really love you.						
You label yourself as "useless" for not meeting a goal.						
You blame yourself for things that happen in your environment, even when they are not your fault.						
You feel life is unfair when you experience many challenges or difficulties.						
You feel dissatisfied because your family does not change their habits to accommodate you.						

You focus on a negative aspect of your appearance and forget the positives.						
You often minimize your abilities and talents and magnify your weaknesses.						
You feel lost when you are not entirely sure about something.						
You feel dissatisfied because you are not doing what you feel you "should" be doing.						
You assume your coworkers think you are incompetent because you made a mistake.						

Interpretation of Results

For each cognitive distortion, the scores assigned to each corresponding item must be summed. Before adding, it is crucial to reverse the scores of items indicated with an asterisk (*). Subsequently, this total sum should be converted into a percentage relative to the maximum possible score, which is 20 points. This percentage will represent the degree of prevalence of the cognitive distortion, where 0% would indicate a complete absence of the distortion and 100% a significantly high presence, though not absolute. 60% would correspond to the threshold of the degree of prevalence.

For example, assume that the total sum of your scores for the "Mental Filtering" cognitive distortion is 12 points. To obtain the corresponding percentage, you must divide 12 by 20 and then multiply the result by 100. In this case, your percentage would be 60%.

It is important to remember that the scoring scale has values assigned as follows: 0 points mean that the described behavior is "never" carried out, 1 point indicates that it is done "almost never", 2 points suggest that the behavior occurs "sometimes", 3 points denote that it is "usual", 4 points imply that the behavior is presented "almost always", and 5 points indicate that it is "always" executed. The scoring system is on the following page.

Cognitive Distortions	Behaviors				Scores					Results
1. Mental Filtering.	1	16	31	46						
2. Overgeneralization.	2	17	32	47						
3. Arbitrary Inference.	3	18	33	48						
4. Personalization.	4	19	34	49						
5. Catastrophic Thinking.	5	20	35	50						
6. Emotional Reasoning.	6	21	36	51						
7. Labeling.	7	22	37	52						
8. Control Fallacy.	8	23	38	53						
9. Fallacy of Fairness.	9	24	39	54						
10. Change Fallacy.	10	25	40	55						
11. Selective Abstraction.	11	26	41	56						
12. Maximization and Minimization.	12	27	42	57						
13. Polarized Thinking.	13	28	43	58						
14. "Should" Statements.	14	29	44	59						
15. Mind Reading.	15	30	45	60						

Cognitive Distortions Present in the H-BCDS

- *Mental Filtering:* This refers to paying exclusive attention to the negative aspects of a situation, ignoring any positive aspects. This can lead to a biased and negative view of the world and limit the ability to see solutions or alternatives.

- *Overgeneralization:* This refers to the habit of making broad, general rules from a single incident or piece of data. This can lead to negative and sweeping conclusions about future situations based on a single past event.

- *Arbitrary Inference:* This involves coming to conclusions without sufficient evidence or even in contradiction to the evidence. It can lead to misunderstandings and unnecessary conflicts.

- *Personalization:* This is the tendency to assume that one is the cause of external events without evidence to support that belief. This can lead to feelings of guilt, shame, and low self-esteem.

- *Catastrophic Thinking:* This pattern involves always thinking of the worst-case scenario, often magnifying the importance of negative events. This can lead to significant anxiety and avoidance of situations due to fear of a possible negative outcome.

- *Emotional Reasoning:* This refers to allowing emotions to dictate how reality is interpreted. If you feel bad, you assume the situation is bad, even if the objective reality is different.

- *Labeling:* This involves applying simplistic and generally negative labels to oneself or others. These labels can limit the perception of one's own and others' complexity and humanity.

- *Control Fallacy:* This is the belief that you have total and undeniable control over every aspect of your life, which can lead to self-inflicted guilt for events outside your control. This can generate unnecessary stress and anxiety.

- *Fallacy of Fairness:* This refers to the feeling that the world should be fair and the disturbance or upset when things do not seem fair.

This can lead to constant frustrations and difficulty in accepting reality as it is.

- *Change Fallacy:* This distortion involves the expectation that other people will change so that you can feel better or achieve what you want. This can lead to tense relationships and the inability to accept others as they are.

- *Selective Abstraction:* This is focusing on a single aspect of a situation, ignoring the broader context. This can lead to a biased and limited view of situations.

- *Maximization and Minimization:* This distortion involves exaggerating mistakes and minimizing accomplishments. This can lead to low self-esteem and a distorted perception of your abilities and achievements.

- *Polarized Thinking or Black-and-White Thinking:* This involves seeing things in absolute terms, with no gray areas. This can lead to unrealistic expectations and the inability to see the subtleties and complexities of life.

- *"Should" Statements:* This distortion refers to using a series of inflexible and unrealistic rules dictated by words such as "should," "must," or "need." This can lead to guilt, frustration, and dissatisfaction.

- *Mind Reading:* This distortion involves assuming that you know what others are thinking without having solid evidence to support these assumptions. This can lead to misunderstandings, conflicts, and unnecessary stress.

Appendix 3: List of Emotions

Basic Emotions

The identification and understanding of basic emotions are fundamental in the process of developing Emotional Intelligence and in the application of CBT and REBT. Below is a list of primary emotions, with a description of their adaptive functions and suggestions on how they can be used to address mood disorders such as stress, anxiety, and depression.

1. **Joy**

   - *Adaptive Function:* Joy arises in response to achievements, success, or any favorable event. It functions as a positive reinforcement, motivating us to repeat actions that produce satisfaction or happiness. Joy strengthens social relationships by sharing and celebrating with others.
   - *Therapeutic Application:* Encouraging the pursuit of pleasurable or rewarding activities can help mitigate the symptoms of depression and increase levels of satisfaction and well-being. Joy can be a valuable resource to reinforce self-esteem and promote a positive outlook on life.
   - *Physiological Reactions:* Increase in the release of dopamine and serotonin, decrease in heart rate, muscle relaxation, and often increased physical energy.

2. **Sadness**

   - *Adaptive Function:* Sadness appears in response to losses, failures, or disappointments, fostering a process of reflection and revaluation of our experiences and goals. This emotion can promote empathy and mutual support by sharing feelings and vulnerabilities.
   - *Therapeutic Application:* Recognizing and accepting sadness without judgment allows for the proper processing of losses and adapting to new realities. In the therapeutic context, the expression

of sadness is essential for grief and emotional recovery, facilitating the resolution of internal conflicts and the reconstruction of personal meanings.

- *Physiological Reactions:* Decrease in neurotransmitter levels such as serotonin and dopamine, reduction of physical energy, feeling of heaviness, and sometimes, a decrease in heart rate.

3. Fear

- *Adaptive Function:* Fear is activated in the perception of threats or danger, preparing the body for flight or fight. This emotion is essential for survival, as it alerts us to potential risks and motivates us to avoid dangerous situations.
- *Therapeutic Application:* In therapy, recognition and management of fear are crucial for overcoming anxiety and stress. Working on irrational perceptions and negative expectations helps reduce the fear response and develop more effective coping strategies.
- *Physiological Reactions:* Increase in heart rate, elevation of blood pressure, dilation of pupils, sweating, and activation of the sympathetic nervous system preparing the body for the fight or flight response.

4. Surprise

- *Adaptive Function:* Surprise allows us to quickly adjust our attention to unexpected events, facilitating adaptation to new situations. This emotion can be positive or negative, depending on the context and interpretation of the stimulus.
- *Therapeutic Application:* Leveraging surprise in therapy can be useful for breaking rigid thought patterns, promoting cognitive flexibility, and openness to new experiences. Surprise can also be a catalyst for motivation and change.

- *Physiological Reactions:* Rapid dilation of pupils, temporary elevation of heart rate, and in some cases, a startle that may include a quick inhalation.

5. **Asco**

- *Adaptive Function:* Disgust arises as a response of rejection to stimuli perceived as harmful or contaminating. This emotion plays a crucial role in protecting against diseases by avoiding substances or situations that are potentially dangerous.
- *Therapeutic Application:* In the therapeutic context, understanding disgust can be relevant for treating specific phobias or eating disorders. Recognizing and revaluating disgust reactions can facilitate gradual exposure and desensitization to feared stimuli.
- *Physiological Reactions:* Contraction of facial muscles, especially around the nose; decreased appetite; and in extreme cases, nausea or vomiting.

6. **Ira**

- *Adaptive Function:* Anger manifests in situations of injustice, frustration, or threats to our well-being or that of our loved ones. This emotion can mobilize resources for defense and the vindication of rights or needs.
- *Therapeutic Application:* Proper management of anger is essential to prevent aggressiveness and promote healthy interpersonal relationships. Therapy can help identify the underlying causes of anger and develop skills for assertive communication and conflict resolution.
- *Physiological Reactions:* Increase in heart rate, elevation of blood pressure, release of adrenaline, increase in body temperature, and muscle tension.

Complex Emotions

Complex, or secondary, emotions are formed from the interaction of basic emotions and are influenced by our experiences, beliefs, and personal values. These emotions reflect a deeper understanding of our reactions to the world around us and play important roles in our psychological and social adaptation. Below are some significant complex emotions, their adaptive functions, and how they can be leveraged in coping with mood disorders.

1. **Envy:** Envy originates from social comparison, a cognitive process in which individuals evaluate their own lives in relation to others. This comparison can awaken a sense of lack or desire for what others possess, whether material goods, relationships, achievements, or personal qualities. Envy can arise from the interaction between the basic emotion of desire and the personal assessment of insufficiency or injustice, shaped by beliefs and values related to success, competition, and fairness. Personal experiences of deprivation or insufficient recognition can also intensify the feeling of envy.

    - *Adaptive Function:* Although often viewed negatively, envy points out areas of our life where we feel something is missing or where we aspire to improve. It can motivate us to achieve personal or professional goals and foster the development of skills or talents.
    - *Therapeutic Application:* Recognizing and exploring feelings of envy can help identify unsatisfied personal goals and increase self-awareness. In therapy, working based on these emotions can foster personal growth and motivation for change, transforming envy into inspiration and action.
    - *Physiological Reactions:* There may be an increase in muscular tension, especially in the jaw and fists, and an increase in heart rate due to emotional agitation.

2. **Pride:** Pride results from a positive self-evaluation of oneself or one's actions, specially concerning personal achievements or meeting personal or social standards and values. This emotion arises from the interaction of basic emotions like joy and satisfaction, influenced by personal beliefs about success, self-efficacy, and social recognition. Personal Experiences of success or external validation strengthen the tendency to experience pride, promoting a positive self-image and reinforcing motivation toward personal fulfillment.

- *Adaptive Function:* Pride arises from personal achievements or the acknowledgment of our capabilities. It reinforces self-esteem and a positive self-concept, motivating us to maintain or exceed our achievements.

- *Therapeutic Application:* Cultivating a healthy sense of pride in one's abilities and achievements can counteract the effects of depression and low self-esteem. In the therapeutic context, encouraging the recognition of one's own achievements and capabilities can be an effective strategy to improve emotional well-being.

- *Physiological Reactions:* Physical expansion or upright posture, an increase in dopamine release, and in some cases, an increase in heart rate associated with positive excitement.

3. **Gratitude:** Gratitude emerges from recognizing and appreciating the benefits or kindnesses received, whether from people, circumstances, or the environment. This emotion is nourished by the capacity for attention and appreciation of the positive aspects of life, integrating basic emotions such as pleasure and relief. Beliefs and values that emphasize interconnection, generosity, and the acknowledgment of others' kindness foster the experience of gratitude. Personal experiences of receiving support or kindness, especially in times of need, can deepen the capacity to feel gratitude.

- *Adaptive Function:* Gratitude allows us to recognize and appreciate what we have, strengthening our relationships and increasing our well-being. It promotes a positive life perspective and improves emotional resilience.
- *Therapeutic Application:* Practicing gratitude can be a powerful intervention in treating anxiety and depression, helping to focus attention on positive aspects of life and decrease negative thoughts. Gratitude fosters a sense of connection and well-being, contributing to more robust mental health.
- *Physiological Reactions:* A feeling of warmth, decrease in heart rate, and in many cases, a sense of relaxation or well-being in the body.

4. **Guilt:** Guilt arises when a person recognizes or perceives that they have made a mistake or acted harmfully towards others, contravening their ethical or moral values. This emotion originates from the interaction between sadness and remorse, deeply influenced by beliefs and values about personal responsibility, morality, and justice. Personal experiences of confronting the negative consequences of one's actions on others can intensify the feeling of guilt, motivating the desire for reparation and behavioral change.

- *Adaptive Function:* Guilt plays a crucial role in the development and maintenance of our social relationships, signaling when we have acted against our ethical or moral values. It motivates us to make amends and improve our behavior towards others.
- *Therapeutic Application:* Addressing guilt constructively in therapy can lead to the recognition of mistakes, the repair of relationships, and personal development. Working on guilt can help resolve internal conflicts and promote greater personal integrity and empathy.

- *Physiological Reactions:* May include a feeling of heaviness, a decrease in physical energy, and in some people, specific muscle tensions associated with restlessness.

5. **Shame:** Shame originates from the perception of being exposed to others as inferior, inadequate, or morally questionable, negatively affecting self-image. This emotion combines aspects of fear, sadness, and disgust, and is shaped by beliefs and values related to self-esteem, social respect, and norms of behavior.

- *Adaptive Function:* Shame can serve as a social regulator, indicating when we might have damaged our public image or not met social expectations. It drives us to improve and adapt our behavior to be accepted.

- *Therapeutic Application:* Exploring shame in therapy can reveal underlying perceptions about the self and social expectations, offering opportunities for personal growth and self-esteem improvement. Recognizing and addressing shame can facilitate the development of a more compassionate and accepting relationship with oneself.

- *Physiological Reactions:* Blushing of the skin (especially on the face), avoidance of eye contact, and in some cases, a decrease in posture (slouching) indicating a desire to "hide".

Appendix 4: Emotional Literacy

Application of Emotional Literacy

"Emotional literacy" is a process involving several interconnected steps, designed to enhance the awareness and management of our emotions. This process not only improves Emotional Intelligence but also provides a solid foundation for the development of emotional coping strategies and emotional regulation. Continuous practice in identifying and labeling emotions facilitates a better understanding of our own emotional reactions and improves our ability to face emotional challenges healthily. Below is a detailed guide to delve deeper into each step of the process:

1. Reflection and Recognition

- *Allocate Time and Space:* Choose a quiet moment and a place without distractions to reflect on your emotions. Tranquility helps to focus and be more receptive to memories and sensations.
- *Detailed Recall:* Recall a recent experience that elicited negative emotions. Try to relive that situation in your mind as vividly as possible, paying attention to the details of the environment, the people involved, and especially, how you felt at that moment.
- *Emotional Recognition:* Ask yourself which emotions were present. Was it anger, sadness, frustration, fear, shame, guilt, or a combination of these? Try to name the specific emotions without judging them.

2. Identification of Signals

- *Physical Observation:* Note the physical reactions that accompanied the emotions. Did you feel tension in any part of your body, an increase in heart rate, sweating, or any other physical sensation? These signals are important clues to identify the emotion.
- *Associated Behavior:* Reflect on how these emotions influenced your behavior. Did you respond aggressively, withdraw from the situation, or freeze? Behavior can be an external manifestation of the internal emotion.

3. Recording

- *Emotional Journal:* Write down the identified emotions, the associated physical sensations, and the observed behaviors in a journal. Writing helps to clarify and organize thoughts and emotions.
- *Detailed Description:* Include details about the context in which these emotions arose. What triggered the reaction? Was there any external factor or specific thought that intensified the emotion?

4. Analysis

- *Impact on Decisions:* Reflect on how these emotions affected your decisions and actions. Did you make impulsive decisions, avoid necessary confrontations, or react in a way you later regretted?
- *Identification of Triggers:* Recognize the specific triggers of these emotions. This can reveal important patterns and help you to better anticipate and manage similar situations in the future.
- *Management Strategies:* Based on this analysis, consider what strategies you could develop to manage these emotions more effectively. This could include relaxation techniques, cognitive restructuring, or simply allowing yourself to feel the emotion without acting impulsively.

5. Practical Implementation

- *Conscious Practice:* Try to be more aware of your emotions and physical reactions in real-time. Awareness in the moment can help you apply the management strategies you have considered.
- *Support and Feedback:* Share your observations and strategies with a trusted friend, mentor, or therapist. Feedback can provide new perspectives and support in your process of emotional literacy.
- *Review and Adjustment:* Emotional literacy is an ongoing process. Regularly review and adjust your emotional management strategies based on new experiences and learnings.

Appendix 5:
Negative Emotions
(Appropriate and Inappropriate)

Functionality of "Negative" Emotions

Lazarus's theory on the functionality of emotions emphasizes the adaptive importance of emotional responses, even those traditionally considered negative. Understanding these emotions from the perspective of their adaptive functionality provides a valuable framework for managing emotional responses. This understanding allows us to address negative emotions constructively, recognizing their essential role in our adaptation and personal growth. Below is a review of these, adapting the descriptions to align with Lazarus's perspective of functionality:

1. Anxiety

Adaptive Function: Anxiety serves as an anticipatory signal that alerts us to potential future threats, allowing for proactive preparation and planning. This emotion is essential for survival, as it facilitates risk assessment and the implementation of appropriate coping strategies before encountering potentially dangerous situations.

2. Fear

Adaptive Function: Fear activates the fight-or-flight response to immediate dangers, preparing the body for quick and effective action. This emotional response is crucial for protecting us from physical and psychological threats, ensuring our safety and well-being.

3. Sadness

Adaptive Function: Sadness allows us to process and reflect on experiences of loss or failure, facilitating introspection and personal growth. It promotes the seeking of support and social connection, reinforcing community ties and fostering empathy among individuals.

4. Anger

Adaptive Function: Anger motivates us to confront and resolve conflicts or injustices, serving as a catalyst for change and personal affirmation. This emotion can be a powerful driver for action, promoting the defense of our rights and values.

5. Shame

Adaptive Function: Shame acts as a social regulator, encouraging behaviors and actions that align with social norms and expectations. It fosters self-assessment and the modification of behaviors, contributing to the development of personal morals and ethics.

6. Guilt

Adaptive Function: Guilt promotes the repair and maintenance of healthy interpersonal relationships, motivating corrective actions when our behaviors have harmed others. This emotion underscores the importance of responsibility and empathy in our social interactions.

7. Disillusionment

Adaptive Function: Disillusionment helps us adjust our expectations and goals to reality, facilitating adaptation to new contexts or situations. This emotion can be a starting point for reevaluating goals and seeking new paths towards success and personal satisfaction.

8. Envy

Adaptive Function: Although uncomfortable, envy can be a stimulus for self-improvement and motivation to achieve personal goals. It alerts us to unsatisfied desires or aspirations, prompting reflection and action towards the achievement of comparable objectives.

9. Desperation

Adaptive Function: Desperation can force a fundamental reconsideration of our strategies and approaches, leading us to explore creative alternatives and innovative solutions to complex problems.

10. Resentment

Adaptive Function: Resentment underscores the importance of addressing and resolving interpersonal conflicts, acting as a reminder of our needs for respect and justice. This emotion can serve as a defense mechanism that protects us from future disappointments or harm, by reminding us to be cautious in our relationships and to establish healthy boundaries.

Appropriate and Inappropriate Emotions

Determining the "appropriateness" of an emotion is a complex concept that can depend on multiple factors, such as social context, cultural norms, and individual circumstances. However, there are some guidelines supported by research in psychology and Cognitive Behavioral Therapy that can be useful for assessing or better understanding the "appropriateness" of an emotion (Gross, 2015; Greenberg, 2015):

- **Contextual Relevance:** An emotion is generally considered appropriate if it aligns with the current context, like feeling fear when facing an imminent danger rather than a routine situation.
- **Example:** Suppose an individual is in a work meeting where upcoming project goals are being discussed. Here, a certain degree of enthusiasm or interest would be considered emotionally appropriate, as this is a situation with significant implications for the person's future. In contrast, if that same individual felt overwhelming fear in this environment, it could

be considered that the emotion does not match the context, as there is nothing that poses a real danger to the individual.

- **Intensity:** The intensity of the emotion should also be proportional to the situation. Feeling an overwhelming amount of fear over a minor risk would not be considered appropriate.
- **Example:** Imagine someone feeling ecstatic about finding a parking spot closer to the entrance of a store. Since the event is relatively minor in the grand scheme of life, the intensity of the emotion seems disproportionate.

- **Duration:** Emotions that persist for a period disproportionate to the triggering event might be considered inappropriate.
- **Example:** Consider an individual who feels deeply embarrassed for tripping in public. It's fine to feel embarrassment in awkward moments, but if this sense of embarrassment persists for weeks and affects their overall well-being, the duration of the emotion would be inappropriate relative to the original event.

- **Utility:** If an emotion facilitates or interferes with a person's ability to respond effectively to a situation, this can also be an indicator of its appropriateness.
- **Example:** Think of someone considering a career change. If this person feels fear to the point of paralysis and, as a result, takes no action to explore new opportunities, the utility of this emotion is questionable since it hinders potentially beneficial behavior.

- **Internal Congruence:** Emotions should also be consistent with one's beliefs and values to be considered appropriate. Feeling guilt for carrying out an action that is in line with one's values might be considered an inappropriate emotional response.

- **Example:** Imagine an individual who values independence and self-sufficiency but feels immense guilt for taking time for themselves away from their family. Given that this personal time is aligned with their core values and is potentially beneficial to the subject, the emotion of guilt would be incongruent and inappropriate in this context.

- **Behavioral Outcomes:** If an emotion leads to behaviors that are harmful to oneself or others, it might be considered inappropriate.
- **Example:** Visualize someone who feels intense anger during a couple's argument and decides impulsively to end the relationship. Later, this person realizes that the action was extreme and has regrets. Here, the emotion led to a quite harmful behavioral outcome and, therefore, could be considered inappropriate.

Appendix 6: Mindfulness

Conscious Breathing Exercise

- *Find a Quiet Place:* Select a space where you can be undisturbed and quiet for a few minutes. It could be a corner of your room, a comfortable chair, or even an outdoor spot you find relaxing.

- *Adopt a Comfortable Posture:* Sit with a straight but relaxed back. You can sit on a chair with your feet on the ground or in a meditative position on the floor. Ensure your posture is comfortable yet alert.

- *Center Your Attention on Breathing:* Gently close your eyes and direct your attention to your breath. Notice how the air enters and exits your body. Feel the movement of your abdomen and chest as you breathe.

- *Observe Without Judging:* As you practice, thoughts and emotions are likely to arise. Instead of reacting to them or judging them, simply acknowledge them as a neutral observer. Label them if it helps, such as "anxious thought" or "feeling of calm". If you find your mind has wandered, which is completely normal, gently redirect your attention back to the original focus, whether it be the breath, body sensations, or sounds. Then repeat the process.

- *Duration:* Continue with this exercise for 5-10 minutes. With practice, you can gradually increase the time dedicated to conscious breathing.

Body Scan Exercise

- *Begin in a Comfortable Posture:* You can perform the body scan lying down or sitting. Make sure you are in a place where you can completely relax without falling asleep.

- *Breathe Deeply:* Start with a few deep breaths to center your attention and begin to relax.

- *Conscious Attention to the Body:* Start by focusing your attention on your feet. Note any sensations you are experiencing, such as warmth, coolness, tension, or relaxation. Do not try to change these sensations, just observe them.

- *Shift Your Attention:* Gradually move your attention up through your body: to your ankles, knees, thighs, hips, abdomen, chest, hands, arms, shoulders, neck, and finally, your head. Spend time observing sensations in each part of your body.

- *Observe Without Judging:* If you discover areas of tension or discomfort, acknowledge them without trying to change them. The key is conscious observation and acceptance.

- *Conclusion:* After scanning through the entire body, take a moment to feel your body as a whole. Observe any overall effect of the exercise on your mood or emotions.

- *Duration:* The body scan can last between 5 and 20 minutes, depending on your preference and available time.

Appendix 7:
Absolutist or Irrational Thoughts

Absolute or Irrational Thoughts

Albert Ellis, in his ABC model of Rational Emotive Behavior Therapy, identified a series of absolutist or irrational thoughts that are common in thought patterns contributing to emotional distress. These absolutist thoughts are often recognizable by their key phrases, such as "should", "need", "have to", and are based on rigid and uncompromising beliefs about how oneself, others, or the world "should" be.

These irrational thoughts and beliefs can be challenged and replaced with more rational and flexible thoughts using REBT techniques. Ellis emphasized the importance of recognizing these thoughts, questioning their validity and usefulness, and ultimately replacing them with ones that are more realistic and adaptive, which can significantly contribute to improving emotional well-being and mental health. Below is a list of these thoughts along with examples and key statements:

- **Perfectionism:** The belief that one must be perfect in everything they do to be valuable or accepted. *Example:* "I must impress everyone in my presentation to be considered competent". *Key Statements:* "I must be perfect", "I have to do everything right". *Challenge:* "It is humanly impossible to please everyone; what is important is that I am satisfied with my effort and learn from the experience".

- **Need for Approval:** The idea that it is necessary to be loved or approved by all significant people in one's life. *Example:* "If my partner is not happy with me, I am a failure". *Key Statements:* "I need everyone to like me," "I should be liked by people". *Challenge:* "Others' approval is desirable but not essential to my self-worth; I can disagree with others and still value myself".

- **Catastrophizing:** The tendency to exaggerate the negative consequences of an event or situation. *Example:* "If I make a mistake, it will be a total disaster". *Key Statements:* "It would be terrible if", "I couldn't stand it if". *Challenge:* "Making a mistake is not the end of the world; it is an opportunity to learn and grow".

- **Low Frustration Tolerance:** The belief that one cannot endure any difficulty or inconvenience. *Example:* "I can't stand this uncomfortable situation". *Key Statements:* "I can't bear this," "It's unbearable". *Challenge:* "Although this is uncomfortable, I can bear it and work through it; discomfort is part of growth".

- **Self-condemnation:** The tendency to harshly judge oneself for mistakes or shortcomings. *Example:* "I am a complete failure for not reaching my goal". *Key Statements:* "I should have done better," "I am bad for doing this". *Challenge:* "Making mistakes or failing does not define me as a person; I can learn from this and move on".

- **Negative Global Labeling or Global Condemnation:** The belief that one negative experience completely taints an entity or situation. *Example:* "This mistake means all my effort has been useless". *Key Statements:* "Everything is ruined". "Nothing good comes out of this". *Challenge:* "One error or failure does not negate all my previous efforts; I can acknowledge my achievements despite setbacks".

- **Comfort Dependence:** The belief that one must always have comfort and ease. *Example:* "I shouldn't have to work so hard to achieve my goals". *Key Statements:* "It should be easier", "I shouldn't have to try so hard". *Challenge:* "The value of achieving my goals often lies in the effort required; I am willing to work hard for what is important to me".

Rigid Demands: Absolutist beliefs where one thinks certain things "must" be a certain way without room for flexibility. *Example:* "I must meet all my goals without any errors". *Key Statements:* "My friends have to like me", "Everyone needs to go to the party", *Challenge:* "It is human to have ambitions, but error and failure are natural parts of learning and growth. I can strive for my goals without demanding perfection from myself".

Appendix 8:
Challenge of Irrational Beliefs

Challenging and Disputing Irrational Beliefs

The practice of challenging irrational beliefs is central to psychotherapeutic interventions, particularly in Cognitive Behavioral Therapy and Rational Emotive Behavior Therapy. The foundation of these techniques lies in the assumption that distorted beliefs and negative thought patterns underlie various psychological disorders. Modifying these beliefs through rigorous scrutiny, both logical and empirical, is considered essential for symptomatic relief and behavioral change (Beck, 2011; Ellis, 1994).

These cognitive intervention strategies must be adapted to the particularities and context of everyone, always seeking an empathic and collaborative approach in the therapeutic process. The implementation of these techniques, supported by empirical evidence, promotes cognitive restructuring and the development of greater psychological well-being (Hofmann, Asmundson, & Beck, 2013). Below is an optimized and detailed review of the proposed methodologies for questioning and challenging irrational beliefs:

1. Socratic Questioning: Inspired by Socratic dialectic, this method promotes introspection and critical questioning through a series of structured questions. Its goal is to explore the validity and utility of the individual's underlying beliefs, encouraging deep reflection on the logic and evidence that supports them.

Example: An individual harbors the disturbing belief that they are destined to fail in romantic relationships. Through Socratic questioning, they are invited to reflect: "What concrete evidence supports this belief? Has this pattern invariably manifested in all previous relationships? Does this belief contribute to the development of healthy relationships?". This process facilitates the recognition of the lack of a solid empirical basis, allowing for the consideration of more adaptive alternative perspectives.

Utilization for Creating New Beliefs: After recognizing the unstable foundation of a negative belief, Socratic questioning can be directed to explore and construct a new belief based on positive evidence and personal experiences. This process encourages the individual to identify more realistic and self-compassionate assertions that reflect their capacity for growth and adaptation.

Construction of New Belief: "Although I have faced challenges in my past relationships, each experience provides valuable learnings that better prepare me for future healthy relationships".

2. Reality Testing: This approach involves critically evaluating the empirical evidence that supports the truthfulness of a belief. It is particularly useful for countering negative and absolute generalizations.

Example: Faced with the belief of incapacity for professional success, an individual is encouraged to review their history of achievements and recognitions. This empirical review exercise directly contradicts the notion of incompetence, fostering a reevaluation of self-image from a more balanced and justified perspective.

Utilization for Creating New Beliefs: Once the evidence supporting a negative belief has been identified and refuted, reality testing facilitates the identification of evidence supporting a new, more balanced view of oneself and situations. This approach reinforces the formation *of beliefs based on actual achievements and abilities.*

Construction of New Belief: "My achievements and progress demonstrate that I am capable of achieving professional success. Each step forward reflects my competence and dedication".

3. Cost-Benefit Analysis: Through this method, the functional consequences of holding a particular belief are examined, valuing both its positive and negative aspects. This analysis can reveal whether the belief in question turns out to be more detrimental than beneficial to the individual.

Example: A patient who perceives any mistake as an indication of total failure is guided to weigh how this belief impacts their well-being and performance. The conclusion that such a belief promotes anxiety and limits the exploration of new opportunities can motivate the adoption of a more flexible and compassionate approach to error and learning.

Utilization for Creating New Beliefs: By evaluating the disadvantages of maintaining harmful beliefs and considering the benefits of adopting alternative perspectives, this technique promotes the adoption of new beliefs that favor well-being and personal effectiveness.

Construction of New Belief: "Recognizing and accepting my mistakes as learning opportunities improves my well-being and opens me up to new opportunities for growth and success".

4. Reattribution: This technique involves questioning the attribution of negative events to internal, stable, and global causes, considering instead multiple situational or external factors. It favors a more nuanced understanding of circumstances, freeing the individual from undue blame.

Example: In the context of a dissolved friendship, the reattribution process allows the subject to recognize the confluence of external factors, such as geographical distance or changes in life priorities, reducing excessive self-blame and promoting a more serene acceptance of the situation.

Utilization for Creating New Beliefs: By identifying external and contextual factors, this technique allows for the development of a more nuanced understanding of situations, which facilitates the formation of beliefs that recognize the complexity of circumstances and decrease self-blame.

Construction of New Belief: "I understand that multiple factors contributed to the outcome of this situation. This understanding allows me to focus on what I can control and improve".

5. Decatastrophizing: This consists of objectively evaluating the worst-case scenario and how it could be managed, thus decreasing anxiety and irrational fear. This technique is effective for diluting the emotional impact of catastrophic assumptions.

Example: In the face of exacerbated fear of losing a job, the individual is encouraged to carefully contemplate how they would face such a situation. The identification of viable coping strategies and the recognition of personal and social resources mitigate the perception of the situation as insurmountable.

Utilization for Creating New Beliefs: Through the realistic evaluation of the most feared scenarios and planning coping strategies, confidence can be strengthened in one's ability to handle adversities, grounding new beliefs in personal resilience and adaptability.

Construction of New Belief: "Even in difficult situations, I have resources and strategies to face and overcome challenges. My capacity for recovery allows me to face the future with confidence".

Appendix 9: RULER

Instructions for Using the Mood Meter

The Mood Meter is a tool developed by Marc Brackett and David Caruso as part of the Emotional Intelligence approach. RULER is an acronym made up of the initials of the skills to Recognize, Understand, Label, Express, and Regulate emotions, and is a program applied in education and corporate settings to improve emotional well-being (Brackett, Rivers, & Salovey, 2011).

This tool is represented with a graphical quadrant divided into four colors that represent different emotional states. The X-axis represents energy (from low to high), and the Y-axis represents pleasantness (from unpleasant to pleasant). By using this meter, individuals become more aware of their emotional states and are encouraged to explore the causes and consequences, as well as strategies for emotional regulation.

- *Yellow Quadrant (up-right):* Emotions like happiness, optimism, and energy are located here. These emotions are usually pleasant and high energy.
- *Green Quadrant (down-right):* This quadrant houses pleasant but low-energy emotions, such as calm and satisfaction.
- *Red Quadrant (up-left):* Unpleasant and high-energy emotions like anger, anxiety, and stress are located here.
- *Blue Quadrant (down-left):* This quadrant includes unpleasant and low-energy emotions like sadness, disappointment, and fatigue.

The Mood Meter has been implemented in various settings, including schools and organizations, to help people become more aware of their emotions, which in turn allows them to take more informed actions on how to manage them.

Instructions for the Exercise:

- *Quadrant Identification:* RULER consists of four colored quadrants (red, yellow, green, blue). Each quadrant represents a set of emotions correlated with levels of energy and pleasantness. Start by identifying in which quadrant you find yourself at a given moment.
- *Example:* If you are feeling disheartened and low on energy, you are likely in the blue quadrant.

- *Label the Emotion:* Once you have identified the quadrant, the next step is to label the specific emotion you are feeling. This facilitates understanding and communicating your emotional state.
- *Example:* Within the blue quadrant, you could be feeling sadness, loneliness, or despair.

- *Intensity Scale:* Estimate the intensity of your emotion on a scale from 1 to 10. This helps quantify your emotional state, which is useful for tracking and regulation.
- *Example:* If your sadness is overwhelming, you might place it at a 9 on the intensity scale.

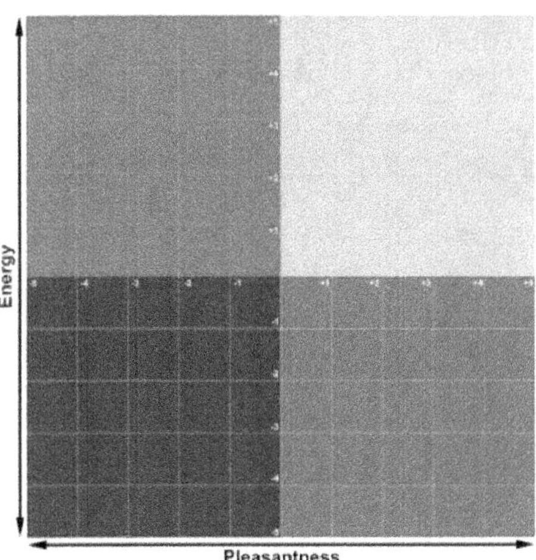

Livid	Panicked	Frustrated	Shocked	Stunned	Energised	Thrilled	Ecstatic	Euphoric	Exhilarated
Enraged	Terrified	Peeved	Worried	Annoyed	Positive	Connected	Joyful	Enthusiastic	Elated
Irate	Frightened	Angry	Nervous	Concerned	Glad	Inspired	Happy	Motivated	Excited
Furious	Anxious	Agitated	Unsure	Excluded	Amused	Focused	Cheerful	Proud	Surprised
Disgusted	Scared	Troubled	Restless	Uneasy	Satisfied	Pleased	Hopeful	Optimistic	Lively
Apprehensive	Ashamed	Guilty	Deflated	Complacent	Easy-going	Safe	Chilled	Respected	Blessed
Sullen	Glum	Disheartened	Discouraged	Bored	Relaxed	Secure	Content	Thankful	Fulfilled
Exhausted	Fatigued	Sad	Miserable	Pessimistic	Thoughtful	Composed	Calm	Grateful	Tranquil
Alienated	Depressed	Disappointed	Tired	Confused	Mellow	Peaceful	Balanced	At Ease	Collected
Despair	Inconsolable	Anguished	Hopeless	Lonely	Listless	Sleepy	Restful	Comfy	Serene

Appendix 10:
Cognitive Distortions

- **Overgeneralization:** Involves the undue extrapolation of a specific negative experience to broad and unrelated situations or contexts. It is characterized by the excessive use of absolute generalizations. *Keywords:* Always, never, everything, none. *Example:* After experiencing a failure, instead of concluding that "I always do everything wrong", one can reflect: "This failure is an isolated learning event, not a verdict of universal incapacity".

- **Catastrophizing:** This distortion involves anticipating the worst possible scenario in a situation, disproportionately magnifying the potential negative consequences. *Keywords:* Terrible, disastrous, impossible. *Example:* Faced with the fear of failing a task with the belief that "my life will be ruined", one can counter by thinking: "Even if I do not achieve the desired result, I have the capacity to learn from the experience and move forward".

- **All-or-Nothing Thinking:** Refers to the conceptualization of experiences in extreme and mutually exclusive categories, without recognizing the existence of intermediate nuances. *Keywords:* Perfect, failure, always, never. *Example:* Against the perception that "if I don't do this perfectly, I'm a failure", one can reason: "There are degrees of success and effort, and every step forward is valuable".

- **Mental Filter:** Involves focusing exclusively on a negative aspect of a situation, ignoring any present positive element. *Keywords:* But, only, except. *Example:* In the face of the idea "it was a failure because I made a mistake", reframe it as "I learned from this mistake and there were many aspects of the situation that I handled well".

- **Disqualifying the Positive:** This cognitive distortion occurs when positive evidence is systematically rejected, minimizing its importance or relevance. *Keywords:* But, only, doesn't count. *Example:* Instead of thinking "I did well in the presentation, but that doesn't count because anyone could have done it", one can value "My success in the presentation reflects my effort and skills, regardless of its perceived difficulty".

- **Labeling and Mislabeling:** Consists of assigning global negative labels to oneself or others based on specific situations, without considering the inherent complexity of human behaviors. *Keywords:* I am, you are, they are. *Example:* Instead of calling oneself "a loser" for a setback, consider "This setback is an opportunity to grow and does not define my worth as a person".

- **Personalization:** Involves unjustifiably attributing responsibility for external events to oneself, ignoring other contributing factors. *Keywords:* My fault, because of me. *Example:* Instead of thinking "My partner is in a bad mood; it must be because of something I did", reflect "My partner's mood can be influenced by many factors that are outside of my control".

- **Mind Reading:** Refers to the assumption of knowing the thoughts, feelings, or intentions of others without sufficient evidence. *Keywords:* I know, for sure. *Example:* Before concluding "I know they think I'm boring", one can think "I cannot know for sure what others are thinking without asking directly; I should avoid making assumptions".

- **Emotional Reasoning:** This distortion is based on the belief that feelings accurately reflect reality, without questioning the validity of these emotions as objective indicators. *Keywords:* I feel, therefore. *Example:* Faced with the thought "I feel scared; therefore, it must be dangerous", one can object "My emotions are subjective responses and do not always reflect the objective reality of the situation".

Fallacy of Should: Involves the imposition of rigid and inflexible expectations on one's own or others' behavior, causing distress when these are not met. *Keywords:* Should, must, ought to. *Example:* Instead of adhering to "I should always be strong and capable", one can adopt "It is human to have moments of vulnerability and each experience is an opportunity for learning".

J.R. Hernández

Bibliography

Aldao, A., Nolen-Hoeksema, S., & Schweizer, S. (2010). Emotional regulation strategies in psychopathology: A meta-analytic review. Clinical Psychology Review, 30(2), 217-237.

American Psychological Association. (2013). Diagnostic and Statistical Manual of Mental Disorders (5th ed.). American Psychiatric Publishing.

Barchard, K. A. (2003). Does emotional intelligence assist in predicting academic success? Educational and Psychological Measurement, 63(5), 840-858.

Beck, A. T., Rush, A. J., Shaw, B. F., & Emery, G. (1979). Cognitive Therapy of Depression. Guilford Press.

Beck, A. T., Steer, R. A., & Brown, G. K. (1996). Manual for the Beck Depression Inventory-II. Psychological Corporation.

Berking, M., Wupperman, P., Reichardt, A., Pejic, T., Dippel, A., & Znoj, H. (2013). Emotional regulation skills as a treatment target in psychotherapy. Behavior Research and Therapy, 51(11), 717-728.

Brackett, M. A., Rivers, S. E., & Salovey, P. (2011). Emotional Intelligence: Implications for personal, social, academic, and workplace success. Social and Personality Psychology Compass, 5(1), 88-103.

Brackett, M. A., & Mayer, J. D. (2003). Convergent, discriminant, and incremental validity of competing measures of emotional intelligence. Personality and Social Psychology Bulletin, 29(9), 1147-1158.

Bradberry, T., & Greaves, J. (2009). Emotional Intelligence 2.0. Google Books.

Butler, A. C., Chapman, J. E., Forman, E. M., & Beck, A. T. (2006). The empirical status of cognitive-behavioral therapy: A review of meta-analyses. Clinical Psychology Review, 26(1), 17-31.

Chapman, B. P., & Hayslip, B. (2005). Incremental validity of a measure of emotional intelligence. Journal of Personality Assessment, 85(2), 154-169.

Chisholm, D., Sweeny, K., Sheehan, P., Rasmussen, B., Smit, F., Cuijpers, P., & Saxena, S. (2016). Scaling-up treatment of depression and anxiety: A global return on investment analysis. The Lancet Psychiatry, 3(5), 415-424.

Clark, D. M., & Beck, A. T. (2010). Cognitive therapy of anxiety disorders: Science and practice. Guilford Press.

David, S. (2016). Emotional Agility: Break free from your blocks, embrace change, and thrive in work and life. Editorial Sirio.

Ellis, A. (2004). Rational Emotive Behavioral Therapy: Works for Me, It Can Work for You. Prometheus Books.

Ellis, A. (2008). Current psychotherapies (8th ed.). Thomson Brooks/Cole.

Ellis, A., & MacLaren, C. (1998). Rational Emotive Therapy: Therapist's Guide. Atascadero, CA: Impact Publishers.

Ellis, A., & MacLaren, C. (2005). Rational Emotive Behavioral Therapy: Therapist's Guide (2nd ed.). Impact Publishers.

Ellis, A., Gordon, J., Neenan, M., & Palmer, S. (1997). Stress Counselling: A Rational Emotive Behavior Approach. Cassell.

Extremera, N., & Fernández-Berrocal, P. (2006). Emotional intelligence and its relationship with levels of burnout, engagement, and stress among university students. Revista de Educación, 339, 345-359.

Extremera, N., & Fernández-Berrocal, P. (2006). Emotional intelligence as a predictor of mental, social, and physical health in university students. The Spanish Journal of Psychology, 9(1), 45-51.

Fernández-Berrocal, P., et al. (2012). Relationship between emotional intelligence and depressive symptomatology in young adults: A person-centered approach. Personality and Individual Differences, 53(3), 250-255.

Fernández-Berrocal, P., et al. (2019). The relationship between emotional intelligence and depression in a sample of young adults. International Journal of Environmental Research and Public Health, 16(13), 2378.

Fernández-Berrocal, P., Alcaide, R., Extremera, N., & Pizarro, D. (2012). The impact of perceived emotional intelligence on mental health among adolescents. Revista de Psicodidáctica, 17(1), 121-139.

Fernández-Berrocal, P., & Extremera, N. (2006). Emotional intelligence and emotional reactivity and recovery in laboratory context. Psicothema, 18, 72-78.

Fernández-Berrocal, P., Alcaide, R., Extremera, N., & Pizarro, D. (2006). The role of emotional intelligence in anxiety and depression among adolescents. Individual Differences Research, 4(1), 16-27.

Greenberg, L. S., & Watson, J. C. (2006). Emotion-focused therapy for depression. American Psychological Association.

Goleman, D. (1995). Emotional Intelligence: Why it can matter more than IQ. Bantam Books.

Hodzic, S., Scharfen, J., Ripoll, P., Holling, H., & Zenasni, F. (2018). How efficient are emotional intelligence trainings: A meta-analysis. Emotion Review, 10(2), 138-148.

Johnstone, K. M., & Walter, F. M. (2020). Emotional intelligence interventions targeting older adults: A systematic review. Journal of Applied Gerontology, 39(1), 3-10.

Kessler, R. C., Berglund, P., Demler, O., Jin, R., Koretz, D., Merikangas, K. R., Rush, A. J., Walters, E. E., & Wang, P. S. (2003). The epidemiology of major depressive disorder: Results from the National Comorbidity Survey Replication (NCS-R). JAMA, 289(23), 3095-3105.

Kessler, R. C., Petukhova, M., Sampson, N. A., Zaslavsky, A. M., & Wittchen, H.-U. (2020). Twelve-month and lifetime prevalence and lifetime morbid risk of anxiety and mood disorders in the United States. International Journal of Methods in Psychiatric Research, 21(3), 169-184.

Koenigs, M., & Grafman, J. (2009). The functional neuroanatomy of depression: Distinct roles for ventromedial and dorsolateral prefrontal cortex. Behavioral Brain Research, 201(2), 239-243.

Kotsou, I., & Leys, C. (2017). Emotional intelligence can make a difference: The impact of principals' emotional intelligence on teaching strategy mediated by instructional leadership. International Journal of Educational Management, 31(2), 163-176.

Kotsou, I., Leys, C., & Fossion, P. (2019). Emotional intelligence and stress in medical students: A closer look at the role of emotional regulation and emotional attention. Journal of Happiness Studies, 20(4), 1037-1050.

Lopes, P. N., Salovey, P., & Straus, R. (2003). Emotional intelligence, personality, and the perceived quality of social relationships. Personality and Individual Differences, 35(3), 641-658.

Lopes, P. N., Salovey, P., Côté, S., Beers, M., & Petty, R. E. (2006). Emotional regulation skills and the quality of social interaction. Emotion, 6(1), 78-84.

Martins, A., Ramalho, N., & Morin, E. (2010). A comprehensive meta-analysis of the relationship between Emotional Intelligence and health. Personality and Individual Differences, 49(6), 554-564.

Martins, A., Ramalho, N., & Morin, E. (2010). A comprehensive meta-analysis of the relationship between Emotional Intelligence and health. Personality and Individual Differences, 49(6), 554-564.

Mayer, J. D., Roberts, R. D., & Barsade, S. G. (2008). Human abilities: Emotional intelligence. Annual Review of Psychology, 59, 507-536.

Mayer, J. D., & Salovey, P. (1997). What is emotional intelligence? In P. Salovey & D. Sluyter (Eds.), Emotional development and emotional intelligence: Educational implications (pp. 3-31). Basic Books.

Nelis, D., Quoidbach, J., Mikolajczak, M., & Hansenne, M. (2011). Increasing emotional intelligence: (How) is it possible? Personality and Individual Differences, 50(1), 36-41.

Prince, M. (2004). Active Learning: A pedagogical approach for knowledge retention and application. Educational Psychology Review.

Rivers, S. E., Brackett, M. A., Omori, M., Sickler, C., Bertoli, M. C., & Salovey, P. (2013). Emotional skills as a protective factor for risky behaviors among college students. Journal of College Student Development, 54(2), 172-183.

Ritchie, H., & Roser, M. (2018). Mental Health. Online publication at Our World in Data.

Rosenberg, M. B. (2016). Nonviolent Communication: A Language of Life. Editorial Acanto.

Ruiz-Aranda, D., Castillo, R., Salguero, J. M., Cabello, R., Fernández-Berrocal, P., & Balluerka, N. (2012). Short and medium-term effects of emotional intelligence training on adolescent mental health. Journal of Adolescent Health, 51(5), 462-467.

Salguero, J. M., et al. (2010). Emotional intelligence and depression: The moderating role of gender. Personality and Individual Differences, 49(1), 29-33.

Salovey, P., & Mayer, J. D. (1990). Emotional intelligence. Imagination, Cognition, and Personality, 9(3), 185-211.

Salovey, P., Stroud, L. R., Woolery, A., & Epel, E. S. (2002). Perceived emotional intelligence, stress reactivity, and symptom reports: Further explorations using the Trait Meta-Mood Scale. Psychology & Health, 17(5), 611-627.

Sánchez-Álvarez, N., Extremera, N., & Fernández-Berrocal, P. (2016). The relationship between emotional intelligence and subjective well-being: A meta-analytical investigation. The Journal of Positive Psychology, 11(3), 276-285.

Schutte, N. S., Malouff, J. M., Thorsteinsson, E. B. (2013). Increasing emotional intelligence through training: Status and future directions. The International Journal of Emotional Education, 5(1), 56-72.

Schutte, N. S., Malouff, J. M., Thorsteinsson, E. B., Bhullar, N., & Rooke, S. E. (2022). A meta-analytic investigation of the relationship between emotional intelligence and health. Personality and Individual Differences, 42(6), 921-933.

Slaski, M., & Cartwright, S. (2003). Training in emotional intelligence and its implications for stress, health, and performance. Stress and Health, 19(4), 233-239.

Thorpe, G. L., & Olson, S. L. (1997). Behavior Therapy: Concepts, Procedures, and Applications (2nd ed.). Allyn & Bacon.

Vos, T., Allen, C., Arora, M., Barber, R. M., Bhutta, Z. A., Brown, A., ... & Coggeshall, M. (2017). Incidence, prevalence, and years lived with disability for 328 diseases and injuries in 195 countries, 1990-2016: A systematic analysis for the Global Burden of Disease Study 2016. The Lancet, 390(10100), 1211-1259.

Williams, J. (2020). Cognitive Behavioral Therapy Made Simple. [NA].

Xiong, J., Lipsitz, O., Nasri, F., Lui, L. M. W., Gill, H., Phan, L., ... & McIntyre, R. S. (2020). Impact of COVID-19 pandemic on mental health in the general population: A systematic review. Journal of Affective Disorders, 277, 55-64.

Zeidner, M., Matthews, G., & Roberts, R. D. (2012). The nexus between emotional intelligence, health, and well-being: What have we learned and what have we overlooked? Applied Psychology: Health and Well-Being, 4(1), 1-30.

Zeidner, M., Roberts, R. D., & Matthews, G. (2002). Can emotional intelligence be schooled? A critical review. Educational Psychologist, 37(4), 215-231.